DATE DUE

DEMCO 38-296

MEDIA SCIENCE BEFORE THE GREAT WAR

Media Science
before the Great War

Peter Broks
Senior Lecturer in Cultural and Media Studies
University of the West of England
Bristol

21 6XS
and London
Companies and representatives
throughout the world

A catalogue record for this book is available
from the British Library.

ISBN 0–333–65638–5

 First published in the United States of America 1996 by
ST. MARTIN'S PRESS, INC.,
Scholarly and Reference Division,
175 Fifth Avenue,
New York, N.Y. 10010

ISBN 0–312–16019–4

Library of Congress Cataloging-in-Publication Data
Broks, Peter.
Media science before the Great War / Peter Broks.
p.   cm.
Includes bibliographical references and index.
ISBN 0–312–16019–4
1. Science—Popular works.   2. Science news.   I. Title.
Q162.B838   1996
070.4'495'09043—dc20   96–7159
                                                            CIP

10   9   8   7   6   5   4   3   2   1
05   04   03   02   01   00   99   98   97   96

Printed and bound in Great Britain by
Antony Rowe Ltd, Chippenham, Wiltshire

For my parents

Contents

Preface

The idea for this book never occurred to me. The work seemed a natural progression and coming together of diverse interests – history, the media, popular science. It occupied an academic space that was, like the magazines themselves, untouched and unexplored. Collecting dust even in the best of libraries and antiquarian shops, bound volumes of magazines still wait the researcher's knife to separate the uncut pages. When we do open them out, we have spread before us the Victorian and Edwardian world. Not a true picture, for nowadays we are too astute to see the media as a window on the world, but at least we have the smell of the times.

I have never liked long lists of acknowledgements. The sincerity seems to diminish with each line of gratitude. I hope my brevity is taken as a sign of true appreciation. First mention must go to John Brooke at the University of Lancaster, whose' phone call prompted a career change from journalism into academic research and whose supervision was as considerate and rigorous as any student could wish to have. The research was funded by the Science and Engineering Research Council, and the book was written during a period of teaching relief provided by the Faculty of Humanities at the University of the West of England, Bristol. However, for a book that is so concerned with the everyday, it is only right that my principal thanks go to those who made the day-to-day writing of it possible: Doreen and Mal, for the support that only parents can give; Kim, for many small kindnesses; and Ilizane for her patience.

Publishing details of illustrations are included in their captions (see pp. 96, 118, 120–1 and 122).

Introduction

In 1902 a Fellow of the Royal Geographical Society told readers of *Pearson's Magazine* about the Tehuelche, a nomadic tribe of Patagonian Indians. Early the previous year he had travelled south from Buenos Aires and had struck the Indian trail that led north from Punta Arenas. The trail ran along under the Cordillera, and for countless generations the tribe had wandered up and down its length following the herds of guanaco, a relative of the llama and the principal quarry of the Tehuelche. These ancient wanderings were now under threat. The article reported a remark from one of the tribe. '"Once," he said, "we had the sea upon the one side of us, and upon the other the Cordillera. But it is not so now; the white man is now ever advancing upon one side and the Cordillera ever unchanging upon the other. And once all the land was ours."' Readers were introduced to the contented lives of the Tehuelche, their customs, religion, ways of hunting, clothes and food. They read of their 'many admirable traits of character' and of how, physically, they were 'one of the finest races in the world', but

> Progress, the white man's shibboleth, has no meaning for the Tehuelche. He is losing ground day by day in the wild onrush of mankind. Our thoughts do not appeal to him. He has neither part nor lot in the feverish desires and ambitions that move us so strongly.... To see a race, so kindly, picturesque, and gifted with fine qualities of body and mind, absolutely at handgrips with extinction seems to me one of the saddest results of the growing domination of the white man and his methods of civilisation.[1]

What are we to make of this? At first glance it is not unlike the global awareness and ethnosensitivity we are accustomed to seeing in television documentaries – the peaceful indigenous population, a vital part of their own environment, forced to come to terms with an alien way of life. Details suggest its age. Terms like 'race' and 'Indians' would only be used in the most circumspect ways today, if at all. Elsewhere in the article we read of how the Tehuelche, 'like other far less intelligent races of uncivilised people', appear to be incapable of much forethought. However, 'in appearance they are splendid fellows', who were 'well built and developed'. Most of them averaged six feet tall or more, and 'their manner of life tends to muscular excellence'. There is clearly something of the 'noble savage' about this vision with its emphasis on height, muscularity and a carefree live-for-the-present mentality. We could explore further and examine how 'subject races' were represented in the British media or how the idea of 'Progress' was popularised. We could pick up on these ideas to look at concepts such as 'civilised', 'savage' or 'natural' and see what they tell us about related issues like science, technology and evolution. We could then trace these themes through a wide range of literature and into the more general culture of late-Victorian and Edwardian Britain.

But there are puzzles here too. What is an attack on the civilising process doing in an imperialist magazine like *Pearson's*? Only three years earlier another Pearson's publication was quite happy to argue that progress only came from the strong conquering the weak and that without an aggressive Anglo-Saxon race the world would lapse into barbarism. Why the difference? Is it because of the different publications or the different times? How do we reconcile divergent views from a single publishing company, or from a single periodical, or indeed from a single issue of a magazine?

The purpose of this book is to understand articles such as this, the magazines in which they appeared and the culture in which they were read. Its principal focus is science (including technology and medicine), yet it concerns people who in all probability were neither scientifically literate nor even scientifically interested. One could call it the zero-option, but it does propose an alternative to the traditional perspective on popular science – to look for science in what was popular rather than popularity in what was science. A truly cultural history of popular science would encompass every aspect of popular culture from leisure and entertainment, to the factory and the classroom. Its source material would be superstitions, folklore, songs, jokes and comic strips as well as advertisements, pulp fiction, newspapers and school textbooks. I have had to content myself with mass-circulation magazines.

1 Popular Culture

There is something very familiar about late Victorian Britain – the neat lawns of suburbia, an urban environment saturated with advertisements, popping down the 'local', watching professional football, eating fish and chips. Much of what is regarded as 'traditional' in British culture is little more than a hundred years old, and despite the cataclysmic events of two world wars the social landscape has remained remarkably untouched. Major transformations in demographic structure, urban and rural life, production and consumption, class identity and civic consciousness all predate the last decade of the nineteenth century, and a good deal of the twentieth century can be read as a coming to terms with this legacy. Historical periods are no more than the historian's sleight of hand, but there is something to be said for the view that the great upheavals of British social history are better placed in the 1870s and the 1960s than at any time in between. In many ways the 'character' of late Victorian Britain resembles Britain of the 1950s more than its early or mid-Victorian persona, and the 'never had it so good' mentality echoes well the brash optimism of the 1890s.[1]

Of course, we must be careful not to overemphasise the continuities, but the real danger is in how we see the changes. We must be careful not to look across the wasteland of the Great War and to believe that the grass really was greener on the other side, the days more peaceful, the summers hotter, first loves sweeter. With its hint of lost innocence, 'before the war' can easily give the period that rosy glow of a Golden Age. We would do well to remember that they were often troubled times and that, with the exception of a few perceptive individuals, when the war did come it was greeted not only with shouts of joy but with what can only be described as a great sigh of relief. Nor were these simply the death throes of Liberal England as recorded by George Dangerfield. The close of the century also, and perhaps quite naturally, brought with it a sense of ending.

'Fin de sìecle,' murmured Sir Henry.
'Fin de globe,' answered his hostess.[2]

Wilde's *The Picture of Dorian Gray* could well stand as a leitmotif for the decadence and dandyism of the 1890s, at least for a section of a cultural elite. In Edwardian High Society such aesthetic sensibilities found a more material expression in an orgy of conspicuous consumption. Armies of servants supported the mad gaddings of those who were, to J.B. Priestley's eye, 'shallow,

1

self-indulgent, stupid'. Making hay while the sun still shines, there was, says Priestley, 'a vague feeling that the end was almost in sight, that their class was now banging away in the last act. So they overdid everything.'[3]

We can catch the same sense of the times from contemporary magazines. It was not that Society was immoral, wrote Lady Violet Greville in 1909, but that it lacked the courage even of its own vices.

> It has not the strength or the ardour to be vicious; it is simply a shifting, struggling mass of unexcited, jaded, restless beings, void of character and dignity, having flung away the attributes which once made it lordly and prosperous, grasping at shifting shadows – puling, crazy, faddy, discordant, and entirely without prestige and power.

Its principal trait was 'vulgarity', the vulgarity of self-advertisement in clothes, wealth and entertaining. It had 'only one desire in common, the desire to get on; only one love, the love of money; only one vice, selfishness'. The great feature of the age, she said, was 'indifferentism' which proclaimed itself in 'a laxity of principle, a disregard of duty, a desire for liberty verging on licence, and a lazy contempt for religion'. There was, it seemed, a fashion for liberty:

> The unemployed loafer who demands an old age pension, the politician who seeks to rob the rich of money, the suffragette who hates man and yet wants his privileges – all are self-seekers. But it is glossed, glorified with the new jargon of liberty.[4]

But we miss the point if we see only decadence and decline. In that 'liberty' we can also detect a new found sense of freedom. Writing in 1913 Holbrook Jackson could see the 1890s as a period of renaissance. It was 'the decade of a thousand "movements"'. Life, dynamism, energy brought the century rushing to a close. 'Everybody, mentally and emotionally, was running about in a hundred different directions. There was so much to think about, so much to discuss, so much to see.' It was an age of experiment, 'an era of hope and action'. Anything might happen and, for the young, as Jackson points out, 'any happening sufficiently new was good'. The 1890s celebrated what was new, what was modern (or indeed what was 'modernist'). There was the New Fiction, the New Realism, the New Drama, the New Unionism, the New Journalism, and, of course, the New Woman. Not to be 'new', it was said, was to be nothing. At times even this was not enough. Not content with what was new, the periodical press sought out what was 'newest'.[5]

It was an age of experiment, exuberance and excess. Decadent and jaded, yet bursting with life and energy; craving novelty and freedom, but somehow weary of the world – the paradoxes pile one upon another. Perhaps we can say little more than the period was complex, pluralistic and transitional, but then what period in history is not. There is, however, one characteristic which historians and Victorians can agree upon. It was a common self-perception that this was the age of the 'masses'. The late Victorians and Edwardians were living in the world's first mass industrial society, and well they knew it.

It was such a commonplace idea. Even Lady Violet Greville saw Society as an 'inchoate mass', and most often for her 'Society' was very much upper case and upper class. More usual was to apply the term to the 'underclass', the submerged one third of the population living in poverty and those desperately trying to avoid it, the multitudes crammed into the recesses of 'darkest England'. Masterman's description is the most vivid.

> Our streets have suddenly become congested with a weird and uncanny people. They have poured in as dense black masses from the eastern railways; they have streamed across the bridges from the marshes and desolate places beyond the river; they have been hurried up in incredible number through tubes sunk in the bowels of the earth, emerging like rats from a drain, blinking in the sunshine.[6]

This was a new force to be reckoned with, 'the creeping into conscious existence of the quaint and innumerable populations bred in the Abyss'. Daily this wave of humanity rolled into and out of London 'as if propelled by the systole and diastole of some mighty unseen heart'.

> A turbid river of humanity, pent up on the narrow bridge, is pouring into London; aged men in beards and bowlers shambling hastily forward; work girls, mechanics, active boys, neat little clerks in neat little high hats shining out conspicuous in the rushing stream. The pace is even lest one should fall; the general aspect is of a harassed but goodtempered energy, as of those driven along ways not clearly comprehended towards no definite goal. The Abyss is disgorging its denizens for the labour of the day.[7]

Even a cursory glance at the work of the 'social explorers' like Masterman, Booth and Rowntree gives a necessary corrective to any ideas of a lost Golden Age. In the 1890s Booth's statistics showed that in the East End of London 35 per cent of the population lived in poverty and, lest it be thought that was a special case, he found that the figure for the whole of London was 30 per cent. Believing that perhaps it was London that had a special problem, Seebohm Rowntree carried out a survey of his own native York. To his horror he found that the level of poverty was comparable to that in London, and yet York was a relatively prosperous town. The wages of unskilled labourers in York were insufficient to provide adequate food, shelter and clothing for a moderate-sized family. Even assuming a diet that was less generous than the one in the local workhouse and making no allowance for any expenditure beyond a necessary minimum, thousands of families were unable to maintain 'merely physical efficiency'. Rowntree was at pains to make clear what that meant. Amongst other deprivations the family

> must never spend a penny on railway fare or omnibus.... They must never purchase a halfpenny newspaper or spend a penny to buy a ticket for a popular concert. They must write no letters to absent children, for they cannot afford to pay the postage.... The children must have no pocket money for dolls, marbles, or sweets. The father must smoke no tobacco, and must drink no beer. The mother must never buy any pretty clothes for herself or for her children.... Finally, the wage-earner must never be absent from his work for a single day.[8]

Many could not forego these simple pleasures and found themselves in what Rowntree classed as 'secondary poverty', but that they were expected to be part of normal family life, no matter how poor the family, is indicative in itself. To be sure, baccy and beer had for long been the traditional solace of the working man, but railway and omnibus fares, newspapers, popular concerts, pocket money for the children are all small pointers to spending power (and expectations) above subsistence level. They may not amount to much in themselves, but they are signs of the times.

If being submerged in the masses was the price to pay for modern life, then at least modern life showed distinct improvements upon that of our forebears. The queen's diamond jubilee in 1897 occasioned many retrospectives of the previous sixty years' progress. One such article set forth the usual record of technological change, of how bicycles, motor cars and 'other hideous machines' had helped supplant the horse, but the writer also noted how the people had changed too. 'The crowd itself is vastly different', and characteristic of the time was the 'monotonous level of equality'. But there were compensations:

> Throughout every class in the country the benefits of trade have brought amelioration of their lot, and national life in England is improving more rapidly than in any other country in the world. If for this fortunate result we must pay in some such monotonous regularity of outward appearance as has just been noticed, it is worthwhile remembering, on the

other hand, that this equalising process has been far more persistent from beneath upwards than in any fall from above towards a lower level.[9]

Nor should this be seen simply as vacuous self-satisfaction; the late-Victorians had good reason to be smug.

For most people the second half of the nineteenth century brought real and substantial improvements in their standard of living. To be sure the Victorians were as well aware as anyone that 'the poor are with us always', but what was equally clear was that the general trend was towards a more comfortable life. Net national income rose so quickly that, despite a population increase, average per capita incomes still experienced an impressive rise. At constant prices, income per head more than doubled in the forty years after 1860. As incomes rose prices fell, resulting in a tremendous increase in average real wages. By 1900 they were one third higher than they had been in 1875 and even allowing for unemployment the real wages of the average urban worker probably rose by 60 per cent or more between 1860 and 1900. The 'Great Depression' of 1873–96 may have expressed a lack of confidence among owners and investors, but it brought a general improvement in the conditions of life for the working class. The cost of food had always taken a large chunk out of small budgets, but now the cheap, imported foods that so worried farmers and landowners eased the burden on low-income families. From the mid-1870s prices of staple products fell as wheat, tea, sugar, lard, cheese and ham poured in from overseas. Not only were imported foods cheaper, but mass-production methods of food processing and an improved distribution system meant that the prices in shops were also brought down. The consequences upon diet are clear to see. Between 1860 and 1910 sugar and tea consumption per head more than doubled while imports of ham and bacon per head more than quadrupled.[10]

Of all the occasions when we can talk of late Victorian Britain as a 'mass' society, it is no more appropriate than here in the new mass market. An expanding population enlarged the pool of potential consumers. Increased spending power pushed horizons beyond mere subsistence. Families now had more to spend on a greater variety of goods and services, not only essentials such as food and clothes, but luxury items, new consumer durables, entertainment and leisure. In short, more people had more money to spend on more things. The result was a second phase of industrialisation, a consumer revolution transforming production and distribution. Most conspicuous was the revolution in retailing to meet the new kinds of demand. The new Co-operatives and multiples set out to

cater for a better-off working class offering new staples of the working-
class diet and products of new mass production technology such as had
been developed in the shoe-making and clothing industries. They were
specifically geared for the mass market, often building on a limited range
of cheap imported goods with small profit margins but a high turnover.
The spread of chain stores is truly remarkable. In 1875 there were 300
shoe-chain shops; by 1900 there were 2600, half of them founded in the
1890s. In 1880 there were 27 branches of grocery firms; by 1900 there
were nearly 3500. Those who succeeded are still familiar names today:
Liptons for groceries, W.H. Smiths for books, Hepworths for clothes, and
Boot's the chemists.[11]

The new managerial and clerical workforce needed to maintain this consumer revolution, together with the legions of shop assistants needed to
serve in it, constitutes one of the most significant elements in British social
and economic life – the expansion of the lower middle class. In many
cases this in itself was a sign of improvement with upwardly mobile
workers joining the ranks of clerks. In the second half of the century the
white collar workforce expanded from fewer than 150 000 employees to
nearly one million. The great mass of shop workers, schoolteachers, commercial travellers and clerks 'constituted the fastest-growing and most
important social category of the time'.[12] Add to these the petty bourgeoisie
of shopkeepers and small businessmen and you have not so much a distinct class as an amorphous grouping united by its aspirational values and
social fears. Small businesses were being squeezed out of the market by
larger businesses. Small retailers faced similar competition from department stores and multiples. Clerks faced competition from each other as
better education made it easier to become a white-collar worker, bringing
an oversupply of men (and increasingly women) to the jobs market.
Upward mobility could easily become downward mobility, and all the
time appearances had to be kept up, middle-class life styles maintained on
lower middle-class incomes.[13] The result was a section of society that was
as frustrated as it was ambitious, a potentially dangerous combination (as
witness interwar Germany) but which in Britain produced Mr and Mrs
Pooter of The Laurels, Brickfield Terrace, Holloway.

Equally significant was the effect upon the working class. A reduction
in working hours and a rise in real wages meant that more time and money
could be spent on the family, home, excursions, sport and entertainment.
The 'remaking of the English working-class' in the late nineteenth century
can be attributed, at least in part, to the decline of a work-centred culture.
In London, for example, traditional artisan culture 'began to yield to a
culture oriented towards the family and the home'. From the 1870s the

migration to the suburbs increased the separation of home from work-place. The regular pub visited would no longer be the 'trade' pub which had been the centre for political discussion and trade union organisation, but the 'local' where conversation was more likely to reflect common interests such as sport and entertainment. The new patterns of working-class life began to take shape from the 1870s and became dominant in the 1890s. By the turn of the century gin palaces had virtually disappeared; free and easies had gone; cock-fighting, bear-baiting and ratting had all but died out; gambling had been driven off the streets; public executions had been stopped. In their place were parks, museums, libraries and four bank holidays.[14]

Raymond Williams once wrote that the 'masses' are always somebody else. They form the alien, threatening 'other', of which we never see our-selves as an undifferentiated part. On close inspection the 'masses' always breaks up into sub-groups, classes, occupations, families, individuals. The idea of 'mass culture' is equally problematic, but in the context of late Victorian Britain I cannot help but feel that it is in some ways appropriate. This is not simply because of the unprecedented numbers involved, nor the historian's inability to identify faces in a crowd. In the realm of consump-tion at least, 'mass culture' conveys the ambiguous suggestion of, on the one hand, individual consumption of mass-produced goods, and on the other, of the consumption of goods en masse. In a football crowd, a music hall audience or a department store filled with shoppers, hundreds or even thousands of people would indulge in the same pleasure in the same place at the same time. The mass market transformed British popular culture by promoting consumption as a form of leisure, and leisure as a form of con-sumption. To call this 'mass culture' may be problematic, but it is as convenient a term as any.

In the last quarter of the century the central feature of the transformation of recreation was that it increasingly depended on consumer goods and services. Leisure came to be expected not as a luxury but as a right, and in the context of an expanding economy with increasing consumer demand those rights were to be met by new leisure industries.[15] We can see this clearly in the development of day trips and seaside holidays. Cheap excur-sions brought hordes of people to the seaside, and although many resorts felt their respectability under threat there was money to be made. The 1880s and 1890s saw a proliferation of piers jutting out into the waters around Britain, and increasingly these were becoming centres for com-

mercial attractions: booths, mechanical devices, theatres. The simple
pleasures of the beach were supplemented by Punch and Judy shows,
donkeys, changing huts, musicians, boatmen, food sellers and a wide
variety of other hawkers. Inland, 'pleasure beaches' followed their
American prototypes and towards the end of the century attractions were
becoming bigger and more elaborate with roller coasters, big wheels and
electric railways.[16] There were winter gardens, pleasure pavilions, music
halls, aquaria and, of course, at Blackpool a 500-foot imitation Eiffel
tower. By 1911 over half the English population were visiting the seaside
on day trips, and 20 per cent stayed long enough to need accommodation.
The impact on the resorts was dramatic. They were the fastest growing
urban centres in the country. Between 1861 and 1911 the population of
Southend grew from 3000 to 63 000, and that of Blackpool from 4000 to
58 000. The growth of Bournemouth was nothing less than explosive,
rising from just under 2000 inhabitants in 1861 to 79 000 in 1911, an
increase of 4000 per cent.[17]

One of the most conspicuous, and regular, forms of mass pleasure was
football. The old game rarely had rules. It was informal, disorderly,
violent and destructive. Not surprisingly it was denounced by the authorities who tried to suppress it. The game that emerged by the end of the
nineteenth century was nationally organised with a sophisticated bureaucracy, large finances, officials, publications and armies of players who
were now often professionals. The game began to be codified in mid-
century when public schools needed the same rules so that they could play
each other. It had been popular in schools for its 'muscular Christianity',
inculcating the virtues of manliness, selflessness and teamwork, and soon
it was seized on as a way of bringing large-scale physical exercise into the
fast-growing cities. Wanting to encourage sport as a counter-attraction to
drinking, gambling or just hanging around, schools and churches started to
organise football teams – like Villa Cross Wesleyan Chapel's 'Aston
Villa' or St Domingo's Church Sunday School's 'Everton'. By the 1880s
particular industries became the bases for other teams, as with the
Woolwich munition workers' 'Arsenal' or the Newton Heath railwaymen
who started Manchester United. As the popularity of the game grew so
did its business possibilities. The result was a spiral of commercialism.
Competitive leagues developed from 1888 meant that clubs tried to hold
on to their best players, and the best way of doing that was to pay them.
To pay the wages clubs needed to attract and accommodate more specta-
tors, and that meant investment in building stadia which in turn increased
costs. To meet the higher costs clubs were forced onto a more commercial
footing with success determined by large crowds paying money to watch

expensive professional players. Over 100 000 people watched Tottenham Hotspur win the FA cup in 1901, and by 1911 the average attendance at the matches of leading clubs rose to 30 000. It all seemed a far cry from the philanthropic visions of mid-century.[18]

Commercialisation was also to be found in the development of an entertainment industry, and here too it meant the introduction of managerial bureaucracy, the rise of professionalism and the consequent exclusion of the masses from cultural production. The economic pattern was the same as for football with a rising income used to pay for better facilities and the higher salaries of performers. From about 1890, for example, working men's clubs shifted from a membership to a business mode of operation, seeking to increase revenue by attracting large audiences for professional entertainment which had at first supplemented then eventually supplanted the members' own amateur turns. Large investments in music halls and variety theatres increased fears for the loss of licences and heightened the concern of proprietors to control both performers and audience. The singing saloons of the 1830s and 1840s with their 'free and easies' drawing on volunteer talent from the audience were to be superseded by the music hall of the 1890s where a tightly timetabled programme would be performed by syndicated artists. Moreover, in the earlier singing saloons, performers were part of and on the same level as their audience, the only distinction being that performers sat at the 'singers' table'. More elaborate design of halls changed that. A stage and proscenium arch distanced performer from audience, and from the 1880s more powerful lighting emphasised the contrast between the two. By this time the strict scheduling of turns prevented acts from hobnobbing with the crowd who were now rooted into fixed stall seats.[19]

In the last two decades of the nineteenth century the impact of technology and commercialisation on leisure and popular culture was more important than any social reform campaign.[20] It was in response to the increasing 'intrusiveness' of workers that middle-class efforts at subordination were directed, in turn, to providing leisure, commercialising it and finally serving it up for mass consumption. By the end of the century a new stage in class struggle can be detected, the making (or projected making) of the English consuming masses, in which an attempt at real subordination of the working 'masses' is as evident in cultural and leisure production as it is in work.[21] Within a complex interlocking of economic, political, social and cultural forces, leisure was active and changing 'in a total situation of dominance and subordination'. Since the late nineteenth century leisure has ceased to be a threat to the establishment and maintenance of hegemony. Provided and controlled by increasingly powerful leisure industries, it became both tamed and legitimate because of its separation from the other concerns of people's lives.[22]

For all their concern to control working-class behaviour, middle-class attempts to do so had been singularly unsuccessful. The working class offered substantial resistance to having their recreation 'rationalised'. Despite the middle-class onslaught on their behaviour the majority of workers in London were neither Christian, provident, chaste nor temperate. The social and economic function of the pub may have been reduced, but it still remained one of the dominant institutions of working-class culture. However, there were, as Robert Gray argues, 'important elements of voluntary consent to the existing structure of society'. What we have is a subtle process of negotiation and accommodation where dominant middle-class values get redefined and reproduced 'spontaneously' by members of the working class. In so far as values were shared, working-class identity could be asserted with divergent interpretations of a consensual language. 'Self-help', for example, might take on collective forms. 'Thrift' might be needed for survival, to keep up appearances or to save for funerals. 'Respectability' might mean independence from middle-class patronage and control. Moreover, the adoption (and adaptation) of dominant language and values was offset by the recognition of working-class independence, and the imposition upon the bourgeoisie of representation of working-class interests, seen, for example, in the middle-class acceptance of unions.[23] The result was the emergence of a new pattern of working-class culture, impervious to middle-class attempts to control it, but which nonetheless displayed an enclosed and defensive conservatism.[24]

Despite any peculiarities of the situation for London's artisans there was a basic consistency of outlook in the new working-class culture which spread over England after 1870. It is generally agreed amongst historians that in the fifty years following the defeat of Chartism a new working-class mentality emerged. The aggressive, even revolutionary spirit of Chartist days and earlier became defensive and acquiescent. From 1850 onwards 'working-class ideology lost its active edge', while working-class culture was 'more inward looking and hermetic'.[25] As reflected and reinforced by music hall, it was a 'culture of consolation'.[26] A study of the songs shows a taste for the concrete and the familiar, confirming the experience of working-class life rather than offering escapes or alternatives. Although often cynical of authority they reveal an acceptance of the class structure and its inequalities.[27] Earlier working-class cultural forms had been less sanguine about the working-class situation, but by the end of the century the keynote of music hall entertainment was 'the celebration of material pleasures'. The political aggression of broadside ballads had been exchanged for the hedonism of Marie Lloyd's 'a little of what you fancy does you good'.[28]

The motivation for consumption, however, might take a variety of forms. Richard Hoggart, for example, recalling the lives of his mother and grandmother believes that:

> to call the working-class attitude towards progress only a form of mate-rialism, as some writers do, is often to underrate it. They wanted these goods and services not out of a greed for possession, a desire to lay their hands on the glittering products of technical society, but because the lack of them made it very difficult to live what they called a 'decent' life...[29]

Robert Roberts remembers possessions as rudimentary symbols of social status. 'Many households', he writes, 'strove by word, conduct and the acquisition of objects to enhance the family image.' Quoting the northern saying 'them as 'as nowt is nowt', he adds the salutary reminder that family ambitions were 'pathetically modest', running as they did to a new piece of oilcloth, a rag rug, a pair of framed pictures, new bedding or underclothes, or even a luxury such as a sewing machine, musical instrument, bicycle, gramophone or watch.[30] Decency, prestige and self-respect were all to find expression in the acquisition of material possessions.

There is much that could be made of this. We could, for example, embark upon a neo-Marxist critique of a consumer society as a successful attempt to integrate the working class into capitalism.[31] We could talk of the 'economisation of the power conflict', and see the search for freedom reinterpreted into an effort to satisfy consumer needs.[32] After all, the department store itself was presented and experienced as an extension of freedom where consumers were 'entertained by commodities' and induced into a 'numbed hypnosis' by their exoticism and grand displays.[33] We might want to explain late-nineteenth-century working-class passivity, at least in part, by the success of reformism in a new age of prosperity, and argue that 'working within the system was a realistic strategy which deliv-ered the goods'.[34] Each of these is worth considering and deserves a closer analysis than I have space for here. However, even without referring to the creation of a consumer 'ethic', or an ideology of 'consumerism' (as in some Marxist sense of false consciousness), I think it does not take much to say that the desire to acquire consumer goods is a stabilising factor in a capitalist society with an expanding economy. What happens when the economy ceases to expand, when the system can, quite literally, no longer deliver the goods? Well, then we have the basis for what has come to be called the Edwardian crisis, when expectations ran ahead of circumstances, and bright hopes had dim prospects. But more of that later.[35]

There is a second aspect of the Edwardian crisis which we need to consider and which will also help us to understand the late Victorian mentality. If we choose not to see consumerism as somehow part of a 'dominant ideology', then we could more easily make such claim for imperialism. From his work on imperialist propaganda, John MacKenzie has concluded that the imperial core ideology was the most effective of all late-nineteenth-century systems of social discipline. If we are to identify a dominant ideology, he argues, then it is to the late nineteenth and early twentieth centuries that we should look, when an 'ideological cluster' of renewed militarism, devotion to royalty, worship of national heroes and racial ideas associated with Social Darwinism was projected by adverts, theatre, cinema and juvenile literature, as well as education and the church. Empire, he says, had the power to regenerate the British, and lead to class conciliation 'by creating a national purpose with a high moral content'.[36]

Morality did not seem high on the agenda for the crowds celebrating the relief of Mafeking in 1900. As witnessed by C.F.G. Masterman

> They blew trumpets; they hit each other with bladders; they tickled passers-by with feathers; they embraced ladies in the streets, laughing genially and boisterously. Later the drink got into them, and they reeled and struck and swore, walking and leaping and blaspheming God. At night we left them, a packed and sodden multitude, howling under the quiet stars.[37]

The riotous behaviour of the jingo crowds brought a new word to the English language, to 'Maffick', but it is open to question as to how far it was an expression of the new imperialism or simply the exuberant release of emotion at a more personal level. With a general distaste for abstractions the working class was, by and large, immune to the more visionary aspects of empire, and in more concrete terms, as Robert Roberts recalls, 'what the undermass got materially from empire, old or new, is hard to see, unless it was the banana'.[38] If they joined the army they often did so because they could find no other work. If they celebrated at imperial high moments, they did so because they had loved ones 'out there'. If they broke up meetings or were arrested after smashing the windows of anti-war shopkeepers, they were most often led on by clerks and students. Henry Pelling finds 'no evidence of a direct continuous support for the cause of imperialism among any section of the working class'.[39]

The working class may have been less than enthusiastic, but the lower middle class seized upon patriotism as an answer to sharpened anxieties about social status and economic insecurity. The expansion of the commercial sector had destroyed the uniqueness of clerical work, much of which was now being done by women, and underemployment brought new divisions of labour and new kinds of social relations with employers. As the hegemony of mid-Victorian respectability declined, demands for a national patriotic consensus allowed one to 'belong' not only to a group but to a code of values which emphasised selfless duty, sacrifice and obedience (the necessary virtues of the clerk). The characteristic concepts of jingo rhetoric in the 1890s (vague appeals to British rights, British superiority and British valour) were the necessary adjuncts of popular political ideology. The jingo crowd sought to enforce this consensus which, in part, was created and represented by the new mass-circulation and inter-class newspapers such as the *Daily Mail*.[40] Imperialism was ideal for the new journalism. Imaginative tales of foreign lands were further spiced by the thrills and passions associated with the possibility of a clash with other great powers. As military potboilers the wars it provided were 'sufficiently distant as not to be too distressing, but successful enough to sustain confidence, with occasional setbacks to maintain tension'.[41]

In late Victorian Britain the new mass media provided the means for transmitting dominant values on a universal scale. In a period of high imperialism the press created and represented a national patriotic consensus. At a time of rising living standards it also encouraged a positive identification with the existing social system by emphasising the freedom of individuals to be consumers.

2 Popular Press

The origins of both mass media and mass market were inextricably bound together. It is one of the more persistent historical myths that the popular press was a response to the Education Act of 1870. A generation before the Act made provision for mass education, there was a reading public large enough to have supported a popular press of considerable size.[1] The indigenous street literature of ballads and broadsheets supplemented by chapbooks, penny novels, Sunday newspapers and Saturday magazines all bear witness to this. Richard Altick, for example, looks to the early nineteenth century to identify a new mass reading public which included skilled workers, small shopkeepers, higher domestic servants, physicians, teachers and an increasing number of white-collar workers.[2] To be sure, a mass press needed universal education, but, as Harold Perkin says, this is 'a truism of egregious triviality'.[3] The new literates were, in any case, often the poorest members of society and so could not afford to buy papers. Overcrowded housing, poor lighting, exhaustion from work, and the lack of spare money and spare time inhibited the growth of the popular press as much as illiteracy did. Only when the opportunities for leisure had been expanded would a popular press be feasible, and then, as with leisure in the new consumer society, it would have to be tailored to meet the needs of the emerging mass market.

More time, more money and more people all helped to increase demand for periodical literature at the same time as legislation and technical improvements were helping to decrease the cover price of publications. The repeal of the 'taxes on knowledge' (abolition of advertisement tax in 1853, stamp duty in 1855, and paper duty in 1861), together with the introduction of steam-driven rotary presses, continuous web-fed paper (now made from wood pulp), linotype composition and the communication revolution brought by the spread of railways and telegraph all contributed to lower production costs.[4] The resulting expansion in the periodical press meant that by 1900 daily papers were read by one adult in every five or six, and the Sunday papers by one adult in three.[5] When Lady Bell visited 200 working-class households in Middlesbrough, she found that in 80 per cent of them were people who could read and had an inclination to do so, with newspapers and magazines being the most common form of literature.[6] It was the penny weeklies which enjoyed the greatest boost in circulation. The Sundays such as *Lloyd's* and the *News of the World* continued to be popular, but by 1900 relative newcomers such as *Tit-Bits*, *Answers* and *Pearson's Weekly* between them were selling over two million copies each week.[7]

Circulation was the sine qua non of commercial success. The aim of publishers was not that papers should necessarily be read, but simply that they should be sold. What the Harmsworth brothers discovered was that in the new mass market the greatest profits for publishers were to be found in selling space to advertisers.[8] Harmsworth did not invent popular journalism (Sunday papers had already done that), but, as Raymond Williams has noted, 'the true "Northcliffe Revolution" is less an innovation in actual journalism than a radical change in the economic basis of newspapers'.[9] Increased revenue from the new display advertising subsidised a lower cover price to boost circulation which in turn attracted advertisers. Circulation thus became the keystone to the new journalistic credo, and it was the Harmsworths who established the system of publishing net sales figures certified by chartered accountants.

As the market expanded running costs increased, driving the industry from its traditional small-scale, multiple, structure towards a large-scale integrated one. From the 1890s onwards the old proprietorial system of publishing was being replaced by the development of groups or chains of newspapers and magazines. The flotation of such corporations as public companies served to change papers from public servants or means of political influence into financial investments. It was, in effect, the commercialisation of the periodical press.[10] By 1897 T.H.S Escott could write that whereas Delane of *The Times* had been 'the interpreter of middle class English thought', modern journalists had become 'the custodians of a commercial interest'.[11] Kennedy Jones, Harmsworth's right-hand man, put it more bluntly: 'The balance sheet is the only honest test of a paper's soundness.'[12]

The changing relationship between newspaper and reader was reflected in the 'new journalism', a term coined by Matthew Arnold and which quickly became the conventional description for developments in the press from the 1880s onwards. It had much to recommend it, wrote Arnold in 1887, 'it is full of ability, novelty, variety, sensation, sympathy, generous instincts', but like the new voters, 'the democracy', it had one great fault. It was 'feather-brained'.[13] Described by Alan Lee as 'a mixture of journalistic and typographical devices, which taken together constituted a new style of journalism',[14] it showed how the reader–paper relationship had changed 'from the ideal one of a tutorial and intellectual nature, to one of a market character'.[15] The old journalism had performed a responsibly critical role summed up by J.R. Scott of the *Manchester Guardian*, 'to

make readable righteousness remunerative'.[16] In the new journalism righteousness was hardly a consideration. Politics was confined to 'opinion'
and usually forsaken for sport and entertainment. Typographically the new
journalism was characterised by cross-heads, shorter paragraphs, larger
and more informative headlines, and the increasing use of illustration. Its
journalistic innovations were the stop press, concentration on the human
interest story, and, possibly its most significant feature, the interview,
which had been introduced from America and was extensively used by
W.T. Stead.[17]

For all the life, energy and downright sensationalism of the new journalism, it was necessary to avoid material that might be objectionable to
readers, proprietors or, more importantly, advertisers. In 1900, soon after
leaving the editorship of the *Daily Chronicle*, H.W. Massingham reflected
upon the 'Ethics of editing'. It was in the interests of advertisers to please
the mass of the readers, he believed, and in the interests of proprietors to
please the advertisers. The result was

> conventional opinion on all subjects...opinion believe[d] to be conge-
> nial to the mass of the people in England who own property, and go to
> the more costly seats in the theatres and opera houses, and accept,
> without question, most English institutions as they exist. It is clear that
> the ideas of these people are in the main shared by less wealthy classes,
> the similarity of views of Englishmen, rich and poor, being one of the
> sources of our national strength.[18]

However, it is precisely because of this conventionality that the press is so
interesting for the historian and worthy of general and systematic study. 'It
represents and articulates, as nothing else does, what was ordinary about
Victorian Britain', according to Shattock and Wolff, and during the
Victorian period the press became 'the context within which people lived
and worked and thought, and from which they derived their...sense of the
outside world'.[19]

Economic reorganisation, therefore, forced the periodical press to identify, represent and articulate consensual interests and values. However, the
public contribution to consensus formation was an illusion of the new
journalism because the relationship of reader to paper was distorted by the
demands of the market.[20] The concentration of ownership and the depend-
ence upon advertisers denied access to the press for the public, especially
if their views were of a more radical nature. By excluding alternative perspectives and 'naturalising' the social and political structure, the modern
press contributed to 'the normative integration of British society'.
Compared with the early militant press the new popular journalism

provided a very different construction of reality. A view of society as a system of class exploitation gave way to a portrayal of different sections of the community being interdependent within a shared 'national interest'. In encouraging a positive identification with the social system, the stress was no longer on class solidarity, but upon the individual who was 'free to obtain the rewards that his own efforts would bring and to participate as a consumer in the growing prosperity of industrial Britain'.[21]

The new periodicals were particularly attractive to advertisers who were increasingly operating through freshly established advertising agencies. The 1902 edition of *Practical Advertising* noted that prominent in the history of modern journalism was 'the sudden and rapid rise to the summit of popular favour of the new style of cheap magazine'.[22] The new magazines were a vast improvement on the old low-priced publications. 'The long dryasdust article, poorly printed, without illustrations, and appealing to one class of reader only is a thing of the past.' We find instead 'pressing topics of the time, treated interestingly, and presented in a vivid fashion comprehensible by all'. In the days before niche marketing, sheer quantity of readers was seen as the key to success, and the possibility of presenting one's goods not to 'one class of reader' but all readers was obviously an enticing prospect.[23] Indeed, for all the differences between individual publications, what most had in common was the generality of their contents.

The fragmentation of the periodicals market into specialist areas has meant the decline of these general family magazines. In terms of their range, appeal and subject matter the nearest modern equivalent would be television. A strong visual element and a family-centred audience; a regular diet of fiction and features; series, serials and one-offs; comedy, tragedy, romance and adventure; social comment, travelogue, science and natural history; celebrities and competitions – a weekday evening's programme schedule bears comparison with an upmarket monthly of Queen Victoria's day.

But what are we to do with this embarrassment of riches?

Acknowledging the great sea of material that lies before us, the most common (and most practical) approach is to take 'samplings and soundings'.[24] The danger, of course, is that through our own selectivity we destroy the very 'ordinariness' we wish to study. On the other hand, if we do not select, and simply 'immerse' ourselves in the subject we are faced with the prospect of drowning. My strategy has been to have a sample that tries to be both wide-ranging and representative – eight titles for close examination and statistical analysis chosen to meet a number of criteria: large circulations and long runs of continuous publication with enough diversity and coherence for comparisons to be made between publishers and across potential markets. This in itself gave a research base of over 6000 individual issues. Add to that a more general, though less systematic, reading of the periodical press and we have a sizeable chunk of turn-of-the-century magazine Britain.

Let me introduce the principal players.

PEARSON'S MAGAZINE AND *PEARSON'S WEEKLY*

Cyril Arthur Pearson was always intently interested in something, but never interested in anything for very long. Once he had established *Pearson's Weekly* he grew bored with going into the office every day. His next passion was to be the *Daily Express*, then after that the Tariff Reform campaign. The key to his character, says biographer Sidney Dark, was a zest for life and hunger for experience. He was not a philosopher, but a man of action. 'Abstract propositions left him cold.'[25] The *Dictionary of National Biography* is a little less coy. 'His opinions were the caprice of his uncriticised intuitions, and he was resentful of opposition, impatient of argument.' His career was, it says, 'perhaps more alarming than edifying. Intellectually he was unfitted to guide, much less to inform, public opinion.'[26]

The *Express*, which Pearson set up in 1900, proclaimed of itself that 'Our policy is patriotic; our policy is the British Empire', and it was Pearson's social imperialism that led him to found the Tariff Reform League with Joseph Chamberlain and act as Chamberlain's publicity manager throughout the campaign. It was for his reputation as a promoter that Baden-Powell enlisted Pearson as business associate, publisher and adviser to market the embryonic Boy Scout movement. For his part, Pearson was, says Dark, 'Immediately attracted by the scheme, by the sport of it, by its open-air atmosphere, and by the fact that it was sure to bring both discipline and interest to growing boys'.[27] No doubt he also saw its financial potential. Pearson organised the publicity campaign for the scheme, put up £1000 to cover scouting's initial expenses, arranged publication of Baden-Powell's *Scouting for Boys*, published the magazine *The Scout*, and even helped in selecting the name of the movement.[28] Percy Everett, who was editorial manager responsible for all of Pearson's magazines, was also a keen scout rising, in the 1940s, to the position of deputy chief scout. At the times of Pearson's boredom with his publications, or, after 1909, his partial retirement from work because of failing eyesight, Everett would almost certainly have ensured that the *Pearson's* stable continued to reflect its owner's concerns.

Advertisements announcing the launch of *Pearson's Magazine* in 1896 claimed that it would be 'clean without being twaddly'. Editorial goals were to create wonder about the ordinary and to tell a good story.[29] The magazine created and satisfied curiosity with the aim of informing and entertaining the reader. ('Infotainment' is a new word for an old ideal.) An editorial in 1904 expressed the belief that a rising circulation was evidence of the magazine's reflecting public taste. Most popular, it said, were the articles on art and the high-quality literature, but the editorial also pointed out that only half the magazine was taken up by fiction:

> There is hardly any range of human thought and activity that has not been covered at one time or another by our articles. If these reflect the public taste, they prove that taste to have a decided leaning towards science. *Pearson's* has been first in the field many times with authentic accounts of science's latest wonders.[30]

Not content with simply reflecting public taste, *Pearson's Magazine* took up a more campaigning stance in 1906 with a series of articles on 'Pressing problems of today'. The titles of the articles exposed the magazine's concerns: 'The prevalence of insanity', 'The waste of infant life', 'How to make a nation of marksmen'.[31]

The motto of *Pearson's Weekly* was carried on its masthead, 'To Interest, to Elevate, to Amuse', and an editorial in the first issue declared: 'It will be our object to impart to the pages of this journal a higher tone than at present exists in the class of literature to which it belongs, without detracting in any way from its interesting and amusing features.'[32] In an editorial retrospect in 1909 Pearson was to write that: 'As popular taste runs at present such a paper as no. 1 of Pearson's Weekly would be voted far too dull and heavy.' The new preference for less informative material was, he said, a change which he deplored.[33] Described by Chamberlain as 'the greatest hustler I have ever known', Pearson used a number of promotional devices to increase the circulation of the magazine. These included insurance schemes, the marketing of various *Pearson's* products, the spraying of eucalyptus oil on the cover as a preventative for influenza during the epidemic of 1892, and competitions (including the offer to his women readers of £100 a year for life and a good husband).[34]

TIT-BITS

Started by George Newnes in 1881, *Tit-Bits* struck upon a successful formula that was to earn Newnes and his imitators Harmsworth and

Pearson considerable fortunes. The formula was for a pot-pourri of information and anecdotes designed to amuse and entertain. When one correspondent complained that there was too much humour in the magazine, the editorial response was an unashamed 'no doubt'. 'There are too many croakers nowadays. We stand for laughter and hope and cheerfulness and brightness all the time.'[35] Moreover, *Tit-Bits* was proud to be a 'pioneer paper', being the first with railway insurance, the first with competitions, and the first with big prizes – having given away houses, £1000 prizes, and even thrown coins from the air on to a grateful public below.[36]

Quite clearly a scissors-and-paste production, it marshalled a miscellany of unrelated facts and figures under headings like 'Tit-Bits Inquiry Column', 'Personal Tit-Bits', 'Tit-Bits of Legal Information', and 'Tit-Bits of General Information'. Its obsession with royalty, sport and the stage was matched only by a fascination for amazing statistics, the cost of things, and marriage and courtship. Its articles were a celebration of the weird and wonderful, and expose a taste for the bizarre, even the macabre – as with 'The romance and reality of a crematorium', or 'Celebrated people whose mothers have been buried alive'.[37]

CASSELL'S MAGAZINE AND CASSELL'S SATURDAY JOURNAL

A former salaried agent of the National Temperance Society, John Cassell set up a wholesale tea and coffee business to give working men cheap substitutes for alcohol. By nature more of a reformer than a capitalist, his philanthropic and business interests were inseparable. He had entered into the publishing industry, he said, 'for the purpose of publications which I believed were calculated to advance the moral and social well-being of the working classes'.[38] It was with a policy of providing good educational and recreational reading for working men that Cassell launched the *Popular Educator*, the *Working Man's Friend*, and, in 1853, *Cassell's Illustrated Family Paper*. It remained company policy long after the sale of the company in 1855 and Cassell's death in 1865.

The 'family' public was, according to Cassell's historian Simon Nowell-Smith, vast and amorphous.

> ...limited both socially and intellectually to a lower level than the subscribers to *Macmillan's* and *Blackwood's*, the *Cornhill* and *Temple Bar*, [it] did not ask for literature: it asked simply for entertainment, and the publishers saw to it that the entertainment should be innocuous, and monotonous.[39]

For the 'greybeards' at the head of the company in the 1890s, the success of a popular magazine was seen to rest upon the avoidance of trouble. The editorial space of the magazine was filled with glowing references to the monarchy, a superabundance of royalty on its birthday pages, numerous articles on 'other courts', and patriotic features on the armed forces. The mainstay of any family magazine, however, was its fiction, and for Cassell's safety lay in those writers who would conform to company rules and whose work 'suited the greatest number of lower and lower-middle class families and [which] could with propriety be given to the sons and daughters of those families to read'.[40]

But by the 1890s the company was in decline and its monthly magazine faced stiff (even overwhelming) competition from the newly established *Strand Magazine*, *Windsor Magazine* and, later, *Pearson's Magazine*. In 1894 the price was reduced by a penny, and in 1896 Bonavia Hunt, editor for over twenty years, was replaced by Max Pemberton to inject new life into the old magazine. The magazine was enlarged, more colour was introduced, and the talents of writers such as Jerome K. Jerome, Kipling and Rider Haggard were bought. The 'Family' was dropped from the title. After Pemberton's departure in 1905, the magazine resumed its decline. In 1912, however, under new editor Newman Flower, its fortunes revived. Renamed *Cassell's Magazine of Fiction*, it was enlarged to more than 260 pages printed on cheap art paper and reduced in price to five pence, with each issue including a complete novel, about twenty short stories, four or five articles, and a fashion section. The circulation increased with every issue.

Cassell's answer to *Tit-Bits*, the *Saturday Journal*, was started with the object of providing livelier reading than had yet been deemed appropriate to the 'family' magazine. Certainly articles like 'The humorous side of wearing an artificial leg' would hardly have been given space in its more upmarket sister.[41] It was, says Nowell-Smith, 'one degree less "bitty" than *Tit-Bits* though several of its pages were made up of instructive or facetious short paragraphs'.[42] The *Journal* often printed the editor's request for 'Smart, Chatty, Anecdotal articles'. As with the monthly *Magazine* its chief appeal lay in its fiction with stories of the Wild West, detective stories, tales of the sea, and 'sensational' serials (a new departure for the traditionally staid Cassell's).

Describing itself as 'A magazine of useful and entertaining literature' it would have been difficult to break the Cassell's mould. In 1902 an editorial retrospective ascribed the *Journal*'s success to the older Cassell's values of 'healthily interesting and entertaining the public'. The editorial expressed pride in announcing that not a single libel action had been brought against the *Journal*, and boasted of the 'miles of sound, whole-some reading' contained in the *Journal*'s one thousand issues to date.[43] The social conscience of the *Journal* could be seen in the 1890s in special features like 'Life dramas of the London poor' and in 1913 in its 'Workers at work' series with its heroic presentation of working-class labours and hardship. The *Journal*'s regular 'Workers' page', started in 1908, was sympathetic to the plight of the working man, but sought improvement through self-help. Articles on the hard lives of workers were mixed with practical hints for small businesses.[44]

From 1911 to 1913 the *Journal* printed a series of full-page drawings under the heading 'The world as it is' (later called 'If Christ came to London'), which give illustrative insights into the Cassell's perspective on the world. Often setting out a polarity between rich and poor, the drawings highlighted the iniquities of modern society (tramps on a bench and a fat vicar in a carriage; poor children in the rain and a rich butcher in a restaurant). The poor may be poor, but poverty was a virtue and many drawings contrasted happy paupers with the sad, empty lives of the rich. Wealth was nothing beside the joys of children and young lovers, and strength could be found in the Cassell's trinity of family, faith and temperance – a rich woman envies the poor woman with children; the shadow of the cross falls on the speculator, gambler, burglar and murderer; the shadow of a bottle falls on a mother and child waiting for the father to come home.[45]

GOOD WORDS

'I wish very sincerely my monthly to do good work', the Right Reverend Donald Macleod told one of his contributors, and it was as a ministry that he saw his editorship.[46] Taking over as editor in 1872, Macleod had a close relationship with his contributors and was careful to state the aims of the magazine when engaging new authors and indicating the sort of material he did not want. Despite such editorial meddling, or perhaps even because of it, Macleod was highly regarded by many authors.[47] His religion, however, was strongly non-denominational. Rising through the ranks of the Presbyterian Church to become Moderator of the General Assembly of the Church of Scotland, he was nonetheless very sympathetic towards the Union of the Church of Scotland and the United Free Church, and brought resentment and protests from his fellow ministers by refusing to differentiate between denominations on his rounds. Revival meetings were another matter. 'The whole thing has too much of Yankee spasmodics about it for my taste', he confessed to his mother.[48]

In an editorial retrospect, Macleod referred to the origins of the magazine and its aim of

> supplying in a cheap form literature and art of the highest class, and, without being religious in the technical sense in which one speaks of 'a religious magazine', would yet be consistent in tone with what is most sacred in Christian conviction.[49]

The 'high purpose' of the magazine's early promoters (Alexander Strahan and Macleod's brother, Rev. Norman Macleod) had been 'anxiously pursued from the first', for

> in addition to papers of a directly religious nature, the contents of Good Words has always embraced healthy fiction, as well as popular articles on science, art, travel and literature contributed by the foremost writers of the day. Good Words has tried to be broad and human in tone and to reflect the interests common to all intelligent and right-minded readers.[50]

This then was the framework for the magazine: not stridently religious but Christian in 'tone' and whose contents would be 'healthy', 'popular', 'broad and human' for 'right-minded readers'.

The decline of the Victorian Sunday and the corresponding fall in demand for respectable material for Sunday reading meant also that the *raison d'être* of the magazine had gone.[51] With the new century the magazine embarked on a desperate search for a wider readership and it does look as though the finances of the magazine were not as healthy as they once were. The days of paying Gladstone 100 guineas an article for his series on the 'Impregnable rock of holy scripture' were over.[52] The services of top scientists were becoming harder to get. Oliver Lodge, for example, wrote to Macleod in 1904, presumably after a request for an article:

> There have been so many articles on the Electric Theory of Matter lately that I hardly feel inclined to write another just now....
>
> I must say that the American magazines or those under American management have a much more attractive system of payment than the old established English ones, and doubtless it is for this reason that they attract such articles as one feels inclined to write.
>
> I think that English publishers will have to mend their ways in this matter.
>
> When one can get £40 for an article it seems absurd to place it where they offer only about £5.[53]

More and more professional writers with a 'racy pen' were replacing the professional scientists as the magazine's contributors, and throughout the 1890s the amount of natural history (the most 'amateur' of the sciences) had risen accordingly.

From 1902 onwards the magazine went through a period of rapid change. Macleod could see the signs of the times in an editorial retrospect of 1904 when he referred to 'a marked tendency towards more sensationalism in much of our periodical literature and art'.[54] It was a new taste that he had tried in some small way to satisfy. The evidence of style and content suggests that the magazine was attempting to become more downmarket with promotional devices such as competitions, and the start of a section titled 'Things and other things', a miscellaneous compilation of information which was little more than an upmarket *Tit-Bits*. But it was not enough. Within eighteen months *Good Words* was merged with the *Sunday Magazine* and changed beyond all recognition. Passing through the hands of various owners, the magazine was finally bought by Harmsworth's Amalgamated Press and turned into a penny weekly. The noble old magazine had finally succumbed to the new journalism.[55]

COTTAGER AND ARTISAN AND *THE CLARION*

More overtly 'ideological' and proselytising than the mass circulation family magazines looked at so far, the *Cottager and Artisan* and the *Clarion* extend our range for useful comparative perspectives.

Published by the Religious Tract Society, the *Cottager and Artisan* was an evangelical temperance monthly. It came in two distinct parts: an outer section with articles of general interest, and an inner pull-out section available for separate (and free) distribution that was more Bible based and 'preachy' – to mix metaphors, the sugar-coating on the pill and the meat in the sandwich. Celebrating its golden jubilee, the magazine proclaimed that: 'For fifty years it has striven to supply wholesome, interesting, and instructive reading for working people.' Articles, it said, were written in simple language 'well adapted to instruct and edify, both in things temporal and spiritual; to comfort and strengthen the poor and tempted; and to make the cottager's home in every respect happier and more prosperous'.[56] Temperance, Sunday observance and the virtues of work regularly found prominent places within its pages. 'Life is for work', declared one article clearly, stating the magazine's own position on the matter. 'God gives to everyone some special work to do...and you cannot be really happy or successful until you get into the very groove for which God designed you, and set yourself with all your might to the task which He makes you to fulfil.'[57]

These were hardly the sentiments of the staff at the *Clarion*. Theirs was a different gospel to be preached.

In 1891, following an argument over his socialist views, Robert Blatchford left the *Sunday Chronicle* to set up his own socialist paper. He took with him his brother Montague, A.M. Thompson and E.F. Fay. The paper they set up was the *Clarion*. In 1912 Blatchford told his readers that the founders of the paper had started the *Clarion* 'in order to get that freedom to advocate Socialism, which was denied to them by other newspapers'.[58] The paper's first leading article, under Blatchford's old *Chronicle* pen-name of 'Nunquam', declared that the policy of the *Clarion* was 'a policy of humanity, a policy not of party, sect, or creed; but of justice, of reason and mercy'.[59] It was, however, an idiosyncratic brand of socialism that Blatchford peddled. 'We were out for socialism and nothing but socialism', he wrote in his autobiography, but added that 'we were Britons first and Socialists next'.[60] This 'imperial socialism' did not find favour with many within the labour movement, and the *Clarion* was to lose face and readers over its support for the war in South Africa and Blatchford's anti-German jingoism prior to the Great War. In 1910 following its attacks on free trade, its warnings about Germany, and its support for compulsory military service, the paper was boycotted by the Labour Party. Blatchford's estrangement from socialism grew ever more complete during the war. In 1924 he voted Conservative.[61]

The *Clarion* called itself a 'labour paper', but it aimed for a wider appeal than this term might allow and, as the paper often lamented, 'labour' did not support it. 'More than half our readers are not working men at all. And if we made the mistake which other labour papers have made, and devoted our columns entirely to labour questions, we should be ruined in three months.'[62] The answer to why a socialist paper could not thrive was, according to Blatchford, quite simple – there were not enough socialists. 'Moral: make more socialists.'[63] This 'educationalist' strategy of Blatchford informed the intellectual, moral and political stance of the *Clarion*. The paradox for an educationalist paper, however, is that once the readers become educated they move on to read other things. Nevertheless, the paper became a movement in itself, and Harrison's opinion that 'the *Clarion* movement was always bigger and better than its admired but vain and immature leader' seems to be a fair assessment. Around missionary vans, cycling clubs, 'Cinderella clubs', *Clarion* choirs, handicraft guilds, field clubs and holiday camps, 'a nationwide society of hopeful people came together in the name of human fellowship'.[64]

Taking the magazines together, and others like them, they fall into two clear categories. Monthlies like *Pearson's Magazine, Cassell's Magazine* and *Good Words* were most often well illustrated with drawings and photographs (sometimes even in colour) and printed on high-quality paper. They usually cost sixpence an issue and had between 72 and 120 pages. Weeklies like *Pearson's Weekly, Cassell's Saturday Journal, Tit-Bits* and the *Clarion* were poorly illustrated with only occasional line drawings and printed on low-quality paper. They were a penny each and had between eight and 24 pages. The *Cottager and Artisan* was unusual in being a well-illustrated 12-page penny monthly.

Circulation figures are notoriously hard to work out not least because of the cultivated confusion between print run, sales and readers. There are, however, some indications. In 1891 the circulation for *Pearson's Weekly* was given as 100 000 and rising, but this was raised by a missing word competition in 1892 to a certified figure of 305 000. *Tit-Bits* averaged around half a million copies a week and regularly topped the 600 000 mark. During its best years in the 1870s, *Good Words* sold more copies than any other monthly with a circulation of between 80 000 and 130 000. Ellegard puts the figure at 100 000 and rising, but in 1895 *Practical Advertising* lists the circulation as 50 000 and, as we have seen, there is reason to suspect that the figure may have been falling further after 1900.[65] Circulation figures for the *Clarion* indicate that its readership was far from loyal. Starting off at 30–40 000 in the early 1890s, sales rose to 60 000 following the publication of the penny edition of Blatchford's *Merrie England*, but dropped with the paper's support for the South African War. After the 1906 general election had returned 29 Labour MPs, the circulation was regularly above 50 000 and reached a peak of 82 000 in 1908 before Blatchford's jingoism alienated his readers, whose numbers plummeted to around 10 000 with the outbreak of war in Europe.

Readers are equally difficult to identify. It is easy to imagine that a six-penny monthly would fit middle-class patterns of consumption and that conversely a penny weekly would be predominantly bought by a more working-class readership. To some extent a study of magazine content bears this out. A lengthy article in *Pearson's Magazine* on 'The crushing of the middle class' which attacked the burdens of rates and taxation was hardly designed for a sympathetic working-class reading.[66] Cassell's historian Nowell-Smith writes of the readership for *Cassell's Magazine* as being 'lower and lower-middle class families'. Similarly it has been said of *Good Words* that its fiction was accepted for family reading 'by the broad mass of respectable, church going people in the Victorian middle class'.[67] We have firmer evidence of readership when we turn to the weeklies. Published correspondence to *Pearson's Weekly* from tradesmen, clerks, grocers' assistants, book-keepers, plumbers, servants and employees of servants suggests a wide-ranging readership probably centred on the lower middle class. Of course, this is only indicative of people who wrote to the magazine and not necessarily of those who simply read it. A more random, and perhaps more representative, sampling can be found for *Tit-Bits*. Lists of prizewinners in competitions based on pure chance include clerks, assistants, labourers, businessmen and civil servants, together with their wives and daughters. *Tit-Bits* had come to be regarded as the traveller's paper, and a higher circulation in the summer months might have reflected increased demand for light entertainment from holidaymakers.[68] It may be that all one can safely say is that the monthlies were 'upmarket' publications compared with the 'downmarket' weeklies.

Even so, the popularisation of science seems to have been a more upmarket pursuit. A quantitative content analysis of non-fiction editorial space shows that the monthlies were willing to devote to science over twice as much space as the weeklies (10 per cent as against 4 per cent). Associated with this upmarket presentation is a preference for articles on technology and nature compared with the downmarket concern for the human sciences. In part this is explained by the weeklies' more practical interest in the 'diet and hygiene' type of material, but it also reflects a desire for articles of 'human interest' in those magazines with a greater inclination towards the new journalism. The characteristics of each market are dramatically illustrated by the experience of *Good Words*, which changed from a monthly to a weekly under the same editor. As an upmarket monthly 12 per cent of its editorial space could be classified as 'science', with a great preponderance of natural history. To be a downmarket weekly meant a minimal amount of science (2 per cent), less natural history and more articles on health matters. It was also science that, like *Tit-Bits*, became more concerned with the curious, the strange and the bizarre.

3 The Popularisation of Science

Two men in a pub, one has just come from a science lecture and talks of the world before Adam:

> This yer radium, Charlie, is reely life. On'y life is raely a jelly, what you find in the sea. So this jelly is radium, you see, on'y they can't find the jelly, an radium is scarce, so they invented electricity. And there's radium in electricity, if they could on'y find the way to get it out. But there ain't no jelly in it – see?[1]

This imaginary scene from the *Clarion* of 1905 is a neat vignette of the gulf between the science of the laboratory and the science of the street, home, factory or, indeed, pub. The mishmash of invention, electricity, radium and 'jelly' (protoplasm) exposes some of the more dominant themes in the popular imagination. The garbled account is what many have now come to expect from popularised science, and then was obviously common enough for it to be a source of humour. However, the science lecture, although still popular, was having to compete with other media as a source of perceptions and understanding of science, and not just the media but the very world in which people lived.

It was, as many commentators observed, a 'scientific age'. The late Victorian and Edwardian general public could hardly avoid science even if they had wanted to. The impact of technology upon everyday life would, in a rudimentary way, have given them first-hand experience of scientific innovation, at least in its applied form. Dramatic feats of engineering and the increasingly widespread use of electricity, particularly for lighting, were transforming the environment. An expanding rail network provided an efficient distribution system for a revolution in retailing, while technology not only cheapened traditional products, but also created new ones such as the bicycle, sewing machine, phonograph and camera, which, if not bought, could be eyed avariciously in the shops.[2]

Also unavoidable were the many advertisements for patent medicines. Appliances and applications, pills and potions, remedies and restoratives were all on offer to help keep body and soul together. In a single issue of *Pearson's Magazine* we can find:

28

Noses – the only patent nose machines in the world. Improve ugly noses of all kinds. Scientific yet simple. Can be worn during sleep...

Or, to build up vitality and strength:

The 'Ajax' battery is a scientific device for saturating the nerves and vitals with a steady, unbroken current of electric life, without the least shock or unpleasant sensation.

One would also find the 'Turvey cure for drink and drug habits', a phosphoric remedy from 'Dr Lalor' called 'phosphodyne', and 'Spermin', an organic essence from the 'Organo-therapeutic Institute of Professor von Poehl and sons'. There were others, and they were all in addition to the magazine's regular advertisements for Eno's fruit salts, Kutnow's, Wincarnis, Tatcho, Zam-Buk and Beechams Pills.[3]

Recreation could also have brought the public into contact with science, in a more institutional setting, although how effective this might be was open to debate. It was reported that zoos were becoming increasingly popular, with the animals being given more room, and the move to realism in taxidermy had transformed many museums 'from dreary sepulchres into palaces of pleasure',[4] an opinion, it has to be said, that was not shared by everyone. 'The very word "museum" sends a cold chill to the heart', wrote one contributor to the *Clarion*. 'We know those museums. We know the depressing cracked clay pitchers, the dismal miscellaneous armour, the withered butterflies and beetles gone to seed....We know them, and dread them like taxes and long sermons.'[5] Likewise the state of British aquaria gave cause for concern. Many were without fish, some did not even have any water. As one observer noted, a remnant of school Latin should at least bid the visitor to expect water somewhere in the definition, but at some leading aquariums there was none to be found: 'He finds instead a musical hall, the walls in the distance being ornamented with a dado of tanks, with or without – mostly without – water in them, and one or two, maybe, containing an emaciated fish.'[6]

Much more exciting would have been the 'living picture shows'. Furthering the traditions of the magic lantern show, natural history and scientific 'interest' films were an important part of early British film culture. Charles Urban was to the fore in producing this type of film, making series like *Natural History*, *Marine Studies* and *Unseen World* (this last employing new techniques in microcinematography). The continuing interest in scientific films can be seen in the numerous bird studies in film-makers' catalogues, the nature films of F. Percy Smith, and the success of Herbert G. Ponting's record of Scott's Antarctic expedition. It was only from around 1911 onwards that film-makers became increasingly concerned with drama.[7] Like the cinema, the periodical press combined pictures and stories, fact and fiction, in a mélange of entertainment/ education that was, to use the slogan of *Pearson's Weekly*, designed 'to interest, to elevate, and to amuse'.

The people who were to provide this early form of 'infotainment' often remain invisible to the historian's eye. In the weeklies very few contributions appeared with a byline giving the author's name. The magazines seem to have been largely dependent upon staff writers and, with the notable exception of the *Clarion*, who was on the staff is unknown. The monthlies were more reliant upon outside contributions and here it was common practice to give the author's name, or at least pen-name. If we take our sample of eight magazines we find a total of 484 acknowledged contributors of science content, and I have been able to compile at least basic biographical information for 205 of them. If we concentrate on the more prominent contributors we may still be no nearer in getting a clear picture of what a typical contributor was like. There was no 'typical' science writer. Their diversity makes a nonsense of any attempt to construct a single 'type' of populariser. To take some of the more prolific writers we find: F.G. Aflalo (sportsman and writer), Rev. J.M. Bacon (lecturer and aeronaut), Sir Robert Stawell Ball (Professor of Astronomy), S.L. Bensusan (writer), Emma Marie Caillard (poet and essayist), Harry Lowerison (teacher), E.K. Robinson (naturalist and author), Edward Step (naturalist and author), Dr L. Forbes Winslow (physician), and Marcus Woodward (author and journalist). There is the added complication that any one contributor might have a number of career changes, for example the Rev. J.M. Bacon's moves from clergyman to scientific investigator to popular lecturer and writer.

Such multi-varied careers almost defy classification. What we can do though is simply divide the contributors into those who were brought to science writing through their scientific activities ('scientists'), and those who came to it through their literary activities ('writers'). Even so, there were still a number of contributors who could only be classified as 'science writers', and of course others who fitted none of these categories. On this basis the occupational breakdown for contributors to our eight magazines would be: scientists 36 per cent, writers 40 per cent, science writers 6 per cent, and others 18 per cent. However, the almost equal proportion of scientists and writers belies great differences between publishers. Interestingly, the highest ratio of scientists to writers is to be found in the 'religious' *Good Words*. Its science content came from twice as many scientists as writers, and indeed, twice as many scientists as clergymen. Conversely, *Pearson's* science came from writers rather than scientists, reflecting the magazine's interest in natural history and technology, subjects upon which writers tended to concentrate. Scientists were more likely to write on the pure and environmental sciences, as they did for *Good Words*, or on health and medicine, as they did for the *Cassell's* publications.

For the scientists popularisation was not a youthful pursuit. Their average age was fifty, with nearly one third aged sixty or over.[8] They were commonly men at the height of their careers writing about the field of expertise in which their reputations had already been made, often contributing a single article, presumably at the request of an editor. Nor should it be thought that these were men of little consequence. Over one in four merit entries in the *Dictionary of Scientific Biography*. Together with men like Wallace, Lodge, and Ramsay, they included W.F. Barrett (founder of the Society for Psychical Research); Sir William H. Flower (director of the British Museum (Natural History)); and Richard T. Glazebrook (director of the National Physical Laboratory). In addition there was a high proportion of professors and lecturers supplemented by keepers, curators and assistants from museums and botanical gardens.

The science writers, however, were a much younger breed. Nearly all were in their thirties or early forties.[9] Popularisation was part of their profession not something to be turned to in their twilight years. Included among them were men like Richard Gregory (extension lecturer and assistant editor of *Nature*) and Richard and Cherry Kearton (nature photographers, authors and lecturers). The non-scientists were also younger men and women. The lecturer and writer Gertrude Bacon, for example, was only 27 when she first wrote for *Good Words*. Moreover, it is with the non-scientists that the diversity of contributors is most clearly seen. Frank T. Bullen, for example, was a junior clerk at the Meteorological Office when he first started writing for *Good Words*, but later became a full-time author. In those classified as being 'other' than scientists or writers we can find numerous clergymen together with barristers, members of parliament, and the keeper of oriental books at the British Museum. Among them were the ex-governor of Borneo writing about the silkworm; a baronet and retired captain in the Royal Navy writing about microbes; and a 32-year-old company secretary telling 'The story of the field vole'.

About one in eight of the contributors were women. This may not sound much to modern ears, but for the period I believe it can be regarded as a notable proportion. Moreover, the science that these women contributed should not necessarily be thought of as being the more 'soft' sciences such as natural history. This is made quite clear if we look at the three most prolific women writers: Emma Marie Caillard (physics), Grace Frankland (microbiology), and Gertrude Bacon (technology). The subject is certainly one worthy of further study. It may be that journalism provided women opportunities to work in science that were, perhaps, denied to them elsewhere. This may even be true for all forms of journalism and not just science writing. A full survey of magazine contributors is something that awaits the attention of an enterprising researcher. In the meantime I can only offer suggestive hints. The highest levels of women science writers are found in the more proselytising publications. For the *Cottager and Artisan* (where over a quarter of the science contributors were women) and for *Good Words* it may be that a tradition of female religious activism, for example in charity work, increased the likelihood of female journalistic activity. For the *Clarion* on the other hand, accepting or commissioning contributions from women would have been a simple extension of its egalitarian world-view.

However, most of the contributors were historical nonentities. For most of them (58 per cent) even basic biographical information is unavailable. They do not merit any references in biographical dictionaries, and many do not even rise to the heights of a single publication listed in the *British Museum Catalogue*, or a single article recorded in either the Poole or the Wellesley index.[10] But the lack of evidence is indicative in itself. For here we seem to be in 'New Grub Street', the world of literary hacks, wraiths of the reading room at the British Museum mechanically producing their quota of words before disappearing into the shabby gentility of late Victorian London.[11]

We can get some idea of how the Grub Street scientists worked from the advice to would-be authors given by an old hand. 'How I write my *Pearson's Weekly* articles' appeared in 1903 and sets itself the task of researching a piece on 'Why we don't sneeze in our sleep'. True to form, the place to begin is the reading room of the British Museum where the author consults the *Index Catalogue of the Library of the Surgeon General's Office of the United States Army*:

> Here, as I expected, I find innumerable references to the bibliography of sneezing. Books have, it would appear, been written about it, around it, and concerning it, in almost every language under the sun.
>
> But they are mostly too technical.
>
> 'On the inhibitory arrest of the act of sneezing, and its therapeutical applications.' No good that.
>
> 'Sneezing, an obstinate case cured by the galvanocautery, and the cold-wire snare.'

Worse and worse.

Ah! 'Sneezing, snoring, and sleep – a monograph.' This looks promising.[12]

Getting the book and about a dozen others (unspecified), the author then turns to *Poole's Index to Periodical Literature* to gain a more general point of view. Fanciful as this account might seem, it may not be too far from the truth. *Poole's Index* was also one of the reference sources listed by one of the *Pearson's* staff when they described 'Books writers write from'. Other sources included the *Zoological Record*, the *Catalogue of the Royal Geographical Society*, *Quain's Dictionary of Medicine*, *Tuke's Dictionary of Psychological Medicine*, and *Taylor on Poisons*.[13]

Paradoxical as it may seem, journalistic practice was not necessarily conducive to simplification. It was not uncommon, for example, particularly in scissors-and-paste productions like *Tit-Bits*, to lift reports from *Nature*, source unacknowledged, often reduced to a single sentence, and degutted of all but the barest details. Methodology and experimental data would be discarded. Only the result, the 'fact', would remain, copied verbatim from the original, complete with all technical terminology and void of all explanation. Such rewrites were usually taken from *Nature*'s 'Societies and Academies' section or from its 'Notes' column, these being less specialised and less technical than other sections, and more concise, more readable and presumably more accessible to the average journalist. Consequently, since the work of British scientists received fuller coverage in the rest of the magazine and tended not to appear in these sections, the impression one gets from these lifted pieces is of science being an activity peculiar to foreigners. How far this might have fuelled the debate over the 'bankruptcy' of British science is a matter for conjecture.

Naturally such downmarket science journalism did not find much favour with the more upmarket periodicals devoted to popular science like *Science Gossip* which often took great delight in pointing out the inaccuracies of newspaper 'scientists'. Usually there was a supercilious air about the way it reported the scientific errors of others, but a more serious tone was struck when the editor John T. Carrington reproached the *Daily Mail* for a 'silly' article on butterfly-hunting:

There is, however, a responsibility as a teacher of the crowd attached to the editing of such a paper....We would recommend the writer to get his facts before committing his teachings to the wide world. When will there be a science censor for news-papers?[14]

Journalistic ignorance, however, was regarded as a vital element in the process of popularisation. The editor W.T. Stead gave the following advice to readers of *Cassell's Magazine*:

> In editing a newspaper, never employ an expert to write a popular article on his own subject, better employ someone who knows nothing about it to tap the expert's brains, and write the article, sending the proof to the expert to correct. If the expert writes he will always forget that he is not writing for experts but for the public, and will assume that they need not be told things which, although familiar to him as ABC, are nevertheless totally unknown to the general reader.[15]

One contributor put it more succinctly. He always asked people lots of questions, he said, because 'a healthy ignorance is useful to the purveyor of hastily collected facts'.[16]

How much the readers understood is almost impossible to judge. Certainly public ignorance was noted by the magazines. Both *Pearson's Weekly* and *Tit-Bits* found it worthwhile to print articles on 'popular errors' like believing that stones grow, that drowned bodies float when the gall bladder breaks, or that shingles is fatal if the rash encircles the body. Some were probably genuine errors, and can still be found today, but the intention of the articles may simply have been to flatter readers into thinking that they knew better, didn't they?[17]

Rather than give too much credence to such flattery and prejudice, a better guide to scientific literacy (although still an inadequate one) might be to see what contributors assumed their readers already knew. The writer of an article on Edison's work on X-rays, for example, thought it necessary to explain the term 'fluorescent', but not 'specific gravity' or 'atomic weight'. Similarly in *Pearson's Magazine* a feature on underwater telegraph cables explained the term 'ohm' and put 'conductor' and 'resistance' in quotation marks as if they might be unfamiliar, but an article on astronomy mentioned 'spectroscopic studies of the stars and nebulae', 'variable stars', 'motions of the sidereal system', and 'double stars' all without further explanation.[18] *Good Words* seems to have been the magazine that expected most from its readers. A series of articles by Professor A.W. Rucker on underground magnetic rocks, which appeared in 1890, was a complex and abstruse argument with complicated diagrams and tables of figures. Likewise articles on 'Phosphorus and phosphorescence' and 'Natural mineral waters and bacteria' were both quite technical and used difficult language.[19]

The problem of literacy, in a more narrow sense, was a real and important one since language was often seen as separating scientist from layman.

Common to all magazines was an association of science with strange, technical language, the use of which was frequently accompanied by a qualifying 'to put it scientifically' or 'termed by scientists'. We find, for example, a reference to the aniline compound methyltribromofluorescine immediately followed by an apology for the 'eccentricities of chemical nomenclature' and a promise not to inflict on the reader the scientific name for 'methyl violet'.[20] In *Pearson's Weekly* Thomson's description of cathode rays was reproduced with the suggestion that it could be used as a sinker to drown a cat, and even in an article on cave exploration we find the cry: 'Speleology! The word has a forbidding scientific look.'[21] To the ordinary man, claimed an advertisement for the *Harmsworth Popular Science*, the jargon of science was 'a meaningless arrangement of words that neither impress nor instruct'.[22] Nonetheless, it could amuse. Botanists might assert that roses do not have thorns, only 'modified setaceous processes of the epidermis', but as E. Kay Robinson pointed out in *Good Words*: 'It is good moral training, when you have a few buried in the epidermis of the back of your hand, to try and remember this.'[23]

Language not only separated scientist from layman, but also presented what seemed insurmountable difficulties for the populariser. 'It is not easy to make so very dry a subject as structural botany interesting', confessed John J. Ward. 'It is too full of terrifying technical terms.'[24] Modern meteorology may have explained old weather lore, but as one writer lamented, 'unfortunately these explanations can never be popularised. The philosophy of weather prognostics can only be known to those who are prepared to grapple with the difficulties of "isobars", of "cyclones", and of "anti-cyclones".'[25]

The solution was to avoid all 'nomenclature' and to simplify 'technicalities', a process which, in the eyes of scientists, could leave the populariser open to charges of adulteration and distortion. It was, after all, by no means an easy task. As one contributor noted, science was too often expounded by writers who either could not write simply or could only attain simplicity by stripping their subject of all its interest.[26] The limitations this imposed upon contributors was clearly recognised and acknowledged. Professor Andrew Gray admitted that Lord Kelvin's scientific discoveries 'do not lend themselves easily to popular description'. Undeterred, he pressed on with his biographical article on Kelvin's theoretical and abstract work with the caveat that 'of course only the very slightest discussion, couched in the most general and untechnical terms, will be possible'. Nonetheless he still managed to explain the conservation of matter and of energy, dynamics, thermodynamics and the dissipation of energy.[27]

But given that there was so much else to read in the magazines – articles on the royalty of Europe, on politics, on the stars of music hall and theatre, as well as fiction for all tastes – is it likely that there would have been much interest in the features on science and the natural world? Robert Blatchford at the *Clarion* certainly had his doubts. Reviewing *Mutual Aid*, he urged the common man to read not only Kropotkin but also Darwin, Morris, Kidd and Robert Ball to awaken the public conscience and arouse social and political energies. However, for all his belief in his readers' interest in science, he was not so optimistic as to think this would happen. Ask the first hundred men you meet some simple questions like what is a star, what was the glacial epoch, what is socialism, what did Darwin teach, what is protoplasm

> and you will find that they can only tell you about Mr Balfour and Mr Chamberlain, the famous football and cricket players, the price of jute on the market, who played Topsy Gigglewick in 'The Bohemian Boy', and the winner of the Mudshire Handicap. The knowledge of the British crowd is a full century behind the times.[28]

Nevertheless, believing that the road to socialist salvation lay through education, he was keen to associate science with socialism and the working man. In a glowing review of Sir E. Ray Lankester's *Science from an Easy Chair* he makes reference to the number of copies of the *Science History of the Universe* bought by *Clarion* readers, and comments: 'In a paper whose readers have bought 20,000 scientific books in a few months, science is an important matter.' This may well have been true. In 1907 a poll of the magazine's readers to find 'Britain's greatest benefactor' came out with Darwin the clear favourite and other scientists high on the list.[29]

Outside such socialist fervour others were more sceptical. Giving advice on how to sub-edit a daily paper, one contributor to *Pearson's Weekly* told how he learnt to cater for the public taste in news. The opinion of a learned professor on the bearing of radium on the fiscal problem was worthy of a short paragraph, but an article on 'Should society women play marbles?' was marked for half a column.[30] However, radium, like X-rays before it, was one discovery that did appear to have caught the public imagination. In 1904 it was noted in *Cassell's Magazine* that next to the fiscal question and the Russo-Japanese war it formed the very topic of the day, although interest in the substance was thought to be because of its extreme rarity or costliness and the fact that it was obtained by a method new to science, for 'it is scarcely probable that the non-scientific mind is particularly impressed with the importance of the latest contributions to science as such, and, generally speaking, to human knowledge'.[31] This state of affairs was bemoaned by Professor G.G. Henderson in *Good Words*: 'The British public, with all its virtues, can hardly claim for itself that interest in scientific progress which all who have their country's welfare at heart would fain to see.'[32]

The lack of interest, however, may have been due to a basic lack of understanding. In 1898 a book offer of one hundred of the world's most famous books listed only one which might be regarded as scientific (White's *Natural History of Selborne*), explaining that some, presumably including many science books, were left out because the public would not read them and would not understand them if they did.[33] An advert for the *Science History of the Universe* was, understandably, more optimistic, believing that there were few people who did not long to know something of the wonders of science, but felt that in the mind of the average person there was 'a quite unfounded dread of difficulty – an idea that the study of science requires some extraordinary cleverness such as is not required for any other study'.[34] Opening a new science series *Pearson's Weekly* recognised that to many people the very name of science was repellent. There was, it believed, a prevalent mistake of supposing that science was 'dry, difficult, and uninteresting', and that practical science was 'an expensive and rather dangerous pursuit'.[35]

Only very rarely did the magazines invite their readers to be more than passive recipients of the information that they were peddling. The boldest attempt at readership participation was the series 'Science for the unscientific' launched in *Pearson's Weekly* in 1894. Through simple experiments to be performed at home the series explored such topics as electricity, air pressure, optical illusions and the chemistry of salt. However, one series in twenty-five years of eight magazines was hardly a record of feverish activity, and after appearing regularly every fortnight for a year the series degenerated into a collection of tricks and games. Later articles in *Pearson's Magazine*, 'Playing tricks with science' and 'After-dinner science', merely picked up where *Pearson's Weekly* left off.[36] As far as doing science was concerned it was, in the end, to be a form of entertainment, instructive to be sure, but above all simple, inexpensive, novel and amusing.

Common to all the periodicals was the presentation of science not as an approach to the world, but as a collection of facts and feats. In the late Victorian consumer revolution science was another commodity, to be received, not participated in. It was not a process, but a product. In its simplest form 'science as product' joined together technology and consumerism in a marriage which will be more fully discussed in Chapter 8. In a more general sense it was a preference for result over method. Science was, perhaps above all else, practical and useful. For many Victorians any grounds for unease about science were more than offset by its apparent material successes.[37] Scientists themselves may not have looked at their work from a purely utilitarian point of view and may have been, as one article in *Pearson's Magazine* put it, 'more concerned in patiently unravelling the many mysteries by which we are surrounded', but, as the article continued, 'in fact there is hardly a scientific discovery that has not been followed by practical applications of great importance'.[38] Elsewhere in *Pearson's* we can read of the work of the Greenwich Observatory and its use for navigation, and 'see how the most abstruse of the sciences is made of such practical effect that, working hand in hand with commerce, it has conduced to the cheapening of figs and to the putting of tea on the poor man's breakfast table'.[39] The esoteric was firmly rooted (or reduced to) the mundane.

It was just the kind of utilitarian science that all attempts at popularisation would degenerate into, or so the British Association had feared. More important for the Association was the public understanding of scientific method. A focus on method, it believed, not only was recommended on moral and educational grounds, but also, as Richard Yeo has argued, 'offered a point of consensus in the midst of increasing specialisation and allowed the scientific community to promote a unified public image'.[40] However, by the end of the century disagreements on the definition of method, particularly within the Darwinian debates, meant that method was no longer a point of consensus but a point of controversy. Increasing specialisation continued to undermine the unity of science and made it more and more difficult to separate the methods of science from the esoteric knowledge it produced, knowledge which, as we saw earlier, was alien and inaccessible to the general public. In short, for all the hopes of the Association and leading scientists, a focus on method could not narrow the gap between scientific advance and public understanding. Consequently what persisted in the magazines were the most simplistic notions of what constituted scientific practice. Kumatology, or the study of waves, was, said Marcus Tindal in *Pearson's Magazine*, vast, deep and absorbingly interesting, 'yet it is to a great extent made up by the observation of the commonplace'.[41] Science, explained *Pearson's Weekly*, 'is simply a kind of ordered common sense, and scientific observation is little more than making the most of the perception of the senses'.[42]

Science was empirical. It was observation and experiment, Baconian and inductionist. It was only in comparatively modern times, wrote Emma Marie Caillard, that it had become 'considered necessary to verify a scientific theory by systematic observation, or put it to any experimental test'.[43] It was one thing to state a scientific fact, said Sir Robert Ball, but it was quite another to establish that fact with a 'train of reasoning, founded on observation and experiment'.[44] J. Holt Schooling took a similar line in his investigation into dowsing. Urging his readers not to be too sceptical, he argued that the usual process of scientific advance was that 'before a fresh bit of knowledge can be added to the store, its validity is commonly heralded by purely experimental evidences, brought about by empirical tests'. And how was this store of knowledge to be expanded? 'One gets facts before one finds out how the facts come to be facts, and this finding-out process properly belongs to science, while the facts may be, and often are, laid hold of by persons destitute of all scientific knowledge or thought.'[45] The Baconian distinction between empirical research and theoretical speculation was clear, and so too was the division of labour.

By the end of the nineteenth century the 'finding-out process' had increasingly become the preserve of professional scientists. The consolidation of the scientific community was reflected in an increasing emphasis on the conjectural and conceptual features of scientific thinking, thus excluding 'amateur' inductiveness and further enhancing the privileged status of the 'expert'.[46] The role of the amateur in the scientific enterprise had, by and large, been relegated to that of the collector whose function was descriptive, not speculative. In mid-century Robert Chambers could challenge the intellectual authority of the nascent professional scientific community by asserting the rights of the lay public to hypothesise and generalise, but by the 1870s the institutional and educational status of science had become more secure.[47] In the first half of the century popular science periodicals were permeated by an ideology of amateur participation. Emphasising the universal accessibility of the scientific endeavour, the magazines encouraged amateur activity and invoked the image of a republic of science open to all. By the 1860s, however, as Sheets-Pyenson argues, 'a younger generation of scientists began to try to mould the Republic of Science's amateur practitioners into sympathetic supporters of professional high science'.[48] The editors of the magazines, once architects of an alternative 'low scientific culture', became accomplices of the high scientific community, 'replacing the "entrepreneurial ideal" of the self-made science worker with the "professional ideal" of the scientific expert'.[49]

The professionalisation of science and the alienation of the scientists from the public were in line with other developments in popular culture.[50] With the establishment of a segregated professional elite in science, sport and entertainment, the role of those excluded from such circles was reduced to that of spectator, relegated to the touchlines or filling in pools coupons, joining in the chorus but not appearing on stage, and leaving experiments and theories to the 'experts'. Natural history presents a necessary qualification to this general ambience of scientific passivity, and the *Clarion* field clubs are a notable exception to the disinclination of family magazines for encouraging their readers to indulge in scientific pastimes. But the pursuit of nature had wider ramifications than simple participation in the process of science, as we shall see in Chapter 6, and the proposals of Arthur Tansley for 'scientific natural history', or ecology, were as clear a statement of the demarcation between professional and amateur as one could expect to find. Amateur naturalists may well have felt they were being made redundant before then. 'Complaint is made again and again of the approaching extinction of the old fashioned "field naturalist"', wrote one correspondent to *Science Gossip* in 1897 in an attack on 'would-be monopolisers of science'. He had approached a high-ranking official of one scientific institution to ask for help in drawing up a list of flora and fauna of endangered areas around London, but he met only with the reply that 'the members of the society would be much better occupied in counting lamp-posts'.[51]

In the end, it seems, 'Science' was best done by 'Scientists' and popular accounts of science reinforced the idea of a great gulf between the scientist and the public. Inductive amateurs were to leave the 'real' work to be done by theorising professionals. Excluded from the process of science the common reader was left to consume the products of science. Ironically, by setting apart expert from laity, the process of popularisation was in effect a process of alienation.

4 Images

Ignorance, language and the problems of simplification all contributed in making the scientist appear remote (even foreign) and divorced from everyday life. In popular fiction this would lead almost inevitably to the stereotype with which we are now so familiar. Almost to a man (and they were all men) scientists were portrayed as, at best, unemotional and detached, and, at worst, inhuman and insane. Mindless of everyday affairs, fictional scientists were eccentric, unpunctual, slovenly, scruffy. They were cantankerous and short-tempered. Their precision was the precision of the pedant. They actively connived the deaths of others, failed to see the dangerous implications of their work, or were indifferent to the suffering that their research might cause. Lusting after fame or fortune, their dedication often became warped into an obsession leading them from one act of inhumanity to another.

We find, for example, the surgeon ('a doctor of medicine, a master in surgery, a recognised power in the scientific world') who uses his knowledge of anthrax to kill his rival in love. 'If the world but knew to what use I put my knowledge.' He muses over the death of his victim wondering when it will be, but then 'my scientific training getting the ascendency I dropped the humour'. There is the bacteriologist who wants to kill off the working population to solve the problem of poverty. As the narrator notes, 'It was another illustration of the inevitable bee which, sooner or later gets into the bonnet of every scientific man.'[1] The 'earthquaker' Jefferson Collins quite clearly has a bee in his bonnet. He wants to cause an earthquake to test his theory of gravitation:

> 'You don't seem to think of the misery that an earthquake would cause,' said I.
> 'Did you ever know a scientific man who cared a rap about the misery of other folks so long as he could monkey with an invention of his own?' replied Collins.[2]

More light-heartedly, but no less revealing, Professor Peek is determined to make a profit from his discovery of the bacillus of love claiming that: 'I can reconcile anything with my conscience if it fills my pocket.'[3] Detached from the world around them, fictional scientists could display the calmness of meteorologist Professor Henry Tellurin in a story from *Pearson's Magazine*. Tellurin investigates the disappearance of several men and women snatched into the air by mysterious 'sky-folk' for experimentation. When it rains blood the professor is unperturbed and merely hopes that it is not his colleague.[4]

But fictional scientists were not above carrying out their own heartless experiments. Among many of them vivisection was a common practice, even a leisure pursuit, and it should be no surprise to find them experimenting on animals (and men) especially at the height of the anti-vivisection campaign in the mid-1890s. In 1894, for example, *Pearson's Weekly* told the story of Dr Bellingham whose scientific interest is introduced to the reader through a description of his laboratory:

> There is a faint smell of chloroform in the room, and the dark patches of blood on the table, the chisel and mallet, the electrical appliances, and the large cylindrical glass case containing iron pincers and claws with which the operator may grip at pleasure any part of the captive animal's body, and lacerate it and crush it, indicates the nature of the sufferings from which death had not yet relieved the mangled victim of the vivisectionist.[5]

His wife, discovering that he is a vivisector, is disgusted at his cruelty and refuses to give him any more money for his experiments. Thwarted in his ambition for immortal fame he tries to poison her, confessing that 'it is his duty to sacrifice his wife upon the altar of physiology as he has sacrificed the lives of animals on his vivisecting table'.[6] Accidentally taking the poison himself, he has a feverish vision of hell as an animal in a vivisector's laboratory and repents his past sins.

The sense of responsibility among such men was low, verging on the insane. We can see this in the story of Arthur Moore who is obsessed with the idea of creating a lady automaton to show how society ladies are mere dolls. This would not just be a simple toy that performs tricks, but, as he explains to his friend Dr Phillips, the narrator of the story:

> 'I want her to be a lady that would deceive anyone. Not a thing that can only act when lifted into a chair, or stuck upon a platform, but a creature that will guide herself, answer questions, talk and eat like a rational being – in fact, perform the part of a society lady as well as the best bred of them.'
> 'Moore', I said, 'You must be mad.'
> 'Mad or not, I mean to try it.'[7]

In spite of his misgivings, Phillips nevertheless helps his friend in his work. 'I was carried away in a kind of drunken enthusiasm, and almost as feverishly excited as Moore himself. Nothing would now have stopped me. Would Frankenstein have paused the very hour before his creature took life?'[8] Determined to carry on with his project, Moore is indifferent to the feelings of the two men who become engaged to his creation, and it dawns on his friend, the narrator of the story, that his extraordinary success has turned his brain. As witness to these terrible events, it is in fact the narrator who ends up in an asylum, but Moore has a higher price to pay. His own life becomes so bound up with that of his creation that he dies when his automaton is stabbed by a jealous suitor.

For a final taste of the work of fictional scientists here is Dr Alexander Chance and the story of 'The Blue Laboratory' which appeared in *Cassell's Magazine* in 1897. Chance imprisons and mesmerises a man in order to carry out experiments on photographing thoughts. Miss Rennick, the governess, finds out the doctor's secret and comes to the man's rescue. Chance catches her, explains his experiments and states his case:

> I have been able to peer deeper into certain secrets of nature than any other man of my day. Yes, Miss Rennick, I am the greatest scientist at present in existence. What are the tortures of one man in comparison with so stupendous a result?[9]

He admits to being a tyrant and accepts the 'terror' and 'horror' of his experiments, but dismisses her as being 'distinctly human', and tries to kill her in a vacuum chamber. 'I could just catch sight of the fiendish face of my master peering in at me', Miss Rennick recalls. 'It was the face of the devil.'[10]

In the non-fiction of the magazines the treatment was altogether different. The list of virtues attributed to real scientists was, if anything, even more comprehensive than the corresponding list of vices of their fictional counterparts.

Contrast the insane cruelties of the fictional vivisectors with the portrayal of Lord Kelvin, President of the Royal Society. Judging by the amount of press coverage he received, Kelvin must have been a household name, although, as Professor Andrew Gray noted in *Good Words*, 'to perhaps the majority of people he is known as an inventor'.[11] For *Tit-Bits* he was the 'boy prodigy who became a peer', for *Cassell's Saturday Journal* the 'joyful inventor', while for *Cassell's Magazine* he was nothing less than the 'Napoleon of Natural Philosophy'.[12] Unlike the cold, humourless inhabitants of fictional laboratories he possessed much more human and sociable qualities. 'A smile always ready on his lips, warm heart and cheerful disposition' was how *Pearson's Weekly* described him.[13] 'He is not averse from a good comic song', noted *Cassell's Saturday Journal*, 'and now and again he even perpetrates a joke.'[14] He was, according to *Pearson's Weekly*: 'Energetic without being impetuous, quick without any signs of haste, pleased with his own power of cracking philosophical nuts, but never overestimating his own resources, mild and winning in manner, but always decisive.'[15] Donald Macleod, editor of *Good Words*, wrote an article to celebrate the jubilee of 'the greatest scientist of our time, whose nobility and attractiveness of character are as remarkable as his intellectual achievements'. For Macleod, who had been a student of Kelvin, he was a persevering, conscientious, ceaseless worker with everything he did done thoroughly and resting on absolute truth. 'A purer and nobler nature than that of Lord Kelvin's I have never known', wrote Macleod, and, most important for Macleod, 'no one is more reverent as regards all religious questions.' Kelvin's work on cosmogony and the material universe had not shaken his belief in God.[16]

Kelvin was not alone in receiving such glowing press coverage. Scientists were the heroes of the modern age. It was 'resource, pluck, energy and determination' that took Captain E.S. Grogan across Africa in true *Boy's Own* fashion, skirting around volcanoes and fighting off cannibals.[17] Physical endurance, idealism and courage were among the qualities Shackleton said were needed for the making of an explorer.[18] 'Like all heroes, Captain Mikkelsen is a modest man', explained *Pearson's Magazine* in introducing Ejnar Mikkelsen's account of being lost in the Arctic for two years, 'but every line of his direct and simple story vibrates with the glory of superhuman difficulties overcome, and the hard fight won at last.'[19] Nor was the heroic treatment restricted to explorers. In reporting on 'Doctors' experiments upon themselves', *Cassell's Saturday Journal* told of Dr Koch's plans to be inoculated with TB germs and to drink infected milk for a year. 'The five minutes valour which wins a Victoria Cross is a small effort compared with the cold drawn courage which can face death for a year on end for the sake of suffering humanity.'[20]

The scientist was, to use David Hollinger's term, 'the complete Victorian', embodying those virtues thought to be lacking in commercial and political culture, 'a humble and honest man of steady habits, laboring patiently, diligently, selflessly and without prejudice in the interests of truth'.[21] Here, for example, is John Aitkin FRS at work: 'Difficulties unforeseen arose at every stage to thwart the purposes of this indefatigable physicist: yet he returned to the contest with ever renewed courage after every rebuff, and at last succeeded beyond all doubt.'[22] Sir Oliver Lodge, said *Tit-Bits*, was 'an object lesson' for perseverance and energy. Sir John Lubbock, as described in *Pearson's Weekly*, was practical, large-hearted, methodical and an 'indefatigable toiler'.[23]

'Patience' and 'perseverance' were bywords for scientific practice. They stated the obvious. Their use verged on cliché. 'It need hardly be said', wrote one contributor in an article on photographing electricity, 'that these results are only obtained after long and patient research, during which difficulties innumerable crop up and have to be overcome.'[24] The object of such laudable endeavour was neither fame nor fortune, for, as the article continued, there was no more pleasing feature of scientific research than that there were men who devoted themselves to it from pure love of the subject. Likewise, in *Pearson's Magazine*, Orville Wright is quoted as saying: 'We are not inclined to place money above science', while both the Wright brothers and Professor Marey were said to be so modest that they were virtually unknown outside scientific circles.[25] In the international brotherhood of science self-advancement was eschewed for the selfless advancement of knowledge.[26] In *Cassell's Saturday Journal*, for example, we find Marconi described as 'just a plain man who imparts his knowledge freely, so that civilisation may benefit by it', while in *Tit-Bits* it was said that: 'It is characteristic of the unselfishness and modesty of the man that he actually waited nearly a year to give others a chance of taking the palm which he knew he had but to stretch out his hand to make his own.'[27]

Courage, patience, modesty, selflessness, the moral efficacy of scientific practice made scientists ideal material for that genre of moralistic literature that had been so common earlier in the nineteenth century. In the *British Workman* scientists' life stories were retold as moral illustrations in the true Smilesian self-help tradition. Telling of the young James Brindley's rise as an engineer, the magazine comments that 'his self-teaching and hard labour were beginning to tell'. Ultimately his success is as much a triumph of character as it is of engineering talent, a triumph of perseverance, resourcefulness and integrity.[28] The lessons of Nansen's Arctic expedition were even more clearly stated: first, no alcohol was taken; second, 'it showed what pluck and perseverance could do'; and third, 'with the eye of the scientific man and the heart of the poet' Nansen saw the wonders of God's power.[29] These three themes of reverence, temperance and self-help, so dear to magazines like the *British Workman*, were again drawn together in a short feature on the ornithologist Alexander Wilson. Headed 'Labour conquers all things', it described Wilson as a 'poor working lad' who was 'of strong temperance principles and practice, and his morality was pure'. He was also 'fortunate in having a father who was sober and industrious'. It failed, of course, to mention that part of his father's sober industry was employed operating an illicit still, and that Wilson himself was in and out of gaol for two and a half years on various charges of blackmail.[30]

Why should there be this stark contrast between the fictional and factual images? One possibility is that these differences may have arisen from science being presented within two distinct genres of writing – an older literary tradition of Faust, Frankenstein and gothic novels, and the more recent new journalism.

The diabolical associations of science was an age-old theme. It was kin to a belief that science was a black art, that it had links with black magic, that it was knowledge obtained illicitly. The story of Dr Faust would have reinforced these beliefs, as too would the role of alchemy in early science and the building of chemical laboratories underground.[31] Indeed it was often in the description of laboratories that the occult associations of science were brought out in the magazine fiction. Dr Chance's 'blue laboratory', for example, was described as

> ...a splendidly equipped room. A teak bench ran round three sides of the wall, fitted with every conceivable apparatus and appliance, glazed fume chambers, stoneware sinks, Bunsen burners, porcelain dishes, balances, microscopes, burettes, mortars, retorts, and, in fact, every instrument devoted to the rites of the mephitic divinity.[32]

The link with magic was also present in the story of Arthur Moore and his lady automaton, Moore's friend believing that: 'There was a mysterious union between them which gave me an uncanny feeling of sorcery. Could it be that by some unholy means Moore had succeeded in conveying some portion of his own life to this creature of his?' The curious circumstances of Moore's death, as we have seen, could only have strengthened this feeling.

The new journalism, on the other hand, was more than a racy pen. It was personal, domestic, an almost prurient fascination in the private lives of the rich and famous. The interview, or 'chat', was its most favoured device, creating an illusion of intimacy between journalist/reader and the great and glorious. 'I called the other day on Sir Norman Lockyer', wrote the contributor of one chat in *Cassell's Saturday Journal*.[33] Only an introduction from a personal friend, says *Pearson's Magazine*, admits you to Tesla's laboratory, 'a treat that few can enjoy', but presented to all its readers.[34] Regular features like 'In the public eye', 'People of importance', or 'People we hear about' would give readers the personal minutiae of the lives of royalty, statesmen, music hall stars, and also of scientists.[35] Edison, we are told, takes great pains over his handwriting. Kelvin has not read a novel for years. Nansen keeps portraits of his wife and daughter on his writing table.

Interestingly this fascination for the personal is captured in fiction. 'Professor Kenyon' has a low opinion of journalism. The 'Daily Press', he complains, 'gave an account of my new theory of the Diurnal Variation in the Development of a Protozoon that made me a laughing stock', while the 'Weekly Review', he went on,

> 'is the paper which interviewed me and described me as a fat little man with a merry smile and a roguish twinkle in my eye.... It is to that,' said the professor 'that I attribute the cold reception of my recent work. Who,' he asked pathetically 'can be interested in the opinions of a man with a roguish twinkle in his eye?'[36]

Who indeed? But for all the professor's complaints, the new journalism would have done little to damage the public image of scientists. More than that, it may even have helped to enhance the image of the scientist. For one member of the *Clarion* staff the experience of meeting A.R. Wallace was overwhelming.

> When the door opened and I was ushered into the doctor's presence – phew! the inside of my head felt as if it had been stirred up by the tail of a comet, and became like an incandescent floating mass of world material, without form and void. I realised that I was in the presence of a great man.[37]

In the public eye 'scientists' may have been a homogeneous mass of faceless individuals, but through the magazines one learned that Sir Norman Lockyer liked to play golf, or that Lyon Playfair was an interesting conversationalist and 'a favourite with the fair sex'. By creating 'public figures' and 'personalities', the new journalism helped to personalise an otherwise impersonal process. This is not to say that it made scientists any the less remote, but it would certainly have made it harder to fear or distrust them.

There were, of course, exceptions to this simple dichotomy of friend in fact and foe in fiction. In the 1890s a new fictional character emerges, that of the scientific detective, the most famous of whom is Sherlock Holmes, but Holmes's science is of a most singular kind. He is, for a start, plain 'Mister' Holmes, not Doctor or Professor, a dilettante, an amateur, not a professional scientist at all. It is true that he is interested in science, occasionally carries out experiments and Watson's first meeting with him is in a laboratory, but as Watson soon notes his knowledge of science is peculiarly limited. His knowledge of chemistry is 'profound', but his botany is 'variable', his geology 'practical but limited', and his anatomy 'accurate but unsystematic'.

> His ignorance was as remarkable as his knowledge.... My surprise reached a climax, however, when I found incidentally that he was

ignorant of the Copernican Theory and of the composition of the Solar System. That any civilised human being in this nineteenth century should not be aware that the earth travelled round the sun appeared to be to me an extraordinary fact that I could hardly realise it.[38]

By contrast his knowledge of sensational literature is 'immense'. What makes Holmes the great detective is not his science but his powers of observation and deduction. 'You really are an automaton – a calculating machine', Watson tells him. 'There is something positively inhuman in you at times.'[39]

Similar qualities, but better scientific credentials, are to be found in the creation of American author Jacques Futrelle: 'Professor Augustus S.F.X. van Dusen Ph.D., FRS., MD., LL.D., etc etc – logician, analyst, worker of miracles in the exact sciences, intellectual wizard of his time.' First appearing in December 1907, 'Professor van Dusen's problems' became a regular feature of *Cassell's Magazine* in 1908 and warranted a cover picture for the March issue. Popping up once in *Cassell's Saturday Journal* in 1909, he made his final appearance in *Cassell's Magazine* in 1912 (one of the last stories written by Futrelle before he went down on the *Titanic*).[40] The professor's 'problems', in effect, were little more than detective stories, tracking down and outwitting ingenious (and not so ingenious) robbers, smugglers and kidnappers. What characterised the professor's approach, however, was his application of 'logic' to all the crimes. 'Logic', he says, 'will solve any problem – not most of them, but any of them.'[41] He did not, therefore, embark upon remarkable escapades of derring-do, as other detectives might. 'One glance showed that physical development had never entered into the schedule of the scientist's fifty years of life.' Instead he was referred to as the 'foremost brain in science', and commonly known as 'The Thinking Machine'.

Despite being unequivocally on the side of good rather than of evil, his was far from being a sympathetic characterisation:

> He was slight, to the point of childishness, and his thin shoulders seemed to droop beneath the weight of his enormous head....His brow rose straight and dome like and a heavy shock of long yellow hair gave him an almost grotesque appearance. The eyes were narrow slits of blue squinting eternally through thick glasses.[42]

The world chess champion, defeated in van Dusen's first attempt at the game, exclaims: 'Mon dieu! You are not a man; you are a brain – a machine – a thinking machine.' Likewise, when a reporter looked into van Dusen's face, 'he saw no pity, no horror there; there was merely the reflection of brain workings'.[43]

At the heart of nineteenth-century opposition to science, according to I.B. Cohen, lay the perception of science as a dehumanising and impersonal process, seen especially in the fear and distrust of evolutionary theory, reductionist biology and statistics. Man, it was believed, was more than an animal, a machine, or an anonymous average.[44] It seems, therefore, that even when scientists were not the villains of the piece they possessed qualities which were hardly likely to endear them to the reader, qualities which arose from the very nature of scientific practice:

> Seemingly tireless, calm, unemotional...terse of speech, crabbed of manner, and possessed of an uncanny faculty of separating all things into their primal units, he lived in a circumscribed sphere which he had stripped of all illusion. The mental precision which distinguished his laboratory work characterised all else he did. If any man ever reduced human frailties, human virtues, and all human motives, that man was The Thinking Machine.[45]

The scientific detective is also to be found in the non-fiction. In 1902 *Cassell's Saturday Journal* presented a whole series of articles on 'Scientific Detectives of To-day'. The introduction to the series is worth quoting at length:

> Much as we owe to ordinary detectives, we are still more indebted to scientific detectives. As education has spread wrongdoing and crime have taken more subtle and dangerous forms, against many of which Scotland Yard, if it trusted solely to its internal resources, would be powerless. Glorified policemen cannot cope with them; the more skilled and more technically expert watchdogs of civilisation can alone detect them.
>
> The analyst, with his tubes and his microscopes; the chemist who pits himself against that enemy of society who is skilled in every scientific process that can be twisted to nefarious ends; the toxicologist, profoundly versed in poison lore and the diabolically cunning ways of modern practitioners of the secret art; the specialist in photography, armed with his two invaluable handmaidens, the searching eye of the camera, and the still more penetrating X-rays; the expert in legal medicine, the keen clear-headed sleuthhound, whose achievements outvie all fiction and well-nigh stagger belief – these are the men who protect us from the master criminals of to-day...[46]

This was not the only example. In a similar vein we can also find in *Pearson's Weekly* 'Is this stain blood? – How crime experts distinguish human blood from that of animals' and 'How analysts detect murder', or in *Cassell's Saturday Journal* 'Found guilty – by science'.

In looking at the work of the Home Office analytical laboratory, *Cassell's Saturday Journal* noted that in many criminal cases science could be prosecutor and defendant, judge and jury:

> ...in each capacity impartial, dispassionate, unerring; forging the chain of guilt or destroying the links of it one by one; speaking the truth, the whole truth and nothing but the truth, without love and without hate, without fear and without favour.[47]

A public image of neutrality and objectivity was, as Brian Wynne has written, 'part of the social programme of professionalisation under the utilitarian ethos'.[48] To the magazines, science was this and more. Science was serious, precise and truthful. Science spoke with the voice of authority. The claim that all life on Earth would end in four hundred years' time was not, said *Cassell's Magazine*, the prediction of a latter-day prophet or the vision of some romancer, nor even the threat of a frenzied nihilist, but 'the solemn warning of Lord Kelvin, the highest living authority in the domain of physical science'.[49] Meanwhile, true to form, *Tit-Bits* told the story of 'the strangest man in the world' whose rate of mental and physical development was only one sixth that of normal and so would live to be three hundred years old. 'It is scientific, though amazing', declared the magazine as though 'scientific' were a synonym for 'true'.[50]

The authority of science would have been reinforced as much by its perceived beneficence in transforming the quality of life as by its newly acquired status in late-nineteenth-century society. The two went together. 'A triumphalist view of science', Colin Russell has written, 'was much to be encouraged for financial and institutional reasons.'[51] Similarly the British Association increased its public visibility by climbing on the imperialist bandwagon (most conspicuously with its overseas meetings), adding immediacy and potency to its claims for the utility of science and for the need to have increased support for scientists and scientific institutions.[52] Moreover, late Victorian eulogies of science would have served to strengthen scientists' claims to extend the exercise of the authority into spheres beyond their immediate realms of competence. From the 1880s onwards 'public scientists', to use Turner's term, criticised politicians and civil servants for their lack of scientific knowledge, and stressed the necessity of scientific solutions for political and social problems.[53] By 1904 the British Science Guild, in contrast to all previous science organisations, could announce that its purpose was not the promotion of natural knowledge, but rather the use of science 'to further the progress and increase the welfare of the Empire'.[54] The rhetoric of scientific authority had shifted from the values of self-improvement, material comfort and intellectual progress toward values of political elitism, military preparedness and social imperialism.[55]

Moreover, the scientists' drive for status, as David Hollinger has argued, 'served to increase the pressure to view scientists as saints. The more detached from their fellow citizens that scientists became, the more necessary it became for the Victorian moralists...to trust that scientists were subject to an ethical code intrinsic to their practice.'[56] By embodying all those virtues thought to be lacking in men of politics and commerce, scientists were, as we have seen, more appropriately portrayed as soldiers and priests, not politicians and salesmen. Likewise the metaphor of 'temple', applied to many observatories as well as the Natural History Museum at South Kensington, invoked both the seclusion of scientists from the masses and the righteousness of scientific practice.

In the sixteenth century Étienne de La Boétie saw tyranny perpetuated by a mixture of mystery, specious divinity and beneficence.[57] In the nineteenth century the esoteric language, religious imagery and bountiful products of science would likewise ensure the 'voluntary servitude' of its subjects. The deference due to the authority of science might even suggest that a new 'paternalism of the expert' had replaced the earlier paternalism of the factory owner which has been seen as a source of stability in mid-Victorian society.[58] Excluded from participating in the scientific enterprise, the lay public were left to trust that scientists did indeed possess the heroic qualities of their magazine stereotypes. As represented in the magazines men like Kelvin, Lodge, Lubbock and Edison commanded respect. Progress, one was assured, would be safe in their hands. One had only to put one's faith in science and submit to the rise of the expert. The caustic humour of Alex Thompson at the *Clarion* expressed the helplessness that this could entail. Scientists, he wrote in 1910, are busy resolving us to our component essences, and by and by will construct things like us out of the waste products of their laboratories. He concludes:

> They will regulate our characters, our feelings, our aspect, and our whole lives with the accuracy and certainty of a mathematical demonstration. They will leave us no appetites, no desires, no passions, no gratifications, no emotions, no worries, and no ailments; we shall just have to live, they will do the rest.... When we are done with and not wanted any more, they will politely hand us [a] kind of lozenge, and we shall be effectually converted back to the sort of gases they made us from.... Nothing remains to ordinary mortals but to surrender them-

selves blindly to the tender care of the scientists, and let them make of us whatsoever they will.[59]

Submission to the authority of science demanded all the faith, trust and even fatalism that had been called upon by the traditional authority of religion.

5 Science and Religion

There is a very curious feature about the portrayal of scientists in these magazines. The most fulsome praise is to be found in the more religious publications. What then of any supposed conflict between science and religion? In *Good Words* Kelvin was, as we have seen, noble, pure and reverent, Aitkin courageous and indefatigable, but elsewhere we can also read of the labours of Lister, the philanthropy of Perkin, the fearlessness and resource of Ramsay, the perseverance and determination of Edison, and the love of truth and patience of Newton.[1] Even Darwin, of all people, is admired for having 'sound judgement, unwearied industry, absence of prejudice, a passionate love of truth, and withal abounding charity, all different aspects of real religion'.[2] Courage, patience, modesty, selflessness, the moral efficacy of scientific practice made scientists ideal material for that genre of moralistic literature that had been so common earlier in the nineteenth century.

More than this, the religious imagery with which science is depicted is as evident in the more religious magazines as it is in the secular ones, perhaps even more so. Again in *Good Words* we can read of how, on approaching the telescope at the Yerke's observatory, 'we stand at last, wondering and awe stricken, in the dim religious light of the very Holy of Holies of this Western temple'.[3] While from another contributor we have Darwin's Down house described as a 'silent, solitary shrine' which had been 'consecrated' by the genius of Darwin, 'one of the noblest and yet humblest of the high priests of inductive science'.[4] When the trappings of religion are bestowed upon science by a religious magazine, and the last example comes from the pen of a clergyman, it may be small wonder that others, like Mona Caird at the *Clarion*, should borrow one of Spencer's terms and warn of the dangers of 'scientific popery'.[5]

Now here we have a further twist to the problem. The fiercest attacks on science come from the magazine that also published the fiercest attacks on religion. Characteristically it was the *Clarion* that gave the most prominent support to the anti-vivisection movement. In 1894 the magazine provided a good deal of editorial space for anti-vivisectionists to air their views. For example, Edward Carpenter urged the magazine's readers to protect animals from exploitation in the same way as the labour movement protected men. Edith Carrington feared that the 'modern craze for playing at physiological experiments' would demoralise the young, and argued that nothing could be learned about humans by torturing animals.[6]

At the same time Mona Caird protested that animal vivisection was licensed cruelty and was but one step from human vivisection: 'the vivisectors most often come straight from the torture-trough of some mangled animal to the bedside of the patient. Is it surprising that sometimes the experiments commenced in the laboratory are tested in the hospital wards.'[7] These tirades, perhaps, show not so much a concern for animal welfare, as an attempt to arouse 'the basic moral instincts of laymen against an arrogant coalition of scientists, medical men, and legislators'.[8] Likewise it was the *Clarion* that was most sympathetic to the anti-vaccination movement.

So was there a conflict between science and religion in late Victorian Britain? In his history of the Victorian Church, Owen Chadwick has noted that 'in 1900 men talked as though the conflict was over'.[9] We can see this in a series of features on the Marquis of Salisbury which appeared in 1902 and which included an article on 'Religious belief – scientific research'. It explained:

> Not so many years ago it appeared as though the breach between science and religion was past all healing. This state of things has passed away, and thoughtful men rejoice to believe that the revelations of these two great forces are by no means inconsistent one with the other.[10]

Similarly a 'Sunday Reading' in *Good Words* of 1897 dismissed the possible conflict between Genesis and science by commenting that 'the time is past for such controversies'. We have learned, it said, 'that it is a misuse of scripture to treat it as if it were a text-book and primer of Natural History'.[11] It had been an expensive lesson. Peace was established, says Chadwick, 'because religion had abandoned, or was abandoning, an ancient claim to give truths about the physical world'.[12] Significantly, from the 1880s, as Frank Turner has pointed out, the public rhetoric of scientists was no longer directed against obscurantist clergy, but against ignorant politicians and complacent manufacturers.[13]

From her study of the reasons for unbelief among members of the secular movement, Susan Budd concluded that 'the revolution in scientific and theological thinking seems largely irrelevant'.[14] The loss of faith, she argued, was not an intellectual but a moral matter. Of 150 biographical accounts in her survey only two mention having read Darwin or Huxley. As causes of unbelief much more influential books were the Bible, Paine's *The Age of Reason*, and Robert Blatchford's *God and My Neighbour*. But there is something which Budd does not mention and which brings a final twist to our problem. Blatchford's book was in fact based upon a series of articles that appeared in the *Clarion* in 1903 under the heading 'Religion and science'. However sympathetic Blatchford may have been to those voices of 'anti-science', it was still science that was his main weapon in attacking organised religion.

For all the talk of harmony between faith and 'fact' it is quite probable that there were very real and deep anxieties, if not among the clergy then within the congregation. Certainly this is the impression one gets from reading popular periodicals of the time. Calming words from the pulpit may have been sincere, but just as real was the need for reassurance in the first place. This is well illustrated by the problems page of the *Family Herald*. Here we find one correspondent 'unsettled' by 'the most abstract vital question of the age', namely: how is it possible to reconcile the 'acknowledged facts of science' with the 'opinions respecting the Bible' held by our Puritan forefathers and still held by millions of ignorant people? The answer: it is not possible. However, the magazine is quick to point out that this does not make the faith of Christian ministers any the less firm, simply more intelligent, 'because it is adjusted to things as they are'. On the other hand, a minister's flock puts its trust blindly in traditional opinion which is based on ignorance and has very little to do with the 'great verities of religion'.[15]

Is this side-stepping the issue? Maybe. A common strategy to resolve the conflict was to transcend it, to say that with a better understanding of religion (or science) there really was no problem. Likewise there was much talk of separating science and religion into separate 'spheres', into different realms of competence, the material and the spiritual. The task here is to see how these issues and strategies were presented to the common reader, to see in the magazines the full range of science for, with and (not forgetting the *Clarion*) against religion.

There is, perhaps, no better place to start than with natural theology, through nature to nature's God. In its various guises the argument from design has been the most persistent of proofs for the existence of God. We can find it in Cicero's *De Natura Deorum* and as one of the 'Five Ways' of Aquinas. In the seventeenth century a good example would be John Ray's *Wisdom of God Manifest in the Works of Creation*, while in the eighteenth century there is the *Physico-Theology* of William Derham, for whom the world was 'too grand for anything less than a god to make'. Its clearest and most popular expression, however, came in 1802 with the publication of William Paley's *Natural Theology*. The book became a standard text at Cambridge, and was one of the few which Darwin found of any use during his student days there. As late as 1885 there was a fresh edition of Paley's book, edited by a Fellow of the Royal Society, and 'revised to harmonise with modern science', the main revision being an introduction explaining how evolutionary theory and natural theology were not incompatible.[16] Just how compatible will be a recurring theme for this and the following chapter.

Paley's book is a delight to read. Step by step the argument unfolds in the opening pages. 'In crossing a heath suppose I pitched my foot against a stone...' For all I know, says Paley, it could have been there forever. 'But suppose I had found a watch upon the ground...' Now we need a different type of answer. Why? Because 'when we come to inspect the watch we perceive that its several parts are framed and put together for a purpose'. The inference is inevitable, the watch must have had a maker, 'there cannot be design without a designer; a contrivance without a contriver'. Thus stated the argument is then applied, for 'every indication of contrivance, every manifestation of design which existed in the watch exists in the works of nature'.[17] The great bulk of the book then accumulates the evidence to prove not only God's existence, but also His unity and beneficence. 'It is a happy world after all', says Paley.

And it is just such a happy world that we can find evidence of in the pages of *Good Words*. The best example came in 1899 with T.F. Manning's article 'God in Trifles'. Reminiscent of earlier, halcyon days of natural theology, there is a certain timelessness about Manning's presentation of nature. Why do birds not fall off their perches when they sleep? Manning has the answer: 'Kind Providence seeing that it would be their custom to sleep on branches of trees, fixed a wonderful contrivance' – a sinew that contracts their toes when they rest. Why is ice less dense than water? – to stop it sinking and filling up the bottom of lakes. Why is the ocean salty? – to keep sea water at a warm temperature for fish, to prevent the putrefaction of dead sea animals, and to cause the ocean currents like the Gulf Stream, 'so that, but for the salt in the ocean, England would be as cold as icy Labrador and would never have become that glorious nation that it is'.[18]

By examining the 'thoughtfulness of the Creator' it is quite easy for Manning to argue that: 'Contrary to what is generally believed scientific men are the most truly religious people in the world.' The marvels that one meets in chemistry, biology and physics mean that: 'A man may work all his life at journalism, or book-keeping, or carpentry, or painting, or even preaching, without seeing any special reason for believing in Divine Providence. But the scientist in his daily labour can never get away from God.'[19] What is striking is not so much the sentiments or the ideas, as the innocence with which Manning expresses them. It is as if nothing had happened in the preceding half century to undermine the theological grounds upon which they were based. However, while 'God in Trifles' may be dismissed (particularly by modern readers) as simplistic or even simple-minded, this is less easy to do with the tradition of natural theology as a whole. As John Brooke has shown, nineteenth-century natural theology was notably resilient, quite probably because of its doctrinal imprecision.[20] It could be all things to all believers (even non-believers). What we find in *Good Words*, and indeed what is more common, is the tradition being continued at other, less pronounced, levels of rhetoric.

At the lowest level is what might be called the religious punchline. Here a seemingly straightforward and factual account ends with a sudden, throwaway, concluding paragraph to the effect that the marvels of nature that have just been looked at can only make us marvel at Him who created them. An article on structural botany, for example, comprises a lengthy description of algae, cells and cell formation before ending abruptly with the comment: 'Any portion of any plant, when microscopically examined, reveals the marvellous pencilling of its Creator.' Similarly, in astronomy, it is not until the final paragraph in a series of four articles that Sir Robert Ball refers to the 'great prime cause' which originated the development of the universe described in the series.[21]

At a second level we find such references to the Creator, together with His love and His wisdom, recurring throughout an article, sometimes explicitly, sometimes implicitly, but always through the general tone of the piece, which uses a lyrical, anecdotal and usually an anthropomorphic narrative style. Such articles often take the form of a country ramble or a day at the seaside. One might include here such articles as 'The Trout of the Chalk Stream' by the Rev. B.G. Johns with its many references to the beauties and peace of nature in its description of a fishing trip, or the Rev. Robert C. Nightingale's 'A muddy corner', a narrative crawl around a puddle.[22]

At the highest level such rhetorical devices are replaced by the simple setting out of the argument, and the beauties and wonders of nature take on a secondary, more illustrative role. Most conspicuous here were Manning's article and those written by the Rev. Hugh Macmillan. For Macmillan design was evident in the growth of a gall on a cranberry. 'How then', he asked, 'is the gall so regular, so beautiful in structure and appearance, and so admirably adapted for the purpose which it serves?' The symmetry of morbid products, he wrote, is a wide and yet unexplained subject, but: 'The phenomenon seems one of those blind unconscious operations of nature, which irresistibly suggest the existence of a conscious Mind working through them.'[23] For men such as the Rev. Hugh Macmillan, nature was to be a source of comfort and encouragement at a time of scientific unbelief. However, what was more important for Macmillan was not so much that nature was designed (this was taken as axiomatic), but that having been designed, nature had meaning. It had a 'moral design'. It was a medium for God's message, supplying man with 'parables of nature' and serving a pedagogic function for theological and moral exegesis. As he explained, next to the study of His own word that which made 'all His ways in providence and grace real and true' was the study of humble wild flowers such as the dandelion or the globe flower. 'It is in this way that we ought to consider the lilies how they grow, to sit down before one of these at a time and try and find out what God meant it to say to us.'[24]

If such overt appeals to nature were one way of handling the potential conflict between science and religion, a second strategy was to reconcile the two. Probably the best-known example of reconciliation to be found in *Good Words* is Gladstone's series 'The Impregnable Rock of Holy Scripture' which appeared in 1890. Indeed this is likely to be the only material in *Good Words* with which many historians of science have any familiarity. However, only two of the seven parts had direct bearing on the issue: paper II 'The Creation Story' and paper VI 'On the Recent Corroborations of Scripture from the Regions of History and Natural Science'. In opening this latter paper Gladstone 'observed' that 'many of the favourite subjects of scientific or systematic thought in the present day are of a nature powerfully tending to strengthen or assist the arguments available for the proof of religion and for the authority of Scripture'.[25] We should dispel from our minds, he said, 'those spectral notions of antagonism between religion and science' raised up by prejudice on one side and boasting on the other. The two sides were not so much to be reconciled as married. 'Of religion and of science, as of man and wife, let us boldly say, "What God hath joined together, let not man put asunder".'[26]

It may have been no more than a marriage of convenience, because for all Gladstone's protestations there is very little by way of corroboration of Scripture to be found in this paper. We have in Genesis, he says, an outline history of our planet, 'and of the first appearance and early development of life upon it, anterior to the creation of man, in many of the principal stages which have been ascertained by geology'.[27] Accepting the conclusions of geology, 'we have found the geology of genesis to stand in such a relation to these conclusions as could not have been exhibited in a record framed by faculties merely human, at any date to which the origin of the Creation Story can now be reasonably referred'.[28]

In other words the close correspondence of Genesis with geology is itself evidence of divine communication. How else would the writer of Genesis know about the main phases of development which are only now being revealed by modern science? This does, of course, beg the question of how close was the correspondence of Genesis and geology. What Gladstone seems to have in mind is the interpretation of the seven days of creation as seven geological epochs – an idea that was at least hinted at by Burnett in the seventeenth century and expanded by Buffon in the eighteenth.

As to detailed evidence, that is notably absent. The cynically minded might expect no more from a politician. We should be more charitable. It was not Gladstone's intention to present a catalogue of facts, rather it was to assume those facts and take the offensive. '...as against those who by arbitrary or irrational interpretation, place Genesis and science at variance, our position is not one merely defensive. We are not mere reconcilers, as some call us, searching out expedients to escape a difficulty, to repel an assault.'[29] For all the rhetoric of marriage, however, Gladstone's perspective remained primarily scriptural, as the title of his paper would indicate. For all the military metaphors, natural (and historic) science 'rendered a service' to the cause of belief, 'underpinning' the structure of divine revelation in Genesis, and in particular 'confirming' the stories of Creation, of the Flood, of the dispersion of peoples, and of the Sinaitic journey.

More interesting than Gladstone's series, but less well known, is Emma Marie Caillard's 'On the use of Science to Christians' which appeared in *Good Words* in 1896. Between 1893 and 1897 Caillard contributed several articles on physics to the magazine, and her six-part series placed a much greater emphasis upon science than did Gladstone's. The two premises of her argument were the truth of the Christian revelation, and the 'reasonable probability' that science would help us to understand that revelation more perfectly.[30] The revelation made in nature 'is not of itself sufficient to our needs', but is rather a complement of the Christian revelation to show us 'more of the mind and purpose of God'. However, the Christian 'too often confronts [science] as a necessary evil, whose existence he would gladly ignore if possible'. Regarding theoretical discoveries as inimical to his faith, the Christian carries on a losing battle against conclusions which he feels are too strong for him because they are based on undeniable fact. The reasons for this Caillard sums up as 'the many-sidedness of truth and the general one-sidedness of the human mind'.[31] The mistake of Christians, she says, is to set up the Scriptures as the standard of scientific and historical as well as of spiritual truth. The result had been 'disastrous'

for it has compelled us either to shut our eyes to demonstrated facts, or
to try and accept two contradictory sets of facts, which make the God of
Truth appear in opposition to Himself. Nearly all the attempts to 'reconcile' Scripture and science are founded on this fallacious supposition.[32]

If men were the channels of divine truth, says Caillard, then that truth
'must bear the marks of the intelligence which apprehended it, and the age
in which it was given out'.[33]

Clearly Caillard is taking a different approach to that of Gladstone. For
her the scriptures are marked by the ignorance of their age. For him, in
Genesis at least, the profound knowledge displayed is evidence of superhuman intelligence and inspiration. Caillard's approach is also more
unorthodox in a further respect. A common tactic to reconcile science and
religion was to divide them into separate spheres, the spiritual and the
material. The one to tell us of our souls, the other of our bodies. Caillard
will have none of this. Every new light thrown by science on the laws and
constitution of the universe should show us more of the mind and purpose
of God, she says, but it cannot do this if we insist on believing that we
already know everything.

> Nor can it do this if we make a hard-and-fast line between the 'natural'
> and the 'supernatural', relegating man's 'body' and all with which his
> body is connected, i.e. the whole 'material' universe to 'nature', and
> man's spirit, his power to say 'I am I', to some occult super-nature,
> which is more closely related to God than nature.[34]

Henry Drummond had also sought to blur the distinction between the two
in his book *Natural Law in the Spiritual World*, seeing in altruism the
'super-natural' selection of those most morally fit to survive.[35] Caillard's
argument, however, is different and because of its sophistication is worthy
of a closer look.

She begins with a concession. For an agnostic or an atheist science does
not show that nature is spiritual and divine. However, if we do accept that
there is any spiritual and divine principle at all, then there is something
which shows it to be present throughout the entire 'material' universe.
That something, she says, is the 'organic unity of nature', 'such a unity as
we find in a plant or in the body of an animal whose "organs", despite
their distinctiveness, are pervaded by a single life'.[36] Unlike Paley's unity
of design as evidence for the unity of God, Caillard's unity is one which is
developed from within and not impressed from without. She specifically
excludes the unity to be found in any building, 'mechanical contrivance'
or indeed anything at all which is made.

Organic unity belongs only to that which is 'made to make itself', and what science shows, as with ever-increasing clearness she points out the organic unity of nature, is just this very fact, that the universe has not been made, but has been made to make itself. It is, so far as we can see, the result of evolution, not of manufacture.[37]

The distance from Paley's vision of a divine watchmaker is striking, but Caillard's God is as Christian as Paley's – indeed, maybe more so in that it emphasises the spirituality of God rather than His ability as a craftsman.

Caillard's use of evolutionary theory is, of course, the distinguishing feature between her vision and that of Paley nearly a century earlier. We shall discuss ideas on evolution later, but it is worth noting here how, for Caillard, they show that spirituality is not simply the final stage in the evolutionary process, a position taken by many of her Christian contemporaries.

On the theory of evolution nothing can be unfolded from the germ which was not potentially there from the beginning, needing time and development only to become actual. If, then, man, a spiritual being, is the outcome of the minute mass of protoplasmic matter which we call an organic cell, to what conclusion can we come save that the life of such a cell, germinal though it be, is a spiritual life?[38]

Furthermore, 'personality' must have been implicit from the start since the highest manifestation of life, man, is personal, that is, has self-conscious intelligence and will. This has tremendous bearing on the faith of a Christian.

God has revealed Himself to us as a personal being the source and reason of all personal life; science teaches us that personal life is the outcome of evolution. Seen from the Christian standpoint, therefore, modern science show us that the whole aim of creation has been the production of beings whose personality stamps them as sons of God.... Man is thus shown to be not a mere inhabitant of the universe, but its expression and its interpretation.[39]

The staff at the *Clarion* thought differently. In 1910 A.E. Fletcher wrote that 'science and christianity as taught in the churches are hopelessly irre-concilable. Every attempt to harmonise them has failed.'[40] In 1904 Robert Blatchford complained of how a recent speech by Sir Oliver Lodge had been misrepresented by apologists: 'Christian apologists, grown humble in adversity, have lately made a good deal of capital – more than it is worth, by far – out of the occasional statements of some leading scientists that there is no antagonism between science and religion.' Lodge's God, said

Blatchford, was not necessarily the Christian God, and besides, he added, Lodge did not know what he was talking about.[41] Blatchford's antagonism towards religion, and more especially towards the Church, was uncompromising. His most sustained attack came in 1903 and reached its culmination with the book *God and My Neighbour* which Budd argues was so influential as a cause of unbelief among secularists.

It began in the *Clarion* of 23 January with a review of a cheap edition of Haeckel's *Riddle of the Universe*. It is a masterly book, said Blatchford, which 'demolishes the entire structure upon which the religions of the world are built'.[42] The following week the *Clarion* printed a number of letters in defence of the Christian faith. Blatchford responded with invective:

> Our sun is but a speck in the universe. Our earth is but a speck in the solar system.
>
> Are we to believe that the God who created all this boundless universe got so angry with the children of the apes that He sent them all to Hell for a score of centuries, and then could only appease His rage by sending His son to be nailed upon a cross? Do you believe that? Can you believe that?
>
> No, as I said before, if the theory of evolution be true, there was nothing to atone for, and nobody to atone. *Man has never sinned against God*. In fact the whole fabric of the Christian faith is a mass of error. There was no creation. There was no fall. There was no atonement. There was no Adam, and no Eve, and no Eden, and no devil, and no hell.[43]

Fearful of estranging thousands of their supporters, Alex Thompson, the managing editor of the *Clarion*, implored Blatchford not to embark on a campaign against orthodox religion. 'I can't help it', Blatchford is reported as replying, but 'it has to be said. It may smash us, but I've got to say it.'[44]

On 13 February the *Clarion* published the first of Blatchford's papers on the subject under the heading 'Science and Religion'. Science, he argued, had not proved that there was no God, but had made it impossible for any reasonable man to accept the account of God, and of God's relations to man, given in any religion of which he had ever heard. He stated his position:

> Science and common sense seem to me to render untenable the Mosaic account of the creation, the doctrines of the fall and the atonement, the doctrines of the divinity and resurrection of Christ, the belief in the efficacy of prayer, and the personal interferences of Providence in

earthly affairs, and the theory of everlasting punishments and rewards...any religion teaching any of these things is a delusion.[45]

All the advances in knowledge, and all the improvements in the Christian religion, he said, were due to scientists and sceptics. Neither Christ nor His Church had made any contribution to our better knowledge of the origin and nature of the universe or of man: 'Step by step, the superstition, the ignorance, and the arrogance of the Christian Churches have been driven back. Step by step, the Christian Churches have retreated, cursing, fighting, and hating. And the retreat continues.'[46] Week by week Blatchford replied to criticisms and elaborated upon his case. By the end of March the arguments were more specifically about religious doctrine rather than about religion and science, but the debates about revelation, the Bible and the Resurrection of Christ continued into July.

Not surprisingly the vehemence of Blatchford's attack did not go unanswered. Some correspondents argued that Blatchford's criticisms could only be applied to dogmatic medievalism in Christianity and not to present-day beliefs. To which the reply was: that if this were so, then why not change the Bible and the Book of Common Prayer?[47] Many wished to point out that the theory of evolution was accepted by most clergy and educated Christians. 'Of what use is it', countered Blatchford, 'to say that the bulk of educated Christians accept the theory of evolution, if the whole of the Christian Churches continue to teach the theory of the Creation?'[48] A theological student added that far from being a hindrance, the theory of evolution was a help to religious belief. Blatchford, however, failed to see how this could be, since Christianity was based upon the ideas of the Fall and Atonement. When was the Fall, he wondered, when man was a monkey?[49] One correspondent ventured to write of the infinite goodness of God shown in directive evolution. Blatchford, however, had an old argument to hand: 'what of the infinite goodness of God in teaching the cholera microbe to feed on man', or, he continued, sharks to eat swimmers, or greyhounds to catch hares. 'I see no infinite goodness here, but only the infinite foolishness of sentimental superstition.'[50] Indeed there was little that was new in any of Blatchford's arguments, and much that was reminiscent of Bradlaugh's attacks thirty years previously.[51]

Unlike Bradlaugh's polemic, however, evolutionary arguments were at the vanguard of Blatchford's attack, and such arguments were a significant strand in socialist thought.[52] For example, by the end of the century mechanics' institutes were helping to spread an evolutionary socialist ideology far from the middle-class ideals of their founding fathers. From his study of institutes in Yorkshire, John Laurent concludes that by the

1880s and 1890s working-class people 'had considerable exposure and access to ideas which might serve as the basis for evolutionary arguments for socialism'.[53] Social Darwinism was as much a phenomenon of the political left as of the right, as we shall see again when we turn to eugenics. At the *Clarion* Harry Lowerison was quite clear about the social implications of Darwin's ideas. As the founder and organiser of the *Clarion* Field Clubs, Lowerison advised readers on the study of nature. One correspondent was told: 'there is a more vital connection between Darwin and Socialism than you can imagine. Once regarded as a complete answer to Socialism, the Darwinian theory is now one of the best armouries that a young soldier in our cause can go to for weapons.'[54]

The pre-eminence given to Darwin in the socialist hagiography is conveniently highlighted by a comparison between the *Clarion* and *Tit-Bits*. In the early months of 1907 both magazines searched for the country's great and glorious, in *Tit-Bits* to name 'England's Roll of Fame' and in the *Clarion* to find 'Britain's Greatest Benefactor'. For *Tit-Bits* this was an excuse for a competition with prizes, readers attempting to match their selection with that of the editor. In the winning combination Darwin was not mentioned in the illustrious top ten which included such worthies as the Duke of Wellington, Cecil Rhodes and General Booth. The *Clarion* was much more democratic about the matter, no competition, no prizes, but a poll of readers. Here Darwin emerged as clear favourite (136 votes), pushing Caxton and Cromwell into second and third places (103 and 52 votes respectively). Stephenson, Watt and Lister also received notable support while Newton, Davey and Edison helped bring up the rear. Copernicus received a single vote, but then so did Guy Fawkes, Satan and Keir Hardie's mother.[55]

Despite the popularity of Darwin among socialists we must not fall foul of the fallacy *post Darwin ergo propter Darwin*.[56] The evolutionary strand in radical thought was neither new nor Darwinian. Adrian Desmond has shown that in the radical street literature of the early nineteenth century, progressive transmutation provided a naturalistic analogy for the moral and economic progress attending political transformation – an atheistic blueprint for social change. 'Lamarckian environmental determinism', says Desmond, 'drove out the deity and legitimated the republican struggle by providing a model of ascent power-driven from below.'[57] In the mechanics' institutes of the later nineteenth century, John Laurent finds socialists rejecting individualism and competition, and arguing instead for organicism and co-operation from their evolutionary science.[58]

Clarion socialists were part of this continuing tradition. One correspondent to the benefactor poll supported Darwin for having replaced a 'supine, looking-to-God attitude' with what amounted to a quasi-Lamarckian substitute in 'man as a creature of heredity and environment, whose material salvation depends upon his own exertions'. A second correspondent preferred simply to vote for Kropotkin. The theory of evolution, she believed, had given rise to a view of life that was harsh and devoid of pity, 'excusing the excesses of that rabid licentious "individualism", which came in with the factory system'. Kropotkin, however, 'afforded humanity a glimpse of what might be accomplished by the application of man's riper knowledge and intelligence'.[59] Likewise Harry Lowerison urged readers to study nature for 'you will find mutual aid here as well as rivalry', and in reviewing Kropotkin's *Mutual Aid* Blatchford argued that it was 'partly an amplification, and partly a correction, of the Darwinian theory'.[60]

It was Darwin's emphasis upon environment and evolution that was important for socialists, not his mechanism of natural selection. Indeed, because it stopped the weeding out of the unfit, socialism was seen by its opponents as going against natural selection, thereby threatening to bring racial deterioration and an end to progress. Significantly, when R.B. Suthers at the *Clarion* replied to this objection, he did so not by reaffirming the importance of selection, but by turning to the role of the environment. It was social conditions, he said, which produced the problem of the unfit, and it was the purpose of socialism not to stop the weeding process, but by changing the environment, to make it unnecessary.[61] Thus a good case might be made for seeing late-nineteenth-century socialist environmentalism not as a recently reworked Darwinism, but as the continuation of older Owenite traditions.

This is a point made by Logie Barrow who sees the Owenite mix of rationalism and millennialism transmitted to the 'new Socialism' of the 1880s, 1890s and 1900s by plebeian spiritualism.[62] Certainly Blatchford's (and the *Clarion*'s) educationalist strategy was characteristic of an Owenite perspective, and although the *Clarion* left the matter open to debate, it did lend a sympathetic ear to spiritualism. It did at least discuss the topic, which was more than the other periodicals in the survey, and it shared a number of contributors with the spiritualist magazine *Two Worlds*. Here we seem to come full circle. Religion, of course, was as fertile a soil for socialism as was science, and it is quite likely that the real intention of Blatchford's series was more specifically to weaken the influence of the Labour Church. But there is also one final twist to the knotty problem of science and religion. Shifting our vision forward into the 1920s we can see Robert Blatchford – materialist, socialist and voice of the people – attending seances and voting Conservative.

6 Nature

'Consider the lilies how they grow.' For the Rev. Hugh Macmillan the intention of Jesus's command was quite clear and specific – to study a single plant and 'try and find out what God meant it to say to us'. Nature was a medium for God's message. It was alive with meaning. It lay as an open book waiting to be read, which, together with the Bible (the book of revelation), would make plain not only God's creation but also His will and purpose. Nineteenth-century religious rhetoric was explicit in its use of such textual metaphors. We, with our semiotic susceptibilities, can be a little more sceptical. Furnished with the latest tools of linguistic analysis, we can claim that the world (and 'nature' in particular) does not have any inherent meaning, but has to be 'made to mean'. Any 'text' is open to multi-various readings. Any 'sign' can explode into a polysemic kaleido-scope. Any 'meaning' jostles with others for ascendancy and acceptance. The Book of Nature was no different, its meaning no more transparent than the work of any earthly author.

But to return to Macmillan. Throughout the second half of the nine-teenth century Macmillan published numerous books which highlighted the harmony between the natural and the spiritual world, using scientific research to illustrate moral truths – books with titles like *Bible Teachings in Nature*, *The Ministry of Nature*, and *The Sabbath of the Fields*. In addi-tion, he was a prolific contributor to scientific and religious periodicals, and in his last years wrote a number of articles for *Good Words* (dying in 1903 at the age of 69). For Macmillan the meaning of nature was most often to be found in moral analogies. For example, in the cranberry we find the following lesson. Tall plants are relatively safe and barren, but the smaller plants are in more danger and bear more fruit.

> They rush to bear an abundance of fruit which will link their own lowly lives with generations to come that may grow in happier circumstances. The moral lesson is not difficult to read. Even in the humblest lives that think more of others than themselves the richest fruits are found.[1]

The lessons to be learnt could be religious as well as moral. The after blossom of the cranberry seems a pointless phenomenon, another example of nature's apparent wastefulness and cruelty, but Macmillan concludes:

> Whatever the physical reason may be, the moral design is evidently to impress us with a sense of our own indestructibleness. Even in the

lowest plants there is a vague sense of immortality, some gropings after a resurrection and much more in us the crown and consummation of all God's work.[2]

Macmillan and *Good Words* were by no means alone in seeking to invest nature with a pedagogic function. The *Cottager and Artisan* could also speak of 'A lesson from the hills', and as late as 1914 was referring to the 'Book of Nature', how Christ turned to it for 'texts' and how 'we too may daily learn most useful lessons from it'. This later article told the story of two birds which defend their young from a marauding squirrel, and proclaimed 'What a lesson we may learn from all this', the 'lesson' being the parental instinct given by God to both birds and man, and the love and care of the heavenly Father for His children.[3]

The *Cottager and Artisan* was also no stranger to the use of moral analogies drawn from nature. A collection of anecdotes on birds and fish being attracted by light and so bringing about their own destruction pointed out the moral that 'all is not gold that glitters, and that many things which we think would be very good for us would really do us harm'.[4] Likewise a *British Workman*'s article on 'Drink and the sensitive plant' centred on the analogy between how the Kuikui plant had overrun Samoa and how drink can take hold of a man, while similar analogies were drawn with the invasion of sparrows in America and rabbits in Australia. 'Now to the thinking mind what a moral lies here', exclaimed the article, telling of the weight of responsibility which must lie on the shoulders of those who introduced the 'drink curse' into the country. The analogy becomes more specific. 'And so, to turn from national to individual life, how carelessly and thoughtlessly are habits introduced and begun which are to prove in the long run the greatest enemies of the soul.'[5]

The liberal use of anthropomorphism helped both *Good Words* and the *Cottager and Artisan* to make their moral points. In this way nature was not so much a system of signs to be deciphered, but more a source of illustrative examples of model behaviour in bestial form. The Rev. Robert C. Nightingale, for example, contrasted the world of nature as an ideal – quiet, fixed and conservative – with the world of men which was assertive, bustling and ever-changing. 'What a beautiful life the birds live...it is a perfect life, and shames altogether the poor, trudging heavy one that we men and women have to bear with.'[6] In this world of the upper air inhabited only by God and birds, it was the yellowhammer, always singing and moving, that held the quintessence of bird nature. 'Like most happy dispositions', explains Nightingale, 'the yellowhammer's is a lowly one', the secret of happiness it would seem lying in accepting one's lot, no matter how poor.

I have no doubt the heart within him is too well set to give place to despondency, and he makes the best of every gleam of sunshine and every stray grain of corn that comes in his way. He is a wise bird, and if there were more who adopted the same rule, it would be a better world both for birds and men than it sometimes seems to be.[7]

In the *Cottager and Artisan* the Rev. John Isabell wrote a series of dialogues between a fictitious shoemaker called George and his friend Dick. In these Isabell explained that the 'great book of nature' had taught George more than his little stock of well-thumbed books. 'The flies and the beetles, the grasshoppers and the butterflies, which other people took no notice of or stepped upon, were to him beautiful little texts from which he preached very short sermons to himself.'[8] These sermons were then passed on to Dick. Their colloquial conversation was recorded in the articles which carried titles like 'A chapter about flies', 'A chapter about spiders', or 'A chapter on earwigs', and which highlighted the finer points of the insect concerned, such as the cleanliness of the fly or the parental care of spiders.[9]

Considering the long history of anthropomorphic moralising, it is, perhaps, hardly surprising to find it surviving in the more religious magazines of late Victorian Britain. Thrifty bees and industrious ants were still being held up as models to push home the kind of moral lessons that were typical of self-improvement journals earlier in the century, but it was not only the religious magazines that turned to the study of nature for moral edification. In *Pearson's Magazine* in 1902 Frank Marshall White wrote a number of articles giving anthropomorphic accounts of everyday insect life with titles like 'One day with a working ant' or 'One day with a busy spider'. If we take a closer look at one such article, 'A day in a bee-hive', we can see that in many respects it was no different from the traditional moral tale drawn from nature. White marvelled at the distribution of labour and described the many types of bee, including ladies of honour, chemists, architects, sculptors, wax workers and amazons of the guard. There were also nurses who were 'industrious', 'patient', 'tender', and who were 'thrilled' at the birth of a princess. White also drew a sharp distinction between the workers and the 'lazy', 'useless', 'foolish', 'sluggards', the drones who were up to their necks in the honey vats, asleep. Justice would, nonetheless, be done and the drones would later be slaughtered.[10]

However, there were signs that with time and overuse such ideas were becoming to be seen as somewhat quaint. In 1892 Frederick Burbidge could enthuse over the 'marvellous organisation and ceaseless energy' of the busy bee, that 'social architect' and 'example of self-abnegation', but in 1905 John Fyvie, noting the average Londoner's ignorance about bees, commented:

> Doubtless, in his youthful days, he has been enjoined to admire, and in his own sphere to imitate, that busy little insect. But the extent of his personal observation on the subject has probably been limited to the discovery that the said bee is an evil-tempered little creature with a sting.[11]

Likewise in *Pearson's Magazine* J. Brand had few illusions about the bee's exemplary moral character:

> From our childhood up, we have had the example of bees cast in our teeth. Their natural history has been made up in portable doses, mixed with trite moralities, and administered for the correction of youthful backslidings. And, after all, bees are no better than they ought to be – they are drunkards, thieves, housebreakers, and murderers. Not a bad record for a little insect that has for generations posed as a model of sobriety and well-ordered industry.[12]

Even in *Good Words* an affectionate look at the toad made no outlandish claims for the creature's morals. 'While he is a philosopher the toad is not a moralist. He leaves preaching and nagging to the bee and the ant and other fussy persons with stings...no one has yet seen the way to fix him into an "improving proverb".'[13] It seems the old anthropomorphic moralising was beginning to look a bit dated, a bit too 'preachy', even for the more religious magazines. It did not seem suited to a more worldly-wise twentieth-century readership.

But far from being rejected out of hand, both anthropomorphism and its accompanying moralisation of nature remained, and indeed flourished. Instead what was changing were the assumptions upon which the two were based. The non-religious magazines now offered an alternative interpretation of nature, still anthropomorphic and still morally charged, but with a different tale to tell.

To help illustrate this here are two stories of a single animal – the beaver.

The first is taken from the *Cottager and Artisan* of 1896 and goes under the title of 'The settlers', and it describes the building of a village in the heart of the American backwoods. The settlers of which it speaks are 'clever, active and industrious', and 'never drink anything but water'. They are well mannered, domestic and enjoy privacy. In their work together all is order and method:

There is no dawdling, no laziness. They do not run against each other;
they never get in each other's way. Every one has his own part to fulfil,
and he is doing it with all his might....If you would but follow their
example, what perfect lessons we should have! what useful men and
women you would grow into by and by![14]

It is only now, over half way through the article, that the writer reveals
that the settlers are not men and women, but beavers. However, there is
much that we might learn from the 'forethought, industry, and skill of
these wonderful animals', namely that they are methodical, do not follow
their own will, and work together. There is nothing much here to distinguish this account from the anthropomorphic moralising of former years.

Now compare it with the second story, 'The story of the beaver', written
by William Davenport Hulbert and appearing in *Pearson's Magazine* in
1901. Again the beavers are 'busy little citizens' who in years of peace
marry, build homes and have lots of children, and again the beaver shows
'the old love of work, and of using the powers and faculties that God had
given him', but Hulbert singles out other qualities too. Whereas the
Cottager and Artisan praises the beaver for his 'forethought, industry and
skill', and for being teetotal, well mannered and domestic, in *Pearson's
Magazine* Hulbert highlights the beaver's 'muscle', 'vigour', 'push',
'strength' and 'determination'. In the *Cottager and Artisan* the beaver
illustrates those qualities desirable for social harmony; in *Pearson's
Magazine* it is those qualities born of the struggle for survival. It is after
all a harsh, cruel world that *Pearson's Magazine* presents us with, a world
of the 'fear and suffering and pain' of a beaver who has to tear off his own
hand to escape from a trap, a world where beavers are crushed by falling
trees, and a world where trappers destroy the beavers' ancient city, slaugh-
tering the beaver's family before his eyes. Man is the relentless foe. The
story is set at a time when the woods were 'less infested with men', but
even so, trappers are a constant threat throughout the story and with a
sense of inevitability it is at the hands of a trapper that the beaver finally
dies.[15]

It should not be thought that this was an isolated example. The stories of
W.D. Hulbert were only the start of a new genre of writing which might
best be described as animal biographies, or, depending on the style of
writing, autobiographies. This was particularly true of *Pearson's
Magazine* which published no fewer than 47 of these stories between 1900
and 1908, or nearly one every two months, and this was in addition to any
other articles on natural history. The first of these was Hulbert's 'Pointers
from a porcupine quill' in 1900 when the style was unfamiliar enough to

need explaining in the article's subheading: 'All about the porcupine and its habits told in the form of an interesting story.' The uncompromising presentation of nature as harsh and merciless was clear from the start. Birds starve to death in winter. The young porcupine shows no remorse for his dead mother. A lynx dies in agony with a quill driven through its eye and into its brain. The porcupine is shot in the mouth by a tourist, is unable to eat, and starves until it is finally shot and killed for fun.[16]

By 1907 the form of the story was so familiar, and popular, that one writer felt a need to apologise to naturalists for it. In the preface to his collection of animal life stories S.L. Bensusan wrote:

> The method is indefensible from many standpoints and, in seeking to credit birds and beasts with a measure of intelligence and power of reasoning to which they are supposed to be strangers, in expressing their experiences through the medium of conversational narrative that comes near to assuming a stereotyped form, I am conscious of having committed a grave offence.[17]

In extenuation Bensusan argued that his long experience of the countryside had given him an insight into the mental capacity of animals which, he believed, was greater than was commonly thought. He therefore felt justified for putting forward stories in which 'developments in the lives of wild creatures are presented in the most popular form'.[18]

Bensusan was by far the most prolific of animal biographers in *Pearson's Magazine*, contributing 31 stories between 1902 and 1910 with titles like 'The autobiography of a partridge', 'The life story of a hedgehog', or 'The biography of a bat'.[19] In 1909 the magazine's editorial column felt able to comment: 'Not least popular among the features of Pearson's Magazine during the last year or two have been the animal and bird life-stories contributed by Mr. S.L. Bensusan.'[20] If such a comment were justified then it was a popularity for a view of nature that was no less cruel than that presented by W.D. Hulbert, and again it was man that was the villain of the piece. One has only to look at the fate of the animals whose life histories he relates to see how far man was depicted as nature's enemy. The eagle, the weasel, the raven, the roebuck, the magpie and the barn owl are all shot. Pheasants are 'massacred'; the porcupine killed by trackers. The hare is coursed; the wild boar, the fox and the otter hunted. Even the foxhound, which one might expect to fare better, is run over by a car.[21]

Hulbert and Bensusan were not the only ones to write animal biographies. Marcus Woodward, William J. Long, F. St Mars, Douglas English and Charles G.D. Roberts all contributed such articles to *Pearson's Magazine* between 1902 and 1913, while Roberts also wrote a series on

'Babes of the wild' for *Cassell's Magazine* in 1911 and 1912.[22] What was common to all of these was their narrative form, they each told a story. The editorial of *Pearson's Magazine* was to comment on William J. Long: 'He is a keen observer, with an eye to all the little tragedies and comedies of wild life.'[23] Nature had become a drama, with plots, setting and characters, both villains and heroes. Nature had a story to tell, and as such its description was not natural 'theology' but natural 'history'.

This is important. We are all familiar with anthropomorphism, but our familiarity should not blind us to its many nuances. We have only to put the 'characters' of Beatrix Potter alongside those of Aesop's Fables, *Animal Farm* or *Watership Down* to recognise a wide range of anthropomorphic styles. However, in the opening years of this century the use of a detailed narrative or 'history' was a significant departure from earlier forms of anthropomorphism: a new style of writing, which, as we have seen, needed to be explained to readers, but also a new dimension to anthropomorphism – the direct identification of reader with animal. This is quite explicit, for example, in Hulbert's story of the beaver when he describes the storing of food in a new lodge and writes: '*We* have much goods laid up for many months; let *us* eat drink and be merry, and hope that the trappers will not come tomorrow.'[24]

So long as animals were symbols encoding God's message, or examples of moral standards, or metaphors for human behaviour, there would always be a conceptual gap between ourselves and the natural world, but narrative demands a different relationship. Narrative demands the identification of the reader with the character and personality it describes, and it therefore also demands empathy.

John Berger has argued that until the nineteenth century, anthropomorphism was integral to the relations between man and animal and was an expression of their proximity. The use of animal metaphors, he points out, can be traced back at least to Greek and Roman times.[25] It is not simply in anthropomorphism, therefore, that we should look for evidence of man's increasing awareness of and sensitivity towards nature. But the empathetic relationship demanded by the narrative style of animal biographies was a major new element in the growing sensibilities of man to the natural world, and the constant emphasis on man as the enemy was, in effect, a call for a new relationship with nature.

In his book *Man and the Natural World*, Keith Thomas argues that between 1500 and 1800 there occurred a number of changes in the way men and women perceived and classified the natural world. These changes, he argues, redefined the relationship of man to other species, challenging his right to exploit those species for his own advantage, and giving rise to 'new sensibilities' towards animals, plants and landscape.[26] For Thomas the period begins with the theological assumption that the world was created for man to subjugate and exploit. Human uniqueness rationalised/justified man's treatment of animals and it was the task of religion and of civilisation to maintain that uniqueness and to control the 'bestial' side of human nature. By 1800, Thomas argues, man's ascendancy over the natural world was still the aim of most people, but by now the objective was no longer unquestioned. Doubts had arisen about man's place in nature and his relationship to other species. The detached, 'scientific' study of natural history had discredited many of the earlier theological and anthropocentric perceptions. A closer affinity with animals had weakened old assumptions about human uniqueness and a new concern for the suffering of animals had arisen. There are, however, a number of criticisms of Thomas that can be made and which are relevant here.

First, in arguing that the growth of the scientific study of birds, animals and vegetation helped erode the anthropocentric view of nature, he takes little account of the strength of natural theology at the end of the eighteenth century, and indeed even in the nineteenth century. Natural theology does not even get a mention in the index, and he dismisses William Paley with a single reference on vegetarianism – short shrift indeed for the author of one of Darwin's textbooks at Cambridge.[27] Moreover, this is at odds, to say the least, with Robert Young's analysis of natural theology providing the common context for intellectual debate in the mid-nineteenth century.

Second, Thomas refers to naturalists discarding many of the anthropomorphic assumptions of the past, and starting to study nature in its own right instead of perceiving it primarily in terms of analogies and resemblances to man. 'The conviction that animals and vegetation had religious or symbolic meaning for men remained an article of faith for many Victorian country folk, but it no longer had the support of the intellectuals.'[28] However, anthropomorphism was far from dead. Gillian Beer has analysed Darwin's personification of nature, and D.R. Crocker has urged modern ethologists to recognise their use of anthropomorphism and to take it seriously.[29] 'We cannot help humanising', concludes Crocker. 'Our understanding of ourselves and our societies is the material we inevitably use to build theories of animal social behaviour.'[30] Moreover, as we have seen, the investing of symbolic meaning upon nature survived in popular magazines into the 1890s and I would be hesitant in calling men such as the Rev. Hugh Macmillan 'country folk'.

Finally it is not clear how widespread the 'new sensibilities' were, or which people were involved. In the introduction to his book Thomas refers to the changing perceptions of men and women 'at all social levels', and later he describes the revolution in perception as having 'a traumatic effect upon the outlook of ordinary people', but we have already seen how he distinguishes between the attitudes of 'intellectuals' and 'country folk' towards the symbolic meaning of nature.[31] Similarly the appeal of wild nature, he says, was more likely to be found among those whose social and economic position could afford them the luxury of leaving land uncultivated, and the attraction of unimproved nature was restricted to the educated classes, 'reflecting the highly literary and intellectual inspiration of the new sensibilities'.[32] Moreover, if we turn to the anthropocentric worldview, far from it being eroded, which I believe is central to his argument, Thomas concedes that: 'Of course this was too much for most people; as the nineteenth century debate on evolution would show, anthropocentricism was still the prevailing outlook.'[33]

This raises a further, but related, question: how complete was the 'revolution' by 1800? Unfortunately the evidence is, for the most part, too circumstantial and contradictory for there to be a conclusive answer. The founding of the Society for the Prevention of Cruelty to Animals in 1824 may well be regarded as a sign of increasing compassion, but the need for such a society must also be indicative of widespread and commonplace cruelty.[34] Victorian kindness to animals would also be less than conspicuous in the extinction of whole species by big game hunters, in the ritualised hunting of the fox and other animals, and in the regular shipments of old horses on the 'sausage boats' to the continent.

Let us take the welfare of birds as a case in point. The battue which drove birds over the guns became increasingly popular from about 1840 onwards and laid great emphasis on the numbers of birds killed. Breechloading guns intensified the slaughter and were cheap enough for the new breed of artisan sportsmen who travelled to the coast by excursion train to harry sea birds at close range. The shooting of pigeons from traps, according to one historian, had become a 'national institution' by mid-century and the artificial pigeons introduced in the 1880s were not popular. If not shot for sport birds would be dismembered for fashion, their feathers and wings, or indeed their whole body, being used to decorate hats and dresses. 'At no time had birds been in greater need of protection', writes E.S. Turner. 'Never had they suffered such wanton abuse from the human race.'[35] However, despite this carnage, or even because of it, the concern for bird-life grew. The Society for the Protection of Birds was established in 1889, flourished, soon became a national organisation, and received a Royal Charter in 1904. Meanwhile, towards the end of the century, the practice of putting food out for birds was catching on, especially during the long frost of 1890–1, and wooden nest boxes were beginning to make their appearance in gardens.[36]

Thus, comprehensive as Thomas's account might be, it is still open to question on the nature, extent and timing of this revolution in man's relationship with the natural world. Can we really ignore nineteenth-century natural theology and anthropomorphism? Just how widespread or 'popular' were the new sensibilities? Is 1800 too early a date for seeing the full development of the revolution? To accommodate such problems it might be better to continue the analysis through the nineteenth century, so that Thomas's account gives a broad historical perspective to an understanding of Edwardian attitudes to nature. The carnage of Edwardian shooting parties hardly suggests that the 'revolution' in sensibilities was complete even by 1900, but there is evidence of a new and growing sympathy for the natural world at a truly 'popular' level.

In children's education, for example, attempts were made to foster a compassion for animals. In 1893 *Cassell's Saturday Journal* asked, 'Is cruelty to animals decreasing?', and in reply an officer of the RSPCA was quoted as saying: 'There is no doubt that the more revolting forms of cruelty to dumb beasts are less prevalent than they were a few years back...' This was largely attributed, he said, to the efforts being made among children such as Bands of Mercy and pledges of kindness in *Little Folks*.[37] In 1900 the new subject of nature study was added to the school curriculum, and stressed the importance of preserving all life and of man's maintaining and developing a harmonious co-existence with the natural world.[38] Flora Thompson pointed out the role of schools in educating children about the cruelty of birds' nesting, but was also full of praise for the Boy Scout movement which had 'done more than all the Preservation of Wild Birds Acts to prevent the wholesale raiding of nests, by teaching the boys mercy and kindness'.[39]

It was also at this time that one finds an increasing interest in watching birds rather than in shooting them. Collections became impractical in small London flats, and the efficiency of field glasses had improved, while the growing number of women ornithologists had no taste for weapons.[40] Not only birds but also larger game enjoyed the new fashion. *Cassell's Magazine* noted in 1897 that 'the trapper of the Rocky Mountains has given place to the photographer' who tracks the bighorn and the grizzly bear not to kill them for their peltries, but to photograph them.[41] Similarly in 1902 *Pearson's Magazine* reported how one American sportsman had solved the problem of gratifying the hunting instinct by taking up the camera and 'throwing away the gun he had been so proud of, with a cry of something very like horror, as an instrument that had brought blood-guiltiness on his soul'.[42]

Following early attempts in the 1890s, it was in the Edwardian era that nature photography really took off. Both *Pearson's Magazine* and *Cassell's Magazine* published work by the celebrated nature photographers Richard and Cherry Kearton who in 1895 produced *British Birds Nests*, the first bird book to be completely illustrated with photographs. The attraction of illustrating natural history articles with photographs instead of with drawings was recognised by all the monthlies and soon became the norm rather than the exception. In 1905, under the editorship of *Good Words* contributor E. Kay Robinson, a weekly magazine, *Country-Side*, began publication, crowded with photographs to cater for the new demand in natural history illustration.[43]

The new interest in wildlife was noted and capitalised upon by many of the magazines. *Cassell's Magazine*, for example, introduced a new regular column on flowers, bees and poultry in 1895 with the observation that: 'People in all conditions of life think more of the flowers and country than a few years ago. A healthy awakening to the keen delight of having flowers constantly with us has arisen.'[44]

In 1907 a naval officer told *Cassell's Saturday Journal* about the leisure activities of sailors. 'A great many of the men nowadays are fond of natural history, and when they have a day's leave on foreign stations, numbers of them go hunting for specimens of various kinds, and they chronicle their observations in the log they keep.'[45] Throughout the nineteenth century the 'cult of the naturalist' had been growing. As the 'hard sciences' became increasingly professionalised, natural history still offered a refuge for the enthusiastic amateur.[46] In effect the magazines at the end of the century were simply reflecting, or cashing in on, a rising tide of interest in the subject. *Pearson's Magazine*, for example, encouraged its readers to start botany notebooks, and in the *Clarion* Harry Lowerison regularly gave socialists advice on how best to study nature as well as organising a network of field clubs across the country.

Further evidence of the new concern for nature can be found in the growing desire not only for observation, but also for protection. Environmentalist organisations mushroomed in the second half of the nineteenth century. The foundation of the Commons Preservation Society in 1865 has been described as 'a turning point in the public perception of society's relationship with nature'.[47] Previous suppositions about 'waste' land now faced competing assumptions which gave higher priority to the maintenance of commons as open spaces, emphasising not development but preservation and public access. Other environmentalist organisations were soon to follow: the Lake District Defence Society established in 1883, the Access to Mountains Campaign (1884), the Selborne Society (1886), the National Trust for Places of Historic Interest or Natural Beauty (1895), the Coals Smoke Abatement Society (1898). Of these the Selborne Society was, perhaps, the broadest in its objectives, campaigning for the preservation of birds, plants and forests, as well as being involved in footpaths, commons, ancient monuments, rambling and nature study. Its membership would no doubt have been as diverse as its activities, arising as it did from a merger of the Selborne League founded by George Musgrave, FZS and FRGS, and the Plumage League, jointly founded by the Rev. F.O. Morris (anti-Darwinian naturalist) and Lady Mount-Temple (spiritualist and vegetarian). By 1904 its membership exceeded 1700.[48]

Although many of the organisations were disinclined to seek mass support, their objectives did receive press coverage and, from *Pearson's Magazine* in particular, press support. It was in *Pearson's*, for example, that animal biographer S.L. Bensusan was to write of 'the spirit of protection, the humanitarian instinct, the desire to observe rather than to destroy', as forces striving within everyone, and it was through the pages of the magazine that Bensusan told the story of the Selborne Society's sanctuary 'to counteract the havoc wrought by the "sportsman" and the collector'.[49] *Pearson's* also reported on a code of ethics among sportsmen that made South Africa 'A paradise for big game', and gave space to Linda Gardiner, secretary of the RSPB, to tell of the beneficial role played by birds in the economy of nature.[50] Finally, as part of its series 'Wake up England!' in 1914, the magazine denounced the trade in plumage of rare and wild birds as 'one of the ugliest smears upon the fair fame of our England of today'. Under the heading 'Slaughtered for fashion', the article claimed that the trade had reached the proportions of a 'monstrous crime', and welcomed the forthcoming Importation of Plumage Bill.[51]

If one were to look for evidence of an awakening 'sensibility' towards nature, then the final years of the nineteenth century, and particularly the Edwardian years, would seem to be a fruitful area in which to begin. The upsurge in sentimentalism, the rise of nature study and nature photography, the popularity of life-histories, and the campaigning of environmentalist and animal welfare organisations were all testimony to a new and developing relationship between man and the natural world. Moreover, the magazines of the period bear witness to this growing concern, and may, indeed, indicate that the sense of unease or ambivalence about man's exploitation of nature was felt at a truly popular level. However, that such unease is most conspicuous in *Pearson's Magazine* and that the anti-vivisectionist cause is heard strongest in the *Clarion* suggests that the concern for nature, as widespread as I believe it to have been, was of more importance to some than it was to others, and probably for different reasons. To the anti-authoritarian *Clarion* the importance of the anti-vivisectionist cause was clear.[52] The allegiance of *Pearson's Magazine*, along with that of many individuals, to what might be called the Edwardian nature movement needs further explanation.

The combination of popular journalism and natural history is not one which finds much favour with David Allen.[53] For Allen the personal initiatives of Lord Northcliffe to publish natural history articles were 'subordinate to his instincts as a journalist', and here his training in journalism on the staff of *Tit-Bits* was hardly helpful. Moreover, in the 'peculiar torridness' of the age children's publishers pandered to what they took to be the accepted taste of 'soggy idealism', sentimentalism and mawkishness. 'The study of life-histories, in particular, formed an easy prey for those who felt the urge to view the animal world in human terms, and before long anthropomorphism was rampant.'[54] Allen's attack is also aimed at the addition of Nature Study to the school curriculum in England, the long-term effect of which was 'disastrous'. 'After Nature Study had done its work, a "naturalist" for the average layman no longer conjured up a picture of a rather earnest-looking gentleman tapping on rocks with a hammer or peering at a plant through a lens – but of a grubby urchin with a jam-jar.'[55] Matters were not helped by the emergence of the new range of newspapers and magazines which competed in reflecting the tastes of successive waves of children who now left elementary school. Under the combined impact of nature study and the new journalism, popular writing on natural history soon became 'noticeably more diffuse'. In place of plain factual detail, 'Northcliffe and his imitators prescribed a non-specialised diet, offered in a manner that good professional journalists, rather than good naturalists, were best equipped to accomplish.'[56]

While accepting Allen's account as being a fair representation of turn-of-the-century journalistic representations of nature, I would nonetheless suggest that his polemic is misplaced. True, sentimentalism and a 'diffuse' style are not necessarily conducive to steering natural history on to what Allen calls a 'progressive course', but they are indicative of a developing relationship between ourselves and nature. The journalistic instincts of Northcliffe may have overridden his boyhood interest in natural history, but they would also have alerted him to the growing popular demand for articles on nature, a demand which he attempted to satisfy.

Anthropomorphism may be a poor approach to natural history and so deserving of disparaging remarks, but as I have already argued it can also foster a search for empathy with nature. The publication of life-histories may have been only cashing in on popular taste, but it also shows that the search for empathy (or 'sentimentalism') was widespread enough to make investment in it commercially viable. It may be dismissed as popular taste, but its very popularity suggests that the empathy required by the narrative anthropomorphism of animal biographies really was a major new element in the growing sensibility to nature.

However, Robert Blatchford, for one, took a cynical view of his contemporaries' 'love of nature'. The beauty of nature, he said, had been destroyed in the towns of the North and the Midlands by the pollution of rivers and the tearing up of trees for railway lines. In the *Clarion* of 1912 he wrote: 'We look upon nature as a kind of ornamental adjunct to the serious business of life...we never allow our "love" of nature interfere with trade'.[57] Sportsman and journalist F.G. Aflalo also raised a lonely voice of dissent. In *Good Words* of 1898 he called for deliberate reasoning, not hysteria, in assessing the 'modern protecting craze'. Protection, he argued, was 'the natural reaction from centuries of waste', but it was the height of folly to stop man breeding birds for game and it was unjust for a farmer killing vermin to be judged by 'town dwellers, whose natural history is often limited to what they gather from the perusal of the papers and magazines'.[58]

There is the rub. It was 'city folk' who had the rustic vision. As Richard French has shown, the animal protection movement had an urban power base.[59] Furthermore, of the 'country writing' that was so prevalent at the turn of the century one critic has written: 'Most of the individuals in the "rural" tradition actually lived in the city at various times...more importantly they all wrote for city readers.'[60] The magazine *Country Life* was started in the late 1890s by a country-loving businessman, and *Wind in the Willows* was written by the secretary of the Bank of England. For writer and reader alike, the idealisation of the countryside was an escape from the vice, dirt, smoke and noise of the city, and as such it had a long history. Even before 1800 it had been common to contrast the beauty of the countryside with the horrors of the town. The country was holy, the work of God: the town was corrupt, the work of man.[61] By the end of the nineteenth century the contrasts grew ever more acute as urbanisation proceeded apace, and ever more apparent as the countryside was opened up by motor cars, cheap rail fares, and bicycles.[62]

Paradoxically, at the same time, the spread of suburbia blurred the distinctions between town and country, but it was here, in this land of neat lawns and trimmed hedges, that we can see the concrete realisation of the rural myth, in the rustification of the urban environment. The idealisation of the countryside was not, and never had been, an expression of a genuine desire to live in the country. It did not, for example, stop the migration into towns. It was instead, as Thomas puts it, a 'mystification', an evasion of reality.[63] Significantly the desire to return to what were seen as the simplicities of rural life was almost always expressed by those who were comparatively well off and did not have to face the hardships of agricultural labourers, or the back-breaking toil of farm work.[64] It was to be from the urban middle class and suburbia that the rank and file of the animal protectionists were recruited, and the greatest profits made from rural literature.

This may be little more than symptomatic of what Martin Wiener has seen as the gentrification of the middle classes and the ruralisation of English culture, but two points need to be made.[65] First, there may be more to the middle-class 'love' of nature than simple emulation of aristocratic cultural values. Urbanisation and industrialisation had made nature remote and marginalised. Animals were treated as machines or raw materials in the processes of production and consumption. The explosion in pet ownership in the second half of the nineteenth century turned them into commodities, 'part of that universal withdrawal into the private family unit, decorated or furnished with mementoes from the outside world'.[66] It is the cult of the pet, and in particular its sentimental anthropomorphism, that provides the key to an understanding of anti-vivisectionist fervour and the motivations of other sections of the animal-protection movement.[67] Sentimentalism was not a borrowing from the aristocracy, but may have been a response to an inherent sense of loss within the middle class.

Second, there was an extra facet to the middle-class idealisation of the countryside, especially after the turn of the century, which should be added to Wiener's account. The pursuit of nature not only was one of passive observation and preservation, but was also expressed in a desire to return to nature, a desire which had less in common with English aristocratic culture than it had with the American cult of the wilderness.[68] Nature was to be a source of virility, toughness, savagery, qualities which, like those we saw earlier in Hulbert's story of the beaver, helped define fitness in quasi-Darwinian terms. The wilderness was an aesthetic and ethical resource of beauty and spiritual truth, an escape from the artificialities of the cities to counter the danger of overcivilisation. The sense of return was akin to that of a homecoming. 'For there is now coming to pass a great revival of the study of Nature. More and more, in this age of stress and artificiality, we feel the need of going back to Nature, back to the good land, back to simple pleasures and homely country delights.'[69]

Correspondingly the restlessness for the countryside was not only for the picturesque, but for also the energetic, for camping, hiking, rambling, mountaineering. It was between handsprings and whirligigs that 'The Nature Man' delivered his message to save the world: 'Let suffering humanity strip off its clothing and run wild in the mountains and valleys.'[70] As depicted in the Jack London story, published in *Cassell's Magazine* in 1908, the Nature Man is the epitome of the back to nature devotee. Crawling from his deathbed into the Oregon brush he is revived by the sunshine. He watches the birds and squirrels, envies their health, their spirits, their happy carefree existence, and concludes that 'they lived naturally, while he lived most unnaturally; therefore, if he intended to live, he must return to Nature'.[71] His approach was as extreme as it was simple, stripping off his clothes, running on all fours, eating fruits and nuts, and building a nest of leaves and grass. By 1913, in America at least, fiction became fact. Joseph Knowles went primitive in the woods in Maine, and emerged as a national hero.[72]

In Britain the wilderness ethic would find expression in the nature essays of W.H. Hudson, the popularity of camping, the Boy Scout movement, and the portrayal of nature in animal biographies.[73] Thoreau and Richard Jefferies were recommended reading according to Harry Lowerison in the *Clarion*, but it was in *Pearson's Magazine*, probably the most transatlantic of all the magazines, that the idea of wilderness was most in evidence.[74] It is in *Pearson's Magazine* that we find the greatest interest in natural history, find the most animal biographies (often written by American authors or given American settings), and are most likely to find panegyrics to the virtues of wild nature. The case for returning to nature was presented in 1905 by Marcus Woodward in his article on nature-cure institutes.

> 'Back to nature' is a good little phrase. Apt and concise it stands for a great deal, and so it has won popularity. It represents a movement that has only succeeded in getting under weigh during the last few years, though it has been the dream of thinkers through all the ages since man first turned aside from Nature's paths. For in this movement, in the simple idea of a return to Nature – an end of artificiality, and the beginning again of a rational mode of life – lies the most promising of all signs for the future welfare of our race.[75]

Under the proprietorship of Arthur Pearson, lover of all things American, it may not be surprising that *Pearson's Magazine* appeared particularly susceptible to American influences and ideas, but here we see how such ideas could also be part of Pearson's English context as well. For the belief in a return to nature that is to be found in the magazine, and Pearson's own close association with Baden-Powell and the Boy Scout movement, originated not only in the American wilderness, but also in Pearson's involvement in and espousal of social imperialism.[76]

It has been said of natural theology in the middle of the nineteenth century that its doctrinal imprecision helped it to serve a 'mediating function' at a time of religious dissent.[77] With the demise of natural theology as the common intellectual context, it may be that the 'diffuse' style of the sentimental and anthropomorphic perceptions of wild life helped natural 'history' perform a similar function at a time of social disruption in the Edwardian years.[78] The growth in 'sensibilities' towards nature had a long history, but by the early twentieth century the idealisation of the countryside became firmly established in an increasingly urban society, and we can see in the magazines of the period a genuine search for empathy with nature at a popular level. Nature was in demand. Descriptions and interpretations of it may have differed, but by common consent it was to be pursued, observed and protected. It may be, therefore, that social imperialism and a desire to return to nature are best seen as particular Edwardian responses to the growing pressures of civilisation and part of a broader 'nature movement'. They were, however, responses which affected perceptions not only of the natural world, but also, as we shall see, perceptions of 'man' himself.

7 Evolution

In many respects Darwin's theory of evolution challenged fundamental values of the Victorian era by making natural development an essentially haphazard and undirected process. Consequently in the late nineteenth century there was a massive rejection of Darwinism in favour of alternatives such as Lamarckism and orthogenesis that implied more order and purpose.[1] As Peter Bowler has shown, these years witnessed not only 'an almost complete collapse of the argument from design as it had once been understood',[2] but also the decline of the theory that had done most to undermine it. The demise of traditional natural theology was accompanied by the 'eclipse of Darwinism'. Many Christians found in Lamarckian evolution the 'spiritual dimension' by which they could reinterpret or transform their Darwinist theories.[3] The result was that church acceptance of evolution often amounted to little more than the adoption of a pre-Darwinian, Hegelian belief in spirit progressively dominating matter, and the assimilation of Darwin by late Victorian theologians as often as not turns out to have been the assimilation of Spencer instead.[4]

A sense of purpose in nature provided common ground for both 'providential evolutionists' like Owen, Argyll and Mivart, and 'providential Darwinists' like Lyell, Gray and Wallace.[5] James Moore writes:

> liberal Christians who preserved God's purposes in nature by subjecting natural selection to the components of Lamarckian evolution had, in so doing, embraced concepts of a universal providence through which the divine omnipotence and beneficence could also be preserved.[6]

For Christian Darwinists such as Drummond or Temple progress was not so much a way to avoid the unpleasantness of natural selection as 'a shrewd attempt at reinterpreting natural evils as preconditions for progressively greater goods'.[7] By adulterating Darwinism with the concept of inevitable material, social and spiritual progress, Christians could construct a new theodicy from evolutionary theory.[8] In the doctrine of evolution, Frederick Temple and other liberal Protestant scholars found the basis for what John Durant has called 'a new natural theology of providential progress'.[9]

There were, however, differing responses from pulpit and pew. The consecration of Frederick Temple as the new Archbishop of Canterbury in 1896 might be seen as marking the final acceptance of evolution (as permissible and respectable doctrine) among the divines, clergy and leading laity of the established Church (although John Kent believes that most theologians had not come to terms with evolution even by 1914). 'As a matter of fact', the *Family Herald* told its readers, 'nine out of ten of the most prominent ministers of the day, the representative men of Christianity, are Christian evolutionists.'[10] But for a decade or two after 1896, as Owen Chadwick has written, 'most of the simple worshippers among the chapels of the poor, continued to know nothing of evolution or to refuse to accept it on religious grounds'.[11]

The religious press did its best to reassure readers that all was well. 'Evolution', explained the *British Workman*, 'is only a term invented by certain people because they do not like to use the term creation on account of it being a Bible word.' Life, it said, could only come from pre-existing life, and evolution was as much an act of creation as the making of a creature direct from elementary matter. Both needed the intervention of a creator at every stage. 'Is the argument of design weakened by the theory of evolution?' asked one correspondent to *Good Words and Sunday Magazine*. 'On the contrary', came the reply, 'it seems to me to be strengthened, for whereas before it was proved by isolated illustrations, it is now applicable to the whole order of creation.' Everywhere was evidence of law, it said, and it was impossible to have law without a law-giver. 'Depend upon it', the *British Workman* declared, 'if evolution be proved to be a great natural law it will be equally evident that it is God's law.'[12]

What may have given most comfort was to beat the evolutionists at their own game, not simple assurances that Christian belief and evolution were compatible, but rather the downright appropriation of evolutionary theory for Christian theology. In *Good Words*, for example, Donald Macleod used concepts of heredity and environmental influence to highlight man's moral freedom and duty. Important lessons were to be learned which it was the duty of the Church to recognise: sins of sloth and drunkenness could be passed on from parents to children; through faithful struggling the heredity of evil could be resisted; and there was a heritage of blessing which it was incumbent upon every man and woman to bequeath.[13] Gladstone in his 'Impregnable rock' series made the same point: 'Thus the doctrine of birth-sin, as it is sometimes called, is simply the recognition of the hereditary disorder and degeneracy of our natures; and of all men the evolutionist would be the last to establish a title to object to it in principle.'[14] Appropriation could even be pushed to the point of claiming to be more 'Darwinian' than the Darwinians. In *Good Words* F.G. Aflalo remarks that the differences between men and monkeys [sic] are far more puzzling than the supposed similarities, 'but I suppose they are less attractive to that element in the population that is pleased to affect what it calls "Darwinism", fathering on the Master Thinker a theory of direct descent from apes that might well make him turn in his grave'.[15] This is not to say that critics of Darwin are not to be found – an article on Lord Salisbury takes great delight in recounting his presidential address to the British Association and quotes at length Kelvin on design[16] – but rather that the most common position was the incorporation of evolution into a pre-existing Christian framework.

Even natural selection could be taken into account. The Rev. Hugh Macmillan's description of the struggle for life in a tropical forest would have satisfied the most hardened of Darwinians. As a consequence of this terrible struggle 'everything that has life is cruel and pitiless'.[17] Everything regards only its own well-being, taking advantage of its weak neighbours to make room for itself. The competition between shoots inside a Brazil nut is a 'miniature representation of the terrible selfishness of nature and its carelessness of the single life'. The struggle of the successful shoot is carried on in a 'calm, passionless indifference – like the law of gravitation'. 'It seems to have no moral character. The will has nothing to do with it. It is the law of natural selection, the survival of the fittest, which is as unmoral as any other law of nature...'[18] But far from trying to reconcile Christian ethics with nature's amorality, Macmillan attempted to transcend the problem. The law of natural selection, he said, was not the only law under which he was placed.

That lower, cruel selfish law may mould my material nature, and affect my purely physical actions in ways of which I am not conscious and cannot help. But my being is under a higher law...the law of Christ – that law of supernatural selection which makes the strong consider the weak, the rich the poor, and the fortunate brother of high degree the unfortunate brother of low degree.[19]

The same separation of the spiritual from the material, the religious from the scientific, is to be found in a 'Sunday reading' of 1897 which raised the thorny topic of evolution and the creation of man. If man's physical nature is subject to the law of evolution, it argued, it does not follow that his spiritual nature must have no other source. Without any loss to religious faith, it said, we can make a present of the body to the anatomist and physiologist to examine and propound any theory they please as to the place it occupies in evolution.

There can be no likeness to God – who is spirit – in these physical organs which can be dissected and compared with those of other animals....The animal part, the corruptible which returns to corruption, may belong to poet and apostle in common with the beasts that perish, but what constitutes Man is not there. The part which has been created in the image of God cannot be touched by the scalpel or resolved in the crucible. It belongs to a different sphere.[20]

By 1907 the position of the magazine was made all the more clear in its replies to readers' queries. One correspondent, for example, asked: 'Did God directly create man, or did God produce him from the lower animals?' The magazine's answer, presumably penned by Macleod, was that while evolution may explain the physical development of man, the mind of man, his mental, moral and spiritual facilities, are so great as compared with the lower forms of life, that they afford evidence of direct creation. 'Man is not body', says the magazine, 'but mind, soul. This we believe came direct from God.'[21]

But these issues were old hat. For the general reader, evolutionary controversies were the stuff of yesteryear. In the popular press of the 1860s, Alvar Ellegard found that 'the Darwinian theory was hardly referred to at all except in its relation to religion'.[22] By the 1890s this was no longer the case. In the 1860s, says Ellegard, 'to the general public Darwinism was at least as much a religious as a scientific question'.[23] By the end of the century this was true for the Christian public and almost certainly the case for the socialist public, but for the general public the debate had moved on. Whereas in the 1860s attention had focused upon the concept of evolution itself and very little consideration was given to natural selection or the descent of man:[24] in the 1890s the fact of evolution was taken for granted (even in the more religious periodicals) and interest now centred on evolutionary mechanisms and man's animal history.

Moreover, socialists, Christians and the general reader were of one mind in their preference for non-Darwinian evolutionary theory, especially when such theory was applied to our own species. Disturbed by the prospect that humans were the product of an undirected (and possibly amoral) process, many preferred to see nature as progressive and purposeful with man as the predetermined goal.[25] When the 'Sunday reading' of 1897 discussed the creation of man it dismissed the theory of evolution as of 'comparative little religious consequence', since both it and the theory of separate creation of species 'equally assign to man the position of highest and last in the various ranges of organised existence'.[26] For Emma Marie Caillard, man was not a mere inhabitant of the universe, but 'its expression and its interpretation'. God, she argued, revealed Himself as a personal being and science teaches that personal life is the outcome of evolution. 'Seen from the Christian standpoint, therefore, modern science shows us that the whole aim of creation has been the production of beings whose personality stamps them as sons of God.'[27] The popular survival of recapitulation theory would have further reinforced man's status as the acme of the evolutionary process. 'The life-history of the individual is the life-history of the race in epitome', Caillard wrote, 'because many of the gradations through which the individual passes in his embryonic stage are found as existing forms of adult animal life.'[28]

The theory of recapitulation was the organising principle for a mélange of analogies. Race, gender, crime and child development could all be analogised and cross-referenced within a single framework. Male youths would have to pass through the 'woman stage' of character before developing into men. Women represented the 'lower race' of gender. Children were naturally criminal. The criminal was a savage in civilisation. The savage was a child.[29] In the nineteenth century, as Nancy Stepan has argued,

> By analogy with the so-called lower races, women, the sexually deviate, the criminal, the urban poor, and the insane were in one way or another constructed as biological 'races apart' whose differences from the white male, and likenesses to each other, 'explained' their different and lower position in the social hierarchy.[30]

Inferior intellectualities of both women and the 'lower races' could be explained on the basis of low brain weights and deficient brain structures. Women and negroes, it was believed, shared a narrow, childlike and delicate skull. Both tended to have slightly protruding jaws. Both were seen as innately impulsive, emotional, imitative rather than original, and incapable of the abstract reasoning found in white men. In short, says Stepan, 'lower races represented the "female" type of the human species, and females the "lower race" of gender'.[31]

Certainly the New Woman faced old prejudices. In the last decades of the nineteenth century the male population of Britain was faced with a rising tide of female emancipation. Hard fought and small as the concessions were, women's rights gained ground in law, education and employment. The fight against prejudice and injustice had brought new divorce legislation, Married Women's Property Acts, improved female secondary education, the founding of women's colleges at Oxford and Cambridge, and employment in teaching, the civil service, shops and offices. Male fears were clearly expressed in the humour of the periodical press. *Cassell's Saturday Journal* of 1897 had a 'modern woman' describe her day which included hearing papers on the 'Architecture of the probable capital of Mars' and 'Microscopic insects of Central Africa', as well as attending meetings of the 'Seventeen Great Religions Club' and the 'Society for the Reformation of Murderers' (titles which also highlight other preoccupations to be held up to scorn).[32] In like vein *Pearson's Weekly* in 1892 took a look at 'The fireside of the future' where the wife goes out to a Mahatma seance, the Ladies Trouser League and the Antique Moth-eaten Angels Association, while ('Heaven preserve us from the future') the husband stays at home washing, darning socks and patching skirts.[33]

The male assault upon movements for women's emancipation was actively reinforced by the conduct and attitude of doctors.[34] Smith-Rosenberg and Rosenberg argue that, hopeful of preserving existing social relationships, men 'employed medical and biological arguments to rationalise traditional sex roles as rooted inevitably and irreversibly in the prescriptions of anatomy and physiology'.[35] It was medical orthodoxy, for example, that women were not only frailer but had a finer nervous system which made them more irritable. The 'nervous woman' was a particularly nineteenth-century phenomenon and a vast array of electrical gadgets and patent medicines were on offer to alleviate the problem, but the debate over neurasthenia was only part of a larger ideology defining women's role in society as dependent and subordinate. Women were prisoners of their own bodies, subject to the physical and emotional changes of pregnancy, and controlled by their internal organs, especially the uterus and ovaries. The campaign for women's suffrage met vigorous resistance from doctors who emphasised the conflicting demands of motherhood and intellect, uterus and brain. The body, it was argued, contained only a certain amount of 'vital force' which, if expended in one area (say intellectual activities), would divert energy from other areas (such as the achievement of true womanhood). If a woman were to compete in education then this would disarrange her nervous system, leaving her anxious and open to hysteria. Women were regarded as innately sick, and, for Ehrenreich and English, hysteria 'epitomises the cult of female invalidism'. This, they say, was 'the gynaecologists' solution to the Woman Question'.[36]

In the periodical press we can see such attitudes not only in the humour but also in the medical information that was presented. One source that was often quoted was the Lord Chancellor's Visitor in Lunacy, Sir James Crichton Browne. In *Cassell's Magazine* in July 1892 he was reported as saying that the differences between men and women are founded on the structures of the brain, the male brain being heavier and having a higher specific gravity. Moreover, in the male brain more blood is supplied to the front which is the seat of cognition and volition, but in the female more blood is supplied to the rear which is 'mainly concerned with the senses'. It was from this that Sir James took up the common cry 'against the present tendency to over educate women by instructing them like men'.[37] That same month the 'exhaustive observations' of Dr Crichton Browne and Dr Francis Warner were reported in *Pearson's Weekly* 'to show that the modern girl is being over-educated', on the basis that a female's blood has fewer red corpuscles than that of a male, so resulting in women becoming anaemic if they try to compete with men.[38]

It was, perhaps, this threat of the 'over-educated' woman that most alarmed the late Victorian male who believed the direst consequences would surely follow if women were allowed to develop intellectually. In 1890 *Tit-Bits* asked 'Are women becoming bald?' and answered, yes, most importantly because they were getting more involved in business and politics.

> The fact that women are developing into thinking beings...will undoubtedly tell on their tresses...premature baldness and a high state of intellectuality have much in common, and the more highly a woman's intellect is cultivated the more likely it becomes that the abundance of her hair will suffer.[39]

This twin fear of women becoming more active and less beautiful was given further scientific credibility in *Pearson's Weekly* in 1893: 'The ugliest women in the world are the cleverest according to Sir Crichton Browne. He fears that what woman gains intellectually by the higher education now in vogue she will lose in beauty and grace and often in health too.' The article went on to cite the example of the 'Garo' women. 'They woo the men, they control the affairs of the home and the nation, property descends through them, and in everything they are dominant, but – note the sequel – they are the very ugliest women on the face of the earth.'[40] As an illustration of the dangers of female intellectualism the story proved so convenient that in 1902 it was repeated not only in *Pearson's Weekly*, but also in *Tit-Bits* and *Cassell's Saturday Journal* (although by now these monstrosities of womankind had become the 'Zaro' women of India).[41]

The linearity of recapitulation theory resulted in a temporally determined hierarchy with man (in every sense of the word) at the top and the rest of creation assigned its own 'natural' place beneath. 'Intellectual' women were not only rising above their (evolutionary) station but they were also going against nature. But there is a paradox here which will become apparent when we look at another element in the mélange of analogies – the civilising process and the progress of the 'lower races'.

The most extensive use of recapitulationist ideas is to be found in two articles by palaeontologist S.S. Buckman, both under the title 'Our descent from monkeys', which appeared in *Pearson's Magazine* in 1902 and 1903. Answering the question why a baby is not just a miniature replica of an adult, Buckman explained that each different form of life 'has to pass through the preceding stages of its long history in a condensed and abbreviated manner before it becomes like its own parents'. Thus the human baby is different from the adult, because 'the baby represents the ancestral monkey-like stage – that last stage which is passed through before the real human being is elaborated'. The human baby is not just a miniature replica of an adult man, said Buckman, because it 'represents the ancestral monkey-like stage' of human development. A baby's habits are curious because they are not really human. 'They are modes of action inherited from the monkey-like parents of long ago.'[42] A snub nose, projecting jaw, furrowed upper lip, bow legs, the power to move its toes, and the clasping attitude of its hands were all ancestral features to be found in a baby, while the desire for climbing, destructive habits and predatory instincts were vestiges of tree-top foraging. (In *Cassell's Saturday Journal* even the mental development of a baby was to be explained by reference to simpler life forms, the responses of a baby to looking at a mirror resembling in turn those of a bird, cat, monkey and man.)[43]

Implicit in much of the writing about race was the idea that black Africans suffered from an arrested evolutionary development, a development through which Europeans had passed and whose vestiges could still be seen in children. Prognathism was seen to provide clear evidence of this, as Buckman explained:

> In another respect babies are comparable with monkeys and with other lower animals – namely in the projection of the nose and jaw beyond the line of the forehead. This facial feature is known as prognathism....It is a special character in the physiognomy of negroes: they retain it throughout life. But Europeans do not retain it.[44]

The 'negro', therefore, was at the same time ape-like and child-like. He still resembled a monkey, and had advanced no further than a European child.

There was, however, a further sense in which the black man's development was seen as arrested. His social organisation was likened to that of prehistoric man. Between 1897 and 1900 Herbert Ward, a Fellow of the Royal Geographical Society, wrote a series of occasional articles for *Cassell's Magazine* on the lives of the Congo natives. For the most part they were a sympathetic attempt to understand savage life, but common assumptions still coloured the account they gave, and in one description of the natives dancing at night man's prehistory was put into living flesh: 'The scene is weird, the sounds are barbaric; it is a picture of life in its early Iron Age.'[45] It was no different from the scene painted by Conrad in *Heart of Darkness* – a journey up the Congo and back in time to the dark unrestrained soul of primeval man: 'Going up that river was like travelling back to the earliest beginnings of the world.' 'We were wanderers on pre-historic earth', where the native cannibals 'still belonged to the beginnings of time'.[46]

Evolutionism brought a new dimension and a new scientific authority to racial distinctions and hence to racial stereotyping.[47] A timescale was added to racial descriptions where the black man was now seen not simply as 'savage', but as 'primitive', as 'less evolved' than the civilised white man. Such a belief underlies much of the period's popular fiction. The Bushman, in John Buchan's description, was 'one of the lowest of created types, still living in the Stone Age', and to Bertram Mitford was 'no more than half ape', a 'descendant of the baboons'.[48] The use of evolutionary language to depict native populations was particularly common in *Pearson's Magazine*. Here, for example, is Herbert C. Fyfe's telling of 'The first traverse of Africa', an article in which virtually all the natives are portrayed as ghoulish savages:

> Whilst exploring in the Kako Valley Mr Grogan observed some ape-like creatures, which might be the missing-link in the Darwinian theory.... 'The stamp of the brute,' said Mr Grogan in his recent lecture before the Royal Geographical Society, 'is so strong on these people that I would place them lower in the human scale than any other natives I have seen in Africa.'[49]

But it was not only *Pearson's* which likened Africans to apes. In its section headed 'Scientific notes' the *Clarion* had a short piece titled simply 'Evolution confirmed': 'the king presides and the others sit around in a semi-circle...and some of the sounds uttered by the gorilla and the chimpanzee are identical with certain sounds uttered in the native language.'[50]

That a 'progressive' publication like the *Clarion* should reproduce such ideas is a useful reminder of how extensive racialist assumptions were. Stereotyping was not to be found only in the more sensationalist weeklies. Elsewhere in the *Clarion* we can read a poem by Montague Blatchford attacking Cecil Rhodes, but with the following description of the indigenous population

His nose is flat, his mouth is wide
His air is exceedingly dignified
And his lips are a trifle thickish...

Robert Blatchford's view of the women dockside porters of Jamaica is
hardly less stereotypical: 'with their bold sensuous eyes rolling, and their
white teeth gleaming...[they] gave me the impression of untamed and
untameable diablerie....I am deceived...if they are not as wild as any wild
women in darkest Africa.'[51]

Stereotypes perpetuate a needed sense of difference between 'self' and
'other'.[52] In the periodical press 'natives' of foreign lands were, perhaps
above all else, different, strange, alien. A Tibetan, we are told in *Cassell's
Saturday Journal*, salutes his superiors by raising his hat and sticking his
tongue out three times. According to *Tit-Bits* it is part of Chinese religion
to kill those who are crippled or deformed. In Persia men who laugh are
thought to be effeminate. In Central Africa tribes carry out debates standing on one leg.[53] But it was difference in skin colour that was probably the
most conspicuous racial distinction. The polarity of black and white was a
source of constant interest, especially in the weeklies where it took on
almost proverbial significance. Reports of men and women whose skin
colour had changed (always from black to white, never the reverse) were
as common as stories which refuted such a possibility.[54] In *Tit-Bits* it
became the ultimate test of modern science. One correspondent asked
whether 'science has come to such perfection that it can turn a black man
into a white one and live, by means of electricity'. The magazine's
response was that although this was probably one of the few things that
science would never be able to do, 'many things have been declared by
scientists to be impossible and have afterwards been accomplished'.
Indeed only the previous week *Tit-Bits* reported that a 'well known scientist' was able to 'decarbonise' a black man's skin using electricity, thus
turning him into a white man. However, the article did add that the scientist was still trying to perfect the technique of how to apply the current.[55]

There was an underlying continuity of ideas in the scientific validation
of prejudice, even in the face of profound changes in the natural sciences
themselves. The history of racial science shows a series of accommoda-
tions to the demands of deeply held convictions about the 'naturalness' of
inequalities.[56] Nor was this simply the social use to which scientific
knowledge was put. In literature, fine arts, popular culture, science and
medicine blacks, women, proletarians and children were associated in a
'web of analogies' that linked difference with pathology.[57] Stereotypes
from science existed before imperial rule, but at the end of the century

developments in anthropology strengthened the use of race as a classification and reinforced the belief in the inferiority of 'natives'. Imperial politics, scientific study and popular literature had, what Brian Street calls, a 'unity of consciousness' in the perception of 'primitive man' especially from the 1870s onwards.[58] In vivid imaginative form the novels of Buchan, Haggard, Ballantyne, Mason, Burroughs and others brought to a wider public the ideas and debates being conducted in scientific circles regarding the nature of society in general and 'primitive' society in particular. As Street says, 'we find writers using racial characteristics to stereotype whole peoples in ways for which they could claim some justification since the scientists were doing the same thing'.[59] By the close of the century racism was firmly established in both popular opinion and in science. Racial stereotypes were deeply embedded in Victorian culture. It is not at all surprising, therefore, to find them in the popular periodicals of the time.

In October 1899 *Pearson's Weekly* asked: 'Are we an aggressive race?' The essence of its reply was that the British were indeed an aggressive race, but then so were all nations. Progress, it argued, came only from being strong and conquering weaker states, and progress was seen in the Empire where natives were happier now than they had been before they were colonised. Not all natives were happier though. 'There are coloured races who wither in the presence of civilisation, but that is because they are deficient in that quality which we call adaption to environment.' The article did admit that the British had their faults, but in balance with their virtues:

> It will be found that in all the qualities which go to form a noble people Great Britain stands far ahead from the rest of the world.
>
> Indeed it may be truly said that the future hopes of mankind depend on the Anglo-Saxon race.
>
> With so many nationalities at the present exhibiting signs of decadence, notably the French, it may also be affirmed that were our race to suddenly die out the world would lapse into barbarism.[60]

Published in the same month as the opening of hostilities in the Boer War, the article seems motivated by a desire to reply to possible criticisms of British policy in South Africa and, in some respects, may be seen as a popular, or even populist, form of Social Darwinism.

This may be true to a point, but it obscures as much as it explains. In the first place, Social 'Darwinism' is something of a misnomer since the evolutionary model was most often Lamarckian in shape. In the second place, the evolutionary assumptions behind the imperialism in the magazines did not necessarily have the aggressive connotations found in this article and which modern commentators often associate with Social Darwinism. It was more commonly an ideology of supremacy, not necessarily one of conquest.[61] Ape-like, child-like, prehistoric – the metaphor may have changed, but the cumulative effect was to underline the belief in the inferiority of black races, and the 'natural' role of inferior races was to serve since they were simple, childlike, faithful and gullible. The 'child-like' savage had a long tradition, but within an evolutionary context it took on a new meaning. 'The "primitive-as-child" argument', says Gould, 'stood second to none in the arsenal of racist arguments to justify slavery and imperialism',[62] but the idea of child savages developing into mature adult nations helped foster paternalism and trusteeship.[63] The use of evolutionary assumptions in the popular magazines emphasised the Empire as a civilising process; not the survival of the fittest, but the white man's burden. In this way even such an ardent critic of empire as J.A. Hobson could accept the need for the 'backward people' of the world to be governed by the 'progressive' white races.[64]

The call for 'civilisation' echoed through much of the writing on 'savage' cultures. In *Pearson's Magazine* an article on cannibalism remarked: 'The people who practise it see in it no wrong; so that nothing but punishment and the gradual progress of civilisation can be expected to eradicate the habit.'[65] It is true that the 'punishment' may be pursued with missionary zeal, but the zeal should not be allowed to cloud our perspective of the mission, and it would be a misrepresentation of the magazines to put that mission into simple Social Darwinistic terms. Magazines were more likely to be patronising to natives, rather than simply antagonistic. *Cassell's Magazine*, for example, confessed that 'in truth, we know very little as yet about the capacities of the African tribes for civilisation', but concluded that 'some of the tribes have a degree of artistic skill which is not to be despised, and promises well for the future'[66] – a comment which has the same ring to it as an end-of-term school report.

What was 'civilised', of course, bore a marked resemblance to what was most highly regarded in Victorian society. *Cassell's Saturday Journal*, for example, told its readers that the natives of New Guinea 'number amongst them some of the most backward of the savage races of the world'. They use stone tools, and have cannibal feasts and hideous customs, but 'So strong is the influence of civilisation that these things are growing rarer every year. A striking result of this influence is seen in the fact that the natives, who in their primitive state are extremely indolent, are becoming industrious.'[67] In *Tit-Bits* primitive indolence took on moral overtones of the self-help variety. The Swantians near the Black Sea, it said, were the 'laziest people in the world'. They have holidays four days a week, and 'have made no advance towards civilisation in 2,500 years'.[68]

And here lies the paradox. What better example of self-help could be found than the strivings of the New Woman to improve her own position? Sociocultural evolutionists had an answer to hand. By presenting the monogamous Victorian family not as a 'natural' institution but as the 'civilised' culmination of social evolution, anthropologists 'provided a solid, historical, evolutionary justification for the role of women in their own culture'.[69] The conjunction of anthropological debate over matriarchy with the contemporaneous undermining of patriarchal authority, as George Stocking points out, 'seems scarcely an historical coincidence'.[70] The civilising process of Empire was dragging 'primitive' peoples step by step up the evolutionary ladder; analogously, but to use a modern idiom, sisters were doing it for themselves. The real difference, perhaps, was that the Woman Question was, quite literally, too close to home.

Not that middle-class society (and middle-class men) were always seen as the endpoint of evolution. The start of a new century would see to that. The civilising process would continue, and with it evolution. In the weekly press it was not our past that was of particular interest, but our future. The widespread acceptance of our evolution from ape-like ancestors had removed the novelty value from speculation on the subject, but readers' curiosity could still be stimulated with forward projections of our future (predominantly Lamarckian) development. According to Dr Francis A. Whitely, quoted in *Tit-Bits*, 'the future man's legs will, from lack of use, become very small and atrophied'. In the 'flying age' of the future, man will have a large heart to adapt to the rarefied atmosphere. 'His face will be of the ferrety type', explained Dr Whitely. 'His upper jaw will be greatly developed, and his expression keen, restless, and eternally strained.' Moreover, his eyes 'may become beady and bird-like, with the power to gaze not only before him, but horizontally outwards without movement of the head like a bird'.[71] *Pearson's Weekly* had a different vision. Basing its prediction on the axiom 'What is not needed disappears', the magazine argued that 'the man of the year 1,000,000 AD will be all brain, eyes and hands'. Teeth and hair will decay, it said, while man's jaw, mouth, nose and ears will all become smaller. 'Picture to yourself, then, a vast head, oblong and egg-shaped, supported on two huge sensitive hands with diminished body and tiny feet....The whole muscular system will be shrivelled into mere nothingness, a dangling, degraded, pendant to

1. Evolution guaranteed Progress. Advertisement for *Science History of the Universe*, taken from *The Clarion*, 23 August 1912 (British Library).

the mind.'[72] The effect of modern transport, it believed, was already noticeable in dwindling legs and feet.

Past, present and future were brought together by H.G. Wells in one grand evolutionary pageant. An inductive knowledge of the future was possible, he told readers of *Cassell's Magazine*, and there was no excuse for limited visions.

> We look back through countless millions of years and see the will to live struggling out of the inter-tidal slime, struggling from shape to shape, and from power to power, crawling and then walking confidently upon the land, struggling generation after generation to master the air, creeping down into the darkness of the deep; we see it turn upon itself in rage and hunger and reshape itself anew; we watch it draw nearer and more akin to us, expanding, elaborating itself, pursuing its relentless, inconceivable purpose, until at last it reaches us, and its being beats through our brains and arteries, throbs and thunders in our battleships, roars through our cities, sings in our music, and flowers in our art. And when, from that retrospect, we turn again toward the future, surely any thought of finality, any millennial settlement of cultural persons, has vanished from our minds.[73]

Rhetoric and rhythm sweep the reader along as much as the evolutionary surge, anthropomorphised and purposeful, sweeps man onward to his destiny. 'We are in the beginning of the greatest change that humanity has ever undergone', declared Wells. We are entering upon a progress that 'will go on with an ever-widening and ever more confident stride, for ever'.[74]

An advertisement for the *Science History of the Universe* captured the vision in a single illustration – a temporal slice through the evolutionary panorama. Progressing through time and up the page were the primeval swamp, the sea and the land, each with its respective life forms from evolutionary history. At the top, in the skies, the pinnacle of evolution, was man in the conquest of the air, subduing nature with a flying machine. Evolution was now to be decided by technology. The future was at man's command.[75]

8 Progress

To many people it must have seemed that the future was at the command of one man in particular. The forecasts of H.G. Wells, says Patrick Parrinder, 'were treated more as news than as subjects for critical judgement'.[1] Moving freely between literature and journalism, Wells came to represent a new type, the 'democratic man of letters', seeking to influence the thoughts, feelings, morals and politics of the new reading public. While still a teacher he wrote scraps of journalism for *Answers* and *Tit-Bits*, but what enabled him to devote himself to fiction was the ease of serial publication and the publicity it brought. The main outlet for his scientific romances and stories was the new popular magazines, and he became identified with the 'suburban' and 'half-educated' reader to whom these magazines were supposed to appeal.[2] Both *The War of the Worlds* and *The Food of the Gods* were first published in *Pearson's Magazine*, and *The Invisible Man* was first published in *Pearson's Weekly*.[3] Several of Wells's short stories were published or reprinted in *Pearson's Magazine*, and he also contributed to the *Clarion* and *Cassell's Magazine*. Alternating moods of hope and despair continued throughout Wells's life, but even at his gloomiest the hint of hope never disappeared. Wells was 'consistently utopian'. 'The science fantasies', says Krishan Kumar, 'are offered as so many cautionary fables, so many dreadful warnings to humanity to look to itself, to take stock of its current sick condition and remedy it before it is too late.'[4] As Wells explained in the *Family Herald* in 1899: 'I am strongly of opinion that we ought to consider the possibilities of the future much more than we do....At present we are almost helpless in the grip of circumstances, and I think we ought to strive to shape our destinies.'[5] Over the next six years Wells was to devote much of his creative energy to describing the utopian future for which man would and should strive. Its first full exposition came in 1901 with the publication of *Anticipations*, and drew criticism from A.M. Thompson at the *Clarion* who objected in the main to Wells's concept of 'efficiency'. Wells replied the following week that Thompson had made the 'cardinal blunder' to mistake 'an attempt to calculate the resultant of the forces at work in our present society, for a social Utopia'.[6] But for all his protests that it was intended to be predictive and not prescriptive, Wells's *Anticipations* has much in common with his later, more propagandist book *A Modern Utopia* – the mechanisation of labour, eugenics, the world-state, and the governing of the 'New Republic' by a technocratic elite (the 'Efficients' or the 'Samurai').

Umberto Eco has written that this type of fantastic literature, the 'novel of anticipation', is the most accurate definition of science fiction because its conjecturality is the very essence of all science. Science fiction exists as an autonomous genre, says Eco, 'when a counterfactual speculation about a structurally possible world is conducted by extrapolation from certain tendencies in today's world'.[7] For some reason Eco does not follow this up with a discussion of Wells, but instead dismisses him with a single reference to *The Time Machine* which, with its comments about a visit to a prehistoric people and a lost world, suggests that he has not read the book. Be that as it may, the utopia of Wells is precisely what Eco calls a 'metatopia' or 'metachronia', where 'the possible world represents a future phase of the world as we have it here and now'.[8] The plausibility of any future is the key to the 'conjectural wager' of both scientist and SF writer and the close similarity between the possible and the desirable (between *Anticipations* and *A Modern Utopia*) reveals the basic assumption upon which Wells's inductive reasoning was based. Wells had hope in the future. *A Modern Utopia*, in the opinion of I.F. Clarke, 'remains the most important utopia of the twentieth century, because it made the most complete act of faith in the idea of progress'.[9]

One way of viewing the scientific utopia of H.G. Wells is as a latter-day version of the more specifically Christian metachronia of seventeenth-century millennialism. E.L. Tuveson has argued that in the seventeenth century 'the metaphysical, almost sacred character of the dogma of unilinear progress was connected with a faith in progressive redemption effected through temporal history'.[10] Progress was no longer seen as simply possible, but as inevitable because it had been prophesied in Daniel and Revelation. The method of God's salvation was the progressive betterment of human nature and the amelioration of the cultural and natural environment.[11]

The apocalyptic note is clear in the early science fantasies of Wells. His mother's fervent evangelicalism and the Protestant tracts which were his boyhood literature left Wells with a legacy of religious conceptions which were never far below the surface of his thought. Books such as *The Pilgrim's Progress*, writes Kumar, 'had given him the themes and imagery of millennial Puritanism: the idea of the painful pilgrimage to salvation, the Last Judgement, and the coming of the New Jerusalem of universal peace, brotherhood and wisdom'.[12] One might even see in *The War of the Worlds* a reworking of chapter 9 of the Book of Revelation where a star falls from heaven and opens a bottomless pit out of which emerge monsters bringing death by fire.[13] By the time of his early writings the evangelical religion of his boyhood had taken a secular form with a new Plan of Salvation. Unchecked, the evolutionary process would damn the human species as surely as the Fall. The original sin of man's animal inheritance would have to be redeemed but only the elect (the Efficients, the Samurai) could hope for salvation and establish the Rule of Saints on earth.[14]

The transformation of millennial expectations signalled a new confidence in the historical process, and in the nineteenth century the historical process increasingly appeared in evolutionary guise. If our past was tainted by our animal ancestry, our future was much more promising. 'The myth of evolution', as Frederick Gregory has written, 'fitted perfectly into the general atmosphere of progress that permeated Victorian society.'[15] Evolution seemed to guarantee progress. In 1865 Lubbock wrote:

> The future happiness of our race, which poets hardly ventured to hope for, science boldly predicts. Utopia, which we have long looked upon as synonymous with an evident impossibility, which we have ungratefully regarded as 'too good to be true', turns out on the contrary to be the necessary consequence of natural law.[16]

Spencer's 'Industrial Society' was akin to the utilitarian utopia, although it was arrived at not by legislation or by the ultimate identity of interests, but as the product of the evolutionary process. Social evolutionists conflated what 'ought' to be with what 'will' be, much as the possible and the desirable were interchangeable in the Wellsian vision of the future.[17]

The future was never very far away and Progress was most visible in the onward march of technology. A surfeit of wonders, 'latest improvements' and 'startling developments' had brought a nation to expect a new advance on an almost daily basis. The public were to be thrilled to the point of exhaustion. The seeming inevitability of technological progress meant not only that it was laden with promise, but also that it might be taken for granted.

> the times in which we live may well be called the 'age of invention'. Never before, it would seem, have men so ardently studied the secrets of nature, and turned the knowledge thus acquired to practical account. We have become so accustomed to hearing of new inventions that nowadays they hardly surprise us.[18]

So commonplace had inventions become that in 1898 one correspondent to *Cassell's Saturday Journal* felt able to write: 'We seem to be so up-to-date nowadays that I don't see that there is really much else to be invented.'[19] The building of flying machines, the invention of wireless telegraphy, the development of the internal combustion engine and motor transport, and the application of electricity to almost anything that could be dreamed of, all helped to convince the general public that they were living in a technological revolution. It was a revolution that was extensively covered in the periodical press.

At the turn of the century the problems of flight held a particular fascination for the British public. Articles abound on the history of attempts to fly. There were descriptions of all manner of balloons, airships and flying machines, and biographical pieces on the men who built them, men such as Santos Dumont, Count von Zeppelin, Carl E. Myers, and eventually the Wright brothers. Their experiments and exploits were duly recorded. The problems they faced and the theories they propounded duly discussed. Each small triumph was lavishly praised. There was, indeed, a danger of overexposure. One writer in *Pearson's Magazine* was to comment: 'No doubt the general public has been so saturated with flying machines that it is inclined to look askance upon any more.'[20] *Cassell's Saturday Journal* could see the funny side:

'I have perfected a new kind of airship,' said the inventor.
'Which kind?' asked the cynical friend, 'something to fly or something to write about?'[21]

Nevertheless 'The romance of flying machines', to borrow the title of an article in *Tit-Bits*, is evident in most of what is written in the magazines. This romance, this fascination for flight was fired by promises, hopes and expectations such that the articles become a catalogue of questions: 'Can balloons ever be steered?', 'Will battles be fought in the air?', 'Shall we ever fly to business?', 'Shall we ever fly to New York?', 'Will man conquer the air?', and above and beyond all else 'When shall we fly?'[22]

Achievements in telegraphy, and in particular wireless telegraphy, were as exciting and as promising as those in flight. In *Pearson's Magazine* an article, 'Signalling through space', described the work of Marconi and proclaimed of wireless telegraphy: 'There is nothing, perhaps, in the whole realm of science that more excites the wonder of the layman.'[23] The advent of wireless technology seemed to herald a new age of communication, an age of fantastic possibilities: 'Seeing by wire', 'Talking along a beam of light', 'Talking through the earth', 'Steering torpedoes by wireless telegraphy', and – 'The latest scientific marvel' – 'talking by wireless telephone'.[24] For the *Cottager and Artisan* this new age would be most remarkable for a new unity across the globe, a unity already being realised by the advancement of electric telegraphy of which the magazine wrote: 'Above all, by putting the remotest parts of the world in contact with each other, it tends to destroy the barriers of isolation and prejudice, making indifference give place to sympathy and hatred to loving-kindness.'[25]

Flight and telegraphy can be seen as examples of the slow but steady technological progress that had come to be expected at the turn of the century. However, two scientific discoveries, and their possible practical applications, were so surprising and seemingly fantastic that they burst upon the popular imagination – X-rays and radium. Roentgen's discovery was quickly taken up by the popular press. In 1896 both *Cassell's Magazine* and the *Clarion* had articles on the 'new photography', and the following year *Cassell's Saturday Journal* could write, without too much exaggeration: 'Almost every week brings forth a new practical application of the Roentgen rays.'[26] X-rays, it was reported, were being used to test for food adulteration, to test diamonds and other gems, to detect smuggling, to save sight, and to detect crime. Radium appeared to be the essence of scientific magic. For *Cassell's Magazine* the marvels of radium were to make it the 'modern philosophers stone', and *Pearson's Weekly* seemed particularly spellbound by the new substance. 'Radium revolutioniser' and 'We want more radium' it proclaimed, and in 1904 describing the 'Wonders that Radium is capable of doing' foresaw that: 'In the future our homes will be lighted by it, our motor cars driven by it, our food cooked by it.'[27] As early as 1903 *Pearson's Magazine* was reporting on the 'riddle of radium' and its potential as 'an inexhaustible reservoir of energy'.[28]

But for *Pearson's Magazine* the 'new elixir of life' was to be electricity,[29] and it was, perhaps, the proliferation of fresh applications of electricity that was technology's most obvious public feature. Electricity, it seemed, could be used to do almost anything. Professor Munsterberg, for example, had developed an appliance which, he said, 'will enable all the emotions of a subject to be recorded and all the secrets of the heart revealed'. Meanwhile Professor Mosso had invented a 'thought measuring' machine, said to be so delicate that it could measure the difference in the exertion needed to read Greek from that required for Latin.[30] There were frequent accounts of electricity replacing steam or horse power as the motive force of much machinery, but there were also more exciting possibilities too, such as restoring hearing to the deaf and obtaining nitrates from the air to replenish the earth. This last discovery, reported *Cassell's Saturday Journal*, 'is likely to have a tremendous influence on the food production of the future. It is even suggested that it will ultimately be possible to manufacture food substances directly from the air.'[31] Indeed who could doubt it, especially when men such as Professor J.A. Fleming of University College London could be quoted as saying: 'The future of elec-tricity is absolutely beyond the realm of imagination', and when the engineer-in-chief of the Post Office, William Henry Preece, FRS, says in the pages of *Cassell's Magazine*: 'The word "impossible" has been wiped out of the electrician's vocabulary.'[32]

There was a tremendous feeling of excitement about technological development. This was especially true for *Pearson's Magazine* where the sense of adventure in many ways mirrors the adventure stories of the mag-azine's fiction. However, in all the magazines technology is celebrated, and in turn is itself a celebration of human spirit, endeavour and achieve-ment. More than this, the articles are not only panegyrics to the accom-plishments of man but, by association, are also exaltations of man himself. Technology is, at times quite explicitly, the symbol of man's will. It is not without significance that the development of flying machines is referred to as the *conquest* of the air. One potent symbol of this subjugation of nature was the hydroelectric scheme at Niagara Falls completed in 1896 and which received coverage in many of the magazines. In 1897 the *Clarion*, with what seems a mixture of admiration and amusement, reported that 'the Niagara Power Company are almost ready to open the celebrated Falls as a going concern of a commercial order. After which, I understand, they propose to fence in the sun, and use it for a cooking stove, these Yanks are smart.'[33] It was only three years later that *Pearson's Magazine*, together with other magazines, was reporting on a solar motor, or as *Pearson's* put it 'Tapping the sun's strength', and in 1902 *Pearson's Magazine* was to describe 'A machine which traps sunbeams, and sets them to work to boil water' in an article under the revealing title 'The sun – a servant'.[34] Similarly *Pearson's Magazine*, in telling the 'story of a gigantic engineering feat' (the world's longest trestle bridge), remarked that these days 'the engineer is waging a ceaseless war against the forces of nature, striving to subdue them or to bend them to his will'. In *Tit-Bits* the 'force of the future' was liquid air which was 'another giant caught, imprisoned, and made to work the will of man'.[35] In machine technology the Enlightenment's hopes of achieving mastery over nature were finally realised.[36]

There is another side to this. The glory of God may be seen in the wonders of His creation. Likewise the glory of man may be seen in the wonders of his creation. This much is clear from our survey of natural theology and human technology. But what if the technology has mastery of nature, the human subjects the divine? I have found no explicit evidence for the deification of man (although there is, of course the

H.G. Wells story *Men Like Gods*) but there was a quasi-religious 'framework' implicit in many articles. In this way we find man as god-head, technology as creation, and science as religion with its own priesthood of scientists and hagiography of great men. By setting up this alternative 'religious' framework we may read power over nature as opposition to God. What would be interesting would be to see how far the supposed conflict of science and religion might be construed as a conflict between technology and theology, something which is worthy of further research.

Whether this is the case or not, the technological opposition to God can have important consequences for the use of imagery. Here, for example, is a passage from a *Pearson's Magazine* article describing a visit to a steel mill in Sheffield:

> In a moment [the visitor] steps from calm to storm. The blast of the tempest, the volley of the thunder, the flash of the lightening, seem to fall upon him at once. The whole is one deafening, deadly menace, instinct with diabolical energy.
>
> Before him he sees enormous masses of machinery, gigantic hammers, huge rollers, furnaces grim and glowing, and engines of all kinds, while the crash of falling iron, the screams of the circular saws cutting through the half-molten steel amidst a blaze of golden sparks, the hissing steam, the rumbles and roars of a hundred mechanical devils, confuse and stun his senses all at once. Everywhere men are moving about, guiding, compelling, directing all this titanic and turbulent life....Man, after all, is master here.[37]

This is nothing short of hell, a nineteenth-century echo of Milton's vision. It is the building of Pandaemonium with 'furnaces grim and glowing', 'hissing steam' and 'screams' of saws, and where the references to 'diabolical energy' and 'mechanical devils' are more than apt. It may be no more than ironic, but in an age of what Passmore calls 'secular Zoroastrianism' – where 'Science was symbolised by electricity...and expelled the forces of darkness in a quite literal sense' – it is worth recalling that Christian mythology already had a name for the bearer of light – Lucifer.[38]

The images are powerful but we should not allow ourselves to be misled. These were, after all, triumphalist images born of a belief that among those dark Satanic mills a new Jerusalem was being built. For here lay the ultimate power of the new technology – it created hope. In the language of hope was the simple promise that the future would be better.

Nor should it be thought that this was a cynical, idle promise. One had only to look at the advances in technology made in the recent past, as the magazines took great pleasure in recording, to have hopes that similar advances were in store. A history of inexorable progress and a record of current triumphs gave technology impeccable credentials as a guarantor of better times to come. There was a very strong sense of being on the threshold of a new golden age, or even technological Utopia. 'We are all standing at the open door of a great century', said the *British Workman* in 1897. Scientists, it said, were 'a race of men who have conquered time, space, air, fire, water, nature's deepest secrets'. However, the 'king of the coming age' was to be the engineer, the magazine's depiction of whom is nothing less than heroic:

> A sturdy figure, with thoughtful eyes, gazing out at his vast inheritance from under broad heavy brows. His robe of royalty a suit of grease stained overalls, his throne the mechanic's bench, his stool the footplate of the locomotive, his sceptre a piston-rod, his crown a circlet of electric light, his name – the engineer.
>
> As he advances, there advances with him, step by step, civilisation, knowledge, liberty, comfort, and safety.[39]

What better metaphor could be found for the inevitable technological progress of mankind?

Nor was it a groundless forlorn hope. Although we might dismiss the belief in Progress as blind faith, the late Victorians had every reason to look forward to the new century. It was not so much that there were better times to come, but that they were inevitable. This vision came from layman and expert alike. Richard Kerr, FGS, FRAS, in *Cassell's Magazine*, for example, concludes his article on wireless telegraphy contemplating the future:

> In all this we have a wonderful instance of the power of the human mind over some of the hidden forms of energy that abound in Nature.
>
> In fifty years time still greater things may be achieved. The mind is progressive, always expanding and being amplified, and does it not seem to indicate that it will continue to do so throughout eternity...[40]

For the *Cottager and Artisan* the telegraph was to be a symbol of man's progress and the semaphore towers which it made obsolete were to be 'a monument to the advancement of science and the improvement of everything tending to the well being of mankind, which goes on with ever increasing rapidity as time rolls on'.[41]

Progress is a marriage of the past with the future. If, by its association with progress, technology drew its authority and credibility by an appeal to the past, then it gained its seductive power from visions of the future.

Cassell's Saturday Journal, for example, links past and future in its article on 'Radium and its discoverers': 'The last few years have been rich in marvels, of which the x-rays and wireless telegraphy are not the least. Remembering these things one would need a bold imagination to predict the scientific developments of the near future.'[42] But predicting the future was the stuff of popular journalism and was a pastime commonly indulged in the magazines, particularly the weeklies. Guided by a belief in progress and extrapolating from the past, what a wonderful picture they painted of times to come, ever onward and ever hopeful. Future generations, readers were told, would be able to take an aeroplane to the moon, cross the Atlantic in three days, travel in wagons along pneumatic tubes or on aerial railways, send pictures by telegraphy, make gold, eat pills as food, keep hearts beating with electricity, kill pain with anaesthetics, make the deaf hear, the blind see.[43]

It is worth taking a closer look at these visions of the future, if only because in most cases they are projections forward a hundred years to the present day. Of course they are of more interest than that. In the common conflation of 'will be' with 'ought to be' they reveal the desires and fears of the age. 'Prediction is in the air', said *Cassell's Magazine*.

> Men of science, above all others, have recently shown a disposition to assume the prophetic mantle. One informs us that man is becoming a toothless, toeless biped, all cerebellum, another that the microbe is the true sovereign of the world and will ultimately transform man into a new creature, another confidently asserts that we shall yet send telephonic messages to the planet Mars or see what is going on in Australia without leaving London, and so on ad infinitum.[44]

M. Berthellot, the 'famous chemist', was predicting that by the year 2000 all power would come from the internal heat of the Earth and all food would come from chemical manufacture. The Earth would become a garden. In the meantime 'man, no longer condemned to toil for a coarse livelihood, will feast on the chemical dainties of the laboratory and devote his years to the intellectual works of his love and choice'.[45]

In *Tit-Bits* it was compulsory education that would lead the majority of the country to 'seek brain rather than muscle work', but it was technology that would enable this to happen. 'For a hundred years hence will not all labour be performed automatically or by machinery of some description?' Progress would be nothing less than exponential. In 'Britain a hundred years hence: a peep into 1997' it proclaimed: 'If the world lasts, far more wonderful changes and improvements will be effected in the coming than in the last century, for inventions, knowledge, and progress breed inventions, knowledge and progress.' In the last twenty years the 'germ' had been found for cholera, hydrophobia, tuberculosis, diphtheria, anthrax and a host of other diseases which will, 'under really scientific hygiene, be utterly crushed out of existence'. With the perfection of surgery 'death from ordinary injury will barely be possible'.[46]

Pearson's Weekly, meanwhile, decided to devote a full page to see 'How London will look in 1998'. Everything is run by electricity, nobody walks but transport is by bikes, cars, trams, airships, even roller skates, shopping is done over the telephone and there are telephones on every corner. 'Great and clever as we think ourselves', it remarked, 'what we have achieved in this century is but the shadow of the substance of the next'.[47] It was also *Pearson's Weekly* that in 1907 drew a picture of 'A Christmas house party a hundred years hence'. This was a full-page cartoon of a house with all manner of technological wizardry – air conditioning, double walls for constant temperature and to act as conduits for electric wires and speaking tubes, piped music, meals cooked by electricity and served automatically, electric dishwashers and an automatic laundry, telephones, 'electrical periscopes' and a landing stage for aeroplanes. Again it is to the past that the cartoon's caption looks for its credibility:

> Considering the fact that at Christmas 1807 railway engines, telephones, electric light, and talking machines were practically unheard of, and that even so recently as fifteen years ago the motor-car as we understand it today was unknown to the British public, our Christmas House Party of a hundred years hence is no wild and unpractical dream.[48]

It was by such appeals to the past and projecting progress forward that people could be so optimistic about their technological future. Technology was progress made manifest, pregnant with promises and glorified as a thing of hope. But would such middle-class rhetoric fall on deaf ears? Would its appeal to the past and its heavy emphasis on the future make 'progress' too alien and too abstract a concept for a culture which is often characterised as being predominantly concerned with the present. Hoggart, for example, writes of the working class as being 'substantially without a sense of the past' and having 'little real sense of the future'.[49] Now whether we accept such a characterisation might be a matter for debate, but even if we do then technology still has a particularly important part to play. Technology was the key to material progress, and it was through the products of technology that people were offered the opportunity (however real or imagined) of a better life now, in the present.

Rosalind Williams has written of late-nineteenth-century France that 'never before or since has there been such a concentration of technological change affecting the ordinary consumer'. Her assessment is equally applicable to Britain. There were two interdependent driving forces behind the consumer revolution: first, a steady increase in purchasing power; and second, 'a torrent of technological changes that simultaneously lowered the cost of existing consumer goods and provided entirely new ones'.[50] By standardisation and imitation technology cheapened traditional commodities such as clothes, shoes and furniture, and from 1850 onwards many inventions were themselves consumer products – the bicycle, motor car, typewriter, sewing machine, phonograph, electric lighting and photography. At the same time developments in distribution, particularly multiple retailing, were dependent upon a rapidly expanding railway network to provide an efficient communication system to transport goods to customers or vice versa. Production and distribution were revolutionised, but the transformation was visual too. Electricity, says Williams, 'created a fairyland environment',[51] especially with the use of electric lighting for advertising and with the increasingly popular illuminations at seaside resorts, while the advent of cinema opened up new opportunities for escapism.[52] The almost explosive growth of advertising towards the end of the century made the visual impact of the consumer revolution inescapable. From mid-century onwards production of chromolithographs made possible the mass reproduction of brightly coloured images which, as Mike Featherstone puts it, 'saturated the terrain of consumption with the symbolic promise of luxury, abundance, style, and hedonism'.[53]

Is any of this evident in the magazines?

First, it should be remembered that the magazines themselves were products of the consumer society, and that the presentation of science (and technology) took a commodity form, that is as a product not a process.[54] Second, if we turn to magazine content, what is most obvious is the plethora of advertisements offering all manner of goods and services, many of which were products of new technology. But even on editorial pages one can find a concern for commodities. This is, perhaps, most notable with the numerous articles in many magazines on manufacturing processes, articles like 'How phonograph records are made', 'How linoleum is made', or 'How soap is made'.[55] Interestingly the use of such industrial articles varies characteristically from magazine to magazine. *Cassell's Magazine* and *Pearson's Magazine*, for instance, included articles on the industries behind the Empire and British supremacy such as 'In a dynamite factory', 'How our army is clothed', 'The birth of a battleship', or 'A visit to a gun factory' (this last being part of *Cassell's Magazine*'s 'National defence' series).[56] *Good Words* and especially the *Cottager and Artisan* tended to see such articles as vehicles for more moralistic lessons on the division of labour and self-help,[57] while the *Clarion*, in contrast, preferred to turn its attention to the 'model factory' at Port Sunlight to highlight workers' welfare schemes.[58] However, whatever the tacit intention of these articles they continually and inextricably linked technology with commodity production so that buttons or biscuits, candles or clothes, the stories of their manufacture, as those of other goods, all helped to reinforce the idea of the technological foundation for the present day's material benefits.

Without wishing to oversimplify or overstate the case, I would argue, nevertheless, that a belief in progress was a source of stability in late Victorian society. If we so wish we could even see it as part of a dominant ideology. Working-class 'progressivism', as Hoggart calls it, is little more than a hundred years old. What right then have we to see it as being 'traditional'? Might it not be that its late-nineteenth-century origins are due to its imposition from above? Pollard implies as much when he writes:

> The nineteenth century was the bourgeois century. Its own progress in power, wealth and culture was plain for all to see. The idea of progress not only fitted its own history best, it also proved a useful instrument with which to stifle the anguished protests of those who suffered, and to weaken the determination of the class that armed itself to supplant its rule.[59]

Unfortunately this is a chicken-and-egg type of question, since it requires an already passive working class to acquiesce to the imposition of an acquiescent ideology.

As an assumption Progress connects with the hopeful pragmatism found not only in Hoggart's study of working-class culture but also in Standish Meacham's exploration of English working-class life at the turn of the century.[60] To surrender oneself to the present and leave the future in the hands of hope and progress fits well with the fatalism that was the resort of many. 'Most accepted events as they came', says Meacham, 'acquiescent, mildly hedonistic, concerned with how life should be, but generally only within the manageable dimensions of their own family's conduct.'[61] The effects of social, political and material progress in the latter half of the last century were beginning to be felt by the working class and presumably would lead many to believe that what was to come was further advance. Hope would put a smile on the face of fatalism.

As rhetoric or experience, the belief in 'progress' (however it is interpreted) was a common response to common historical circumstances. Its interpretation could be negotiated (fatalistically hopeful or aggressively utopian), but it was something that could be agreed upon. It was part of the consensus. In the early nineteenth century the ideological power of natural theology had been recognised by radical street literature. 'Breaking the propagandist image of Paley's happy world', says Desmond, 'was an integral step to altering the collective perceptions of the masses.'[62] By the end of the century one happy world was exchanged for another – man-made, optimistic and with the future at its feet.[63] Where theology had once offered redemption and Providence, science now offered consumption and Progress. By usurping the Christian narrative, science had stolen the future. It was not so much an ideological conflict as a breach of copyright. Progress, and the expectation of its inevitability, was an expression of complacency not dynamism. As Wells was later to write, 'hope in the Victorian period was not a stimulant but an opiate'.

9 New Mentalities

What went wrong?

The statistics are quite striking. From our sample of magazines, if we compare the 1890s with the decade before the Great War, we find that the amount of editorial space given over to science falls by at least 25 per cent. This is true whether we look at different markets, publishers or (with the single exception of the *Clarion*) individual titles. Not only is the overall amount of science shrinking, but also within that amount the emphasis is shifting from articles on technology towards a greater interest in natural history and the human sciences such as medicine, anthropology and psychology.[1]

In 1909 George Bernard Shaw told the Medico-Legal Society: 'At the present moment we are passing through a phase of disillusion. Science has not lived up to the hopes we formed of it in the 1860s.'[2] That same year C.F.G. Masterman felt able to write:

> The large hopes and dreams of the Early Victorian time have vanished: never, at least in the immediate future, to return. The science which was to allay all diseases, the commerce which was to abolish war, and weave all nations into one human family, the research which was to establish ethics and religion on a secure and positive foundation, the invention which was to enable all humanity, with a few hours of not disagreeable work every day, to live for the remainder of their time in ease and sunshine – all these have been recognised as remote and fairy visions.[3]

They catch the rising mood, but they need only have looked back ten years for a time of technological optimism, of days filled with promise and expectation.

What went wrong?

Whatever the depth of popular feeling for Empire, the Boer War dealt a severe blow to the imperial ego. Historians have written of the trauma which the war inflicted on British self-confidence, and of the war giving a fatal jolt to national complacency.[4] After the expansionist euphoria of Victoria's reign, says Bernard Porter, no one in the Edwardian years seems seriously to have advocated that the British Empire should grow any bigger.[5] No longer was the Empire a source simply of pride and pleasure. Foreboding and fear were the characteristic Edwardian attitudes. Latent doubts and feelings of insecurity were brought to the surface by the exposure of Britain's military deficiencies, and the appalling physical unfitness of army volunteers served only to confirm that Britain was at the heart of an empire in decline. 'Over civilisation', it was argued, was destroying the moral fibre of the nation, sapping its virility when it was most needed. A physically and morally degenerate Britain, it was feared, would be no match for the growing economic and military power of America, Germany and Japan. Parallels with the decadence of ancient Rome were as clear as they were alarming.

To stop the rot, it was argued, Britain had to be made into a truly imperial nation, fit (in every sense of the word) to run the world's largest empire. The closing of the imperial frontier thus created the introspective context for the ideology of national efficiency. Demanding new governmental machinery and more technical education, and expressing an elitist preference for professional experts, the efficiency movement embodied the new industrial ethic of science, technology and the corporate society. It was not a homogeneous political ideology, but a convenient label for a complex of beliefs, assumptions and demands.[6] In practice it meant a programme of social reform and training to improve the physique, discipline and organisation of the nation, and could encompass Tariff Reform, Compulsory Military Service, the Boy Scout movement and Eugenics.

At all political levels attempts were made to show the interdependence of imperialism and social reform in order to create a consensus around a single national purpose. As Bernard Semmel puts it, this social-imperialism (or for Blatchford imperial-socialism) 'was designed to draw all classes together in defence of the nation and empire, and aimed to prove to the least well-to-do class that its interests were inseparable from those of the nation'.[7] By setting itself above party politics it sought to bypass the old traditional routes to power and to open the way for 'experts'. Its social base was a frustrated and marginalised middle strata of small shopkeepers, civil servants, the 'new middle classes', and status-hungry intellectuals. Its leadership, says Scally, 'represented a disgruntled "successor elite", impatient but immobilised by the transition from an expanding to a static, and soon to be contracting, empire and economy'.[8]

Economic reversals spread the Edwardian gloom and despondency beyond the realms of petit bourgeois imperialism. Late Victorian prosperity had always been subject to the vagaries of short-time working, unemployment, regional and occupational variations, and the vicissitudes of family life cycles, any of which at any time might throw one into the ever-present 'abyss' of poverty. Nevertheless the general picture is one of substantially improved standards of living for the mass of the population through the 1870s, 1880s and 1890s and a partial setback to this in the

1900s.[9] Gourvish concludes that 'most blue-collar workers in the major industries were able to associate the Edwardian period with some kind of pressure on their economic position'.[10] In addition, the slowing down of the economy's growth exposed high levels of inequality. We can see this in the widening gap between real wages and national income per capita. During the 1890s the two kept pace with each other, but in the 1900s per capita income rose by 5 per cent as real wages fell by 6 per cent.[11] The deceleration of the Victorian economy can be seen as a major challenge to the social stability of Edwardian Britain, and, more specifically, it has been argued that the labour unrest of 1910 onwards arose from a combination of stagnant or declining real wages, increasing inequality and a tighter labour market. These were, in short, the economic roots for what has come to be known as the 'Edwardian crisis'.[12]

The effect upon people's perceptions of what was equitable was probably more important than the objective economic effects of stagnation or decline.[13] Without cancelling out the real material gains of the late Victorian years, the Edwardian setbacks were a challenge to rising expectations, bringing frustration and resentment to people who had learned to take gradual improvement for granted.[14] What made class inequalities such a potent source of social instability was not just their existence but society's awareness of them. The disparities of Edwardian society were made all the more clear to working-class people by the expansion of occupations with higher earnings and the concentration of wealth in London which, although remote from working-class experience, was highlighted by the popular press.[15]

From 1906 to 1914 economic pressures produced a greater awareness of common interests among wage earners who had previously been much divided by skill, earnings, status and patterns of association. Working-class solidarity had been generated by a combination of the halt to real wages, the residential segregation of cities, the concentration of work into larger units, the division of labour and the competition of clerical occupations.[16] The labour unrest of 1910–14 generalised class interests across trades and industries, heightening working-class consciousness and shifting the focus of conflict from wage rates to the control of work itself.[17]

There was, of course, no revolution. From the oral evidence of Edwardian survivors, Paul Thompson concludes that, except for those in authority, there was not even any general awareness of a crisis.[18] But the fears for social stability were quite apparent in the periodical press. Articles like 'Is a revolution coming?' and 'The great unrest', major serial stories like 'The world in revolt', and warnings that the present 'age of strikes' carried the threat of famine, food riots and civil war, all give clear impressions of the troubled times that people saw themselves in.[19] We might quibble over the term 'crisis' (Edwardian 'malaise' might be better), but, as Keith Burgess has argued, the period 1906–14 'posed difficulties for the New Liberalism's capacity to re-establish the hegemony of capital and property in relation to the working class'.[20] In this way, the 'crisis' might be seen as a crisis of hegemony, precipitated, at least in part, by the failure of those undertakings for which consent had been sought – an expanding empire and a consumerist economy.

It would be naive to imagine that there was a complete reversal of opinion after the Boer War, but however it is defined or perceived (be it economically, politically, socially or culturally) the Edwardian 'crisis' is evident in the popular magazines of the time as a changing attitude. What we find is a new, less optimistic view, not replacing the old view, but running parallel and in counterpoint to it. The result is not so much a new pessimism as a new ambivalence, an ambivalence which was becoming more and more widespread, and at a more popular level. It may be as much as one can do to speak in terms of 'tendencies' and 'trends' and to see the whole period of 1890–1914 as one of 'transition'. There is nonetheless a perceptible shift in mentality. The earlier complacency was increasingly being accompanied by a new and growing sense of unease. The days of hope were becoming the days of disillusion.

As early as 1900 the Wellsian mechanised utopia was under attack. In *Pearson's Magazine* W.L. Alden was as perceptive and as opinionated as ever.

> Mr Wells, the late Mr Bellamy, and a number of lesser writers, have given us their conception of the world, as it will be several centuries hence. They all agree that it will be a world of machinery. Flying machines will be as common as cabs now are, and books and newspapers will be superseded by machines of the telephonic and telegraphic species. It will be a world in which everything will be so perfectly ordered that it will run like a well-oiled machine. There will be no poverty and no crime, and everybody will be comfortable, and unspeakably bored.

A new book should be written protesting against the Wells–Bellamy style of world,

> and showing us a world in which science is pushed into the background. In such a world there would be next to no machinery. Beer-engines, bicycles, and hydraulic lifts would probably survive, but the vast hordes of machinery, that even now make life wearisome and dangerous, would cease to exist.[21]

Pearson's Weekly was more strident in its tone. 'You're booked for a violent death' it claimed in 1913, and I would be very surprised to find a similar catalogue of fears published in the 1890s. The article opens:

> Every year the odds against your dying a natural death are becoming greater. It is the inevitable result of the highly civilised and scientific age in which we live, for the tendency of every fresh invention is to hasten death, which is to say practically every new discovery of man produces a fresh form of killing.[22]

Motor vehicles, it says, had killed and injured over 35 000 people the previous year in London alone. Explosions and electrocutions from electricity had killed and injured hundreds, while the fires and explosions caused by petrol fumes had caused accidents unknown to previous generations. Aviation, it admits, had not been a great threat to everyday living. 'But as aircraft become more general, this science will undoubtedly add to the list of accidental deaths. Already disinterested members of the public have lost their lives through being struck by descending aeroplanes.' It is, perhaps, worth noting that in 1910 the magazine started an insurance scheme which paid out a hundred pounds to the legal representative of anyone 'dying as the direct and sole result of injuries inflicted upon him (or her) within the United Kingdom by a falling aeroplane'.[23] This is easily dismissed as a mere stunt safe in the knowledge that the chances of making a payment were remote, but to have been thought worthwhile it must have recognised some very real fears.

Doubts about technology and applied science, however, were many and varied. 'Chemicalised foods' was the target of one article in the *Clarion* highlighting the dangers of food poisoning from unnatural foods, additives and preservatives: 'It becomes more and more evident to anyone who closely studies these matters that it is time that public inquiry should be roused, for the health and vitality of the nation are being slowly but steadily destroyed under the acid rule of scientific chemistry.'[24] *Pearson's Weekly* was to write of 'When electricity runs amok', telling of explosions and of people electrocuted on underground railways. In a later article listing '1914 ailments' the magazine pointed out that 'every great advance in civilisation brings new diseases in its train', including 'wireless anaemia', paralysis from vibration of a car, aeroplane deafness and 'picture-palace headache'.[25] *Pearson's* was also concerned about air pollution. *Pearson's Magazine* carried an article on the damage to health and buildings caused by smog, and *Pearson's Weekly* reported on 'Petrologia', 'a new disease caused by the fumes of motor omnibuses'.[26]

The development of motor transport had a lot to answer for when it came to disaffection with technology. 'When the motor comes into universal use life will not be worth living', moaned W.L. Alden in 1900, again foreshadowing later more widespread sentiments.[27] In 1897 *Pearson's Weekly* could have a humorous piece on 'The modern plague', but as the years passed the subject was to grow ever more serious until in the last years before the Great War it became an important political issue.[28] Pressure of motor traffic upon British roads produced alarming statistics as the number of fatalities from motoring accidents rose from 373 in 1909 to 1329 in 1914.[29] It was not without some justification that *Tit-Bits* could call London's streets 'veritable deathtraps' because of the increase in motor traffic.[30] In 1908 a handbill called to the 'Men of England':

> Your birthright is being taken from you by reckless motor drivers....Reckless motorists drive over and kill your children....Men of England...rise up, join together, and bring pressure on your representatives in Parliament, and otherwise make it unpleasant and costly to the tyrants who endanger your lives and the lives of your dear ones.[31]

Obviously this was not merely symptomatic of a new post-Boer War mentality, but was also, perhaps primarily, a result of the simple fact that there were more cars on British roads. It was, nonetheless, creating a divided nation. 'The era of the horse is over or passing and the age of the automobile has begun', proclaimed *Cassell's Magazine* in 1909, 'the question now is how to reconcile the interests of the motorist and those of the non-motoring public.'[32] This would be a far from easy task. *Cassell's Saturday Journal* reported that 'judging from the shoals of letters written by indignant pedestrians to the papers, a considerable section of the British public would like to see automobiles abolished from the high roads forthwith'.[33]

Of all the problems of technology probably none was as directly related to the wider social ills of the time as that of unemployment. Should machinery be seen as 'labour-saving' or as throwing men out of work? In its usual middle-class manner, *Pearson's Magazine* could still be self-confident in 1902. An article on giant cranes addresses the labour question directly.

> These weight-raising machines – time-saving, labour-saving, and money-saving as they are – have wrought vast revolutions in the world of labour. Where they throw men out of work in one direction, they make new work in another. In these days intelligent workmen are more quick to realise than formerly that because a machine may do the work of a hundred men, perhaps hundreds of men, it is not necessarily

robbing them of their labour, but is rather providing work for more men than were ever engaged in the past.[34]

In 1913 *Pearson's Weekly* saw things differently: 'largely owing to the increase of machinery, which can do the work of hundreds of men, the ranks of crime are larger than ever, their numbers being recruited by desperate members of the unemployed'.[35] Technology was restructuring the working class, turning skilled and unskilled into an ever-growing pool of semi-skilled labour, eroding the status of any 'labour aristocracy', or forcing them to retrain and become increasingly specialised which in turn carried a greater threat of unemployment. Accepting technological change as inevitable, many workers turned to trade unions for help. The *Clarion* was more radical. In 1907 Robert Blatchford suggested that it was no good arguing if machinery was good or bad for the country because it could not be resisted. What was more important was how to make the most of it. The solution for Blatchford was the 'nationalisation of the means of production' so that everyone can benefit from the increased wealth brought by the new machinery.[36]

We can find a good illustration of these changing attitudes to technology in a series of cartoons in *Cassell's Saturday Journal*. The first, 'Why flurry, scurry, or hurry?', appeared in September 1900 and, according to its text, was inspired by the recent invention of a dishwashing machine and an automatic floor polisher. The humour is light, and the technology is not so much a threat as a source of amusement. Any danger from the inventions is safely projected away from the present into the future. This is an entertaining look not at what is, but at what might be. The second cartoon, 'What it is coming to', appeared in July 1903 and has a much darker side to it, not least because what is presented, except for the final panel, is an account of what can be experienced today. The future tense used in the text of the previous article is now replaced by the use of the present tense. The threat from technology is brought much closer to home, although the treatment of this threat still remains a humorous one. The final illustration has no saving graces. Published in June 1912 as part of a series of drawings called 'The world as it is', it is as stark in its message as it is in its depiction. There is a simple contrast set up by two drawings – 'For the inventor, fame: for the worker, poverty'. The story told by a notice in the background leaves no room for doubt. 'Owing to the improvement in machinery 1,000 less hands will be needed.'[37]

Unemployment, pollution, health hazards, the charges against technology had been put before, but I do not believe they had been so widespread at such a popular level as they were in the years immediately prior to the

2. Progress – the lighter side. 'Why flurry, scurry or hurry?', taken from *Cassell's Saturday Journal*, 5 September 1900 (British Library).

Great War. They were also part of a more general context of fears about civilisation, or rather over-civilisation. With the retreat from technology came a corresponding desire to return to nature.[38] As Anglicised in the Boy Scout movement, the wilderness ethic presented nature both as an escape from the debilitating artificialities of city life and as a resource for the moral and physical regeneration of the British people.

The Boer War called into question the common assumption of natural supremacy not only politically by the exposure of military deficiencies, but also racially by evidence of the poor physical quality of recruits and volunteers. Official figures led Rowntree to conclude that approximately half the nation's manpower was unfit for military service. Articles by Major-General Sir John Frederick Maurice in the *Contemporary Review* gave the recruit problem a wider audience. So alarming were the statistics and so great was the importance of the issue seen to be for the future of the Empire that in September 1903 the government initiated its own enquiry by setting up the Inter-Departmental Committee on Physical Deterioration. Lord Rosebery put the matter bluntly: 'It is of no use having an empire without an Imperial Race.'[39]

Fears of deterioration can be traced back to at least the 1880s, and similar alarmist opinions as to the quality of recruits were being voiced at the time of the Crimean War. The immorality of towns and the social problems of unemployment heightened anxieties about Britain becoming an urban, industrial society populated by a new sickly, urban 'type',[40] a people dependent upon stimulants, tonics and patent medicines, and well portrayed by Wells in his novels *The New Machiavelli* and *Tono-Bungay*. What differentiated post-war fears from earlier anxieties was that this vision of a deteriorating nation was shared by, and promulgated by, the daily, periodical and specialised press. Whereas in the 1880s a fear of racial degeneration may have been, as Nikolas Rose puts it, 'marginal and idiosyncratic', by the beginning of the twentieth century it underlay an 'extensive and forceful social strategy'.[41] In addition, a new problem came under the deteriorationist spotlight. In the Edwardian decade general references to degeneracy were being replaced by more particular references to what was widely regarded as the root cause of a variety of pathological conditions: mental defect.[42]

To return to that *Pearson's Weekly* catalogue of fears of 1913. It was not just physical injury that was threatened by new technology and modern life. 'At the present time', it claimed, 'you stand a far greater chance of ending your days in a lunatic asylum than you ever had before.'

Lunacy is increasing to an alarming extent, and any doctor will tell you it is due to the strenuousness of modern life. The struggle to exist, the neglect of physical exercise now that mechanical means of transport is everywhere around and the continual strain on the nervous system,

4. The London road appears specially reserved for the enjoyment of the motorist—when you can see him for dust.

brought about by the noise and hustle of town life, are the main reasons for the increase in insanity.[43]

For the greater part of the nineteenth century the Commissioners in Lunacy reported a steady and seemingly inexorable rise in the numbers of people in asylums. Their explanations suggested that the rise was seen as more apparent than real – increased life expectancy of inmates, improved record-keeping, and better methods of identifying the insane. Andrew T. Scull, who has sought alternative explanations, notes, however, that real or apparent the perceived increase aroused public unease throughout the century and that 'public fear of the legions of crazy men and women that society was apparently spawning at times verged on panic'.[44] A reading of the popular magazines of the time suggests that this was not so, at least for the 1890s, and calls into question just how 'public' the fear was that Scull refers to. It is true that the increase in the numbers of the insane was noted in the magazines, but 'fear' and 'panic' over the issue seem to me to be more part of the post-Boer War Edwardian mentality.

8. But when the airship comes along and folk start dropping things about—well, you won't be able to take the children out at all, that's all.

3. Progress – the darker side. Details from 'What it is coming to', taken from *Cassell's Saturday Journal*, 1 July 1903 (British Library).

In the 1890s media, and one assumes public, interest in the insane was akin to the fascination for freaks that was common in the magazines. One finds articles with titles like 'The insane do not shed tears', 'Strange experiences of madmen', or 'Their queer hallucinations', with stories of the woman who thought she was a cat, or the man who thought he was a cherry.[45] Such articles were more commonly found in the weeklies rather than the monthlies and any increase in insanity was simply noted statistically. For example, in an article in *Cassell's Saturday Journal*, 'Is insanity on the increase?', Dr Forbes Winslow explained the increase in

122

4. Progress as threat. 'The world as it is', taken from *Cassell's Saturday Journal*, 1 June 1912 (British Library).

the characteristically complacent way of the commissioners – in terms of alcohol, more vigilant authorities, and the 'present over pressure and the general competition', noting that insanity was more prevalent in European, educated, civilised countries.[46] In 1897 *Pearson's Weekly* could even afford to be slightly humorous on the matter. Its article 'We shall all be mad in AD2301' noted the increase as reported by the commissioners, but concluded that if the increase continues and the insane predominate then 'the marvellous adjusting capacity of nature will no doubt so arrange things that the condition of madness will then be not only more natural than that of sanity, but more pleasant in every way'.[47]

There was no threat to society in either of these pieces, no shrill tone of fear or panic, and the latter example was published in the same year as the commissioners' special report on the increase in insanity, indicating that if the public were not concerned then at least Parliament was. Compare this with *Pearson's Weekly* in 1905. Again the question was asked, 'Is insanity on the increase?', and again it was Forbes Winslow who was called on to answer, but his earlier complacency had now gone and he concluded: 'The increase is so grave that the time has come when some serious measures should be taken to prevent the whole race degenerating into an insane one.' The measures he called for included the compulsory confinement of habitual drunkards and the prohibition of marriage for the feebleminded, epileptics and insane.[48]

Let us examine this new attitude in more detail and see how the fear of insanity was related to wider issues. In 1906 *Pearson's Magazine* published a lengthy piece on 'The prevalence of insanity' as part of a new series on 'Pressing problems of today'. The problem was set out in its opening paragraph.

> Nothing throws a more ghastly light on the canker that is eating at our nation's strength than the established facts concerning our insane. They prove that there has been an ever-growing accumulation of the insane in our big asylums. I am setting out to show that this is a danger to the state – moreover, that there is urgent necessity for the passing of strong laws designed expressly to check the madness and feeblemindedness of the age.[49]

What was important, and indeed what the article was at pains to stress, was that this incidence of insanity was more prevalent among the 'pauper class', who formed 91 per cent of the whole number of the certified insane. Here we can see how a psychological disorder was presented in terms of and in association with a more general social malaise.

Daily we see and hear how grave are the infirmities in the poorest and lowest strata of the population. Apart from the overflowing asylums, the hospitals for epilepsy and diseases of the nerves show an ever-swelling number of patients. Drunkenness is rife throughout the land. Pauperism is everywhere prevalent. Poverty has led to the rise of prison popula-tion....The percentage of unemployed and unemployable is on the increase. The country is over-run with alien undesirables. Every sign points to the fact that with a rise in civilisation there has been a dispro-portionate rise in the number of the physically and mentally unfit.[50]

Insanity, therefore, was not seen simply as a medical problem; it was, perhaps above all else, seen in social terms. The chief causes of insanity were given as 'drink and hereditary influence', and to support its claim the article cited evidence from the Commissioners in Lunacy and from the asylums at Banstead, Bexley, Claybury and Colney Hatch. It followed that what was needed to counter the problem was a social solution – to stamp out intemperance and the breeding of the insane by the insane. In present-ing the prevalence of insanity as a social problem, the article was not slow to give voice to authorities on the subject (such as Forbes Winslow, R.R. Rentoul and Professor Ernest White) and seized the opportunity to cata-logue all the social ills that afflicted the nation. The result was a scientifically accredited checklist of middle-class fears:

- unfit, neurotic, criminal aliens settling in the country,
- the strain of education and the worries of life on the upper and middle classes,
- early marriages among the poor and late marriages in the upper and middle classes,
- cigarette smoking among boys,
- the migration of people from the country into overcrowded and unhealthy towns,
- the compulsory education of poor and pauper children,
- the removal of women from their natural sphere of domesticity.

In the face of such a widespread threat to racial well-being, suggested remedial actions were necessarily comprehensive and harsh:

- the prohibition of marriage for the insane, feebleminded, paralytics, epileptics, consumptives, drunkards, and those with hereditary insan-ity on both sides of their family,
- the segregation of the feebleminded in homes and colonies,
- the compulsory confinement of habitual drunkards,
- the prohibition of very early and very late marriages.

There were also more philanthropic measures such as hygiene education, better housing, a solution to the problem of the unemployed, and a return to the land.

From the prevalence of insanity, degenerationist anxieties soon came to be centred upon the issue of mental deficiency and the problem of the feebleminded. Again *Pearson's Magazine* took up the cause, this time as part of its 'Wake up England!' campaign, and again it was the fitness of the race that was at stake. 'We are allowing the class of feebleminded degenerates to increase and multiply instead of making a serious attempt to sweep out of existence a class whose lives are a misery to themselves and a menace to the future of the race.'[51] What concerned the magazine most of all was that the feebleminded were being allowed to breed more feebleminded children: 'worst of all, they are free, by marrying and having children, to pass on the taint of degeneracy to the next generation. This last fact is the one of vital importance. An examination of the records shows that mental weakness is almost entirely a matter of heredity.'[52] To exacerbate the problem the feebleminded, it was argued, were likely to have more children than normal people. 'Morality has no meaning for them', said the magazine, and they 'very frequently have erotic tendencies'.[53] This was, in effect, simply echoing the findings of the Royal Commission into the Care and Control of the Feebleminded which had reported in 1908 that feeblemindedness was an inherited disease, that the feebleminded were more prolific breeders than normal, and that therefore they should be segregated. This too was the recommendation of the magazine which proposed the setting up of homes and colonies where the feebleminded could be kept. This was in 1912 and by now the vigorous campaign to control the lives of the mentally deficient was coming to a climax. The following year saw the passage of the Mental Deficiency Act which established compulsory powers to detain and segregate the feebleminded.

Does this desire to restrict the breeding of the feebleminded reveal any influence from eugenics? Not necessarily. To combat the prevalence of insanity the magazine's proposals were as often environmental solutions as eugenic ones (if not more so). The policy of segregation was the weakest of a number of eugenic alternatives on offer and can be seen as more a moral/social solution than a eugenic one. Indeed it was only because many non-eugenicists accepted the principle of segregation that the Mental Deficiency Act was able to be passed.[54]

What is most striking is the simple lack of coverage given to eugenics in any of the magazines. This may be, as Searle notes, because the Eugenics Education Society had very few representatives from the media (journalists, freelance writers or people connected with the theatre),[55] but one of the most active members of the Society was Dr Caleb Saleeby, who was a very accomplished publicist (a point acknowledged by both Searle and Michael Freeden).[56] Saleeby carried out important work for the Society, sitting on committees, suggesting tactics and drafting leaflets. He was also on hand to give medical advice to magazines and was often called on for his expert opinion. In 1907 he wrote a series for *Cassell's Magazine* on 'Worry – the disease of the age'.[57] Here at least one might have thought was a golden opportunity to raise the subject of mental health and the excessive birth rate of mental defectives, but in the whole series there is not a single reference to eugenics or eugenic issues. For the magazine's readers it is quite probable that Dr Saleeby, one of the most outspoken supporters of eugenist ideals, was better known for his endorsement of 'Sanatogen' in the advertisements than he was for his views on selective breeding.

Interestingly, in the meagre coverage that there was, the most strident exposition of eugenics came from a Fabian and appeared in the *Clarion* in 1912. In an article on 'Socialism and Eugenics', Victor Fisher argued that 'eugenist enquiry is of the first importance in building up the Socialist State that is to be. I am convinced that it is essential to eliminate the unfit if we are to secure the triumph of Social Democracy.' To achieve this ultimate goal his proposals included amongst others:

1) Incurable idiots and imbeciles, as well as monsters, should be painlessly extinguished in the lethal chamber as soon after birth as their condition could be certified by a Commission of independent scientists and laymen.
2) Sterilisation of the degenerate and diseased and those otherwise physically and mentally unfitted to procreate a normal healthy stock.
3) Segregation and permanent care of the feebleminded.[58]

He also called for 'the severe punishment of alcoholic child-bearing women', together with the state maintenance of pregnant women and national provision for infants and children.[59]

The evidence from the magazines is far too weak and patchy to make any definitive statements, but if our sample is anywhere near representative then the very lack of material is not without significance. If, as Donald MacKenzie argues, 'eugenics should be seen as an ideology of the professional middle class',[60] why do we not see fuller coverage of eugenics in middle-class magazines?

By focusing on biometricians like Karl Pearson, MacKenzie is able to show how eugenics was an appropriate world-view for rising professionals motivated by meritocratic ambitions.[61] But there was more to eugenics than biometry and the movement was riven by a running feud between biometricians at the Eugenics Laboratory and Mendelians at the Eugenics Education Society. The eugenics movement was far from monolithic, but then so too was support from the class whose interests it was supposed to express. If it is true that most eugenists were professional middle class, then it is equally true that most of the professional middle class were not eugenists.[62] Divisions in the class were nowhere more apparent than in the medical profession. 'Medical men were second only to biologists in their attachment to the eugenics cause', says Searle, who can nonetheless list medical officers and doctors among eugenics' professional middle-class opponents.[63] It is quite compatible, therefore, for MacKenzie to argue that eugenics expressed professional middle-class interests, and for Searle, on the other hand, to highlight professional middle-class opposition.

The relationship between class and ideology is problematic and contentious to say the least, but what may prove useful is to place the class analysis of MacKenzie and the political analysis of Searle within a more general cultural analysis. From this perspective, what a study of the periodical press does, if anything, is to further marginalise the movement. This is not to say that the eugenists were without influence. Eugenic language and assumptions could quite easily be used by the press as they were in the parliamentary debates over mental deficiency,[64] but it was an influence within a much broader frame of reference. Eugenics was only one response to the problems of race and empire, and a response largely restricted to ambitious technocrats. What we find from a reading of popular periodicals is not the narrow advancement of a particular interest group by the promotion of a specific ideology, but rather an attempt to generate a broader consensus. During the Edwardian 'crisis' the meaning of 'race' was changing, taking on new and worrying connotations. For the British people, or at least for their magazines, 'race' was becoming less an extrospective assumption of supremacy over others and more an introspective fear of the degeneration of themselves. At least at a popular level, the social 'Darwinism' of the 1890s, descriptive of racial superiority, was giving way to the social-imperialism of the 1900s, prescriptive for racial regeneration.[65]

Conclusion

At heart, current concerns for the public understanding of science see 'popular science' as a contradiction in terms. What is science is too abstruse to be popular, and what is popular is too vulgar to be science. It stems from the traditional view of popularisation of science as a process of communication whereby scientific information is disseminated to the public at large. The dominant view is of the filtration of knowledge from the scientist in 'his' laboratory to the 'man-in-the-street'. 'Pure', 'genuine' scientific knowledge is contrasted with the 'polluted' popularised version, and communication simplifies, or even adulterates and distorts. Pristine science thus becomes corrupted into a popular account.[1] With such a perspective the study of popularisation becomes framed in terms of 'accuracy' and 'misunderstanding'. It concerns itself with levels of scientific 'literacy' and making sure the public know (and get) the 'right answers'. It sees in the public a deficiency which has to be made good, a gap to be plugged, a hole to be filled.

Such an approach presupposes a 'behavioural' model of communications focusing, as it does, on the role of the media in effecting changes in the behaviour of individuals. If the media have 'effects', so the argument goes, then these should show up empirically in terms of a direct influence on individuals, for example in a switch of choice between advertised consumer goods or from one election candidate to another. Before a campaign behaviour is recorded as x, and after as y. The difference between the two is seen as a measure of the 'effectiveness' of the campaign. Likewise efforts to improve the public understanding of science can be measured as more or less effective depending on 'before' and 'after' levels of literacy, on the numbers of right or wrong answers.[2] Perhaps it is this classical (even Newtonian) idea of cause and effect that makes it such an attractive model for the more 'scientifically' minded.

Within media studies this model of communications is increasingly regarded as outdated. As long ago as the 1960s there was a major shift in communications research from the sociological approaches of behavioural science to a more 'critical' paradigm. Within the new paradigm concern has been not so much with the impact of particular media messages as with the politics of signification, the struggle over meaning, and the production of consent. In recent years, for example, the study of TV news (often seen as the most 'objective' genre in television) has seen a reappraisal of the notion of 'bias', the analysis of news as a socially structured discourse, and an awareness of the audience as participants in the construction of meaning. More generally, the idea of media 'effects' has become a much more complex concept incorporating notions of context, interpretation and negotiation.[3] Mass communication is now seen not as a process of transmission, but as 'a process whereby the terms in which reality is to be publicly apprehended are constructed so as to benefit specific social interests: its ultimate concern is with the role of the media in the maintenance of hegemony'.[4] A key concept here is that of 'ideology'.

Historians of popular science have also concerned themselves with ideologies and hegemony. For example, Steven Shapin and Barry Barnes have shown how early-nineteenth-century mechanics' institutes were intended to be a medium for the dissemination of the entrepreneurial ideal and middle-class morality. However, they have also shown how, given the stated aims of the institutes' founders and the clientele that they targeted, the movement was a failure. In natural theology, political economy and the science instruction of the institutes, it is likely that 'what we have are failed attempts in the construction of ideologies, each successively rejected by those for whom they were intended'.[5] The mechanics' institutes failed because 'people cannot be controlled by ideas',[6] and the lower orders, they say, were as well able as their betters 'to sniff ideology and reject it'.[7]

So it was for a 'scentless' ideology that Roger Cooter searched in his study of early Victorian popular science. Science, he says, was an important component in the organisation of consent to bourgeois rule and was one of the things around which hegemony was constructed. Early Victorian phrenology helped to establish the legitimacy of bourgeois hegemony by 'naturalising' the emergent structures and relations of industrial capitalism.[8] However, far from being a crude ideological rationalisation, phrenology was instead a 'mystified mediation of ideology' which 'interacted reciprocally with emergent subdominant meritocratic interests to sharpen and strengthen the aspiring group's social significance and articulation'.[9]

But there is a problem. There are certain tensions, one might even say inconsistencies, in viewing mechanics' institutes or phrenology as vehicles for (or mediations of) bourgeois ideology. Why, for example, should the demise of phrenology coincide with the triumph of those meritocratic interests which it mediated? Is it only a matter of irony that the years of its decline should be ones of relative social stability compared with the turbulent times of its heyday? A similar case can be made for mechanics' institutes. Why should attempts at social control be seen to be prominent in the 1830s and 1840s when they most obviously failed, and not in the more peaceful years at the end of the century which might indicate they were successful? Are we to discard the notion that the ideological function of popular science was to create a more passive, acquiescent working class?

One answer might be found in how the cultural meaning of popular science is open to negotiation and redefinition. If we recognise the cultural autonomy of the working class, we must also recognise the potential for alternative ideological constructions. As Adrian Desmond has argued, 'we might picture the artisan craftsmen not as passive recipients of bourgeois wisdom but as active makers of their intellectual world, manufacturing their own "really useful knowledge"'.[10] To the popular lecturers (the 'ideological vanguard' of the lower middle class) phrenology provided a 'rationale' for individualist self-improvement within a hierarchically structured division of labour. To the artisan, however, the rhetoric seemed egalitarian, democratic and anti-clerical, and it was this more anti-elitist and anti-intellectualist brand of phrenology that came to predominate in the second half of the century.[11] Significantly the combination of radicalism with evolutionary science in early-nineteenth-century street literature has also been found in later-nineteenth-century mechanics' institutes. By the end of the century the institutes were helping to spread an evolutionary socialist ideology far from the middle-class ideals of their founding fathers. In so doing 'the working class used the scientific education offered to them to transform agencies designed for social control into instruments for emancipation'.[12] The lower orders, it would seem, not only were able to sniff ideology, but also were as capable of appropriating mechanics' institutes as they did working men's clubs and organised sport.[13]

But this still leaves unexplained the relative social stability at the end of the century. If the mechanics' institutes and phrenology were ideologically ineffective, then perhaps we should look elsewhere.

Far from being dismissed as a transitional phase between early and late capitalism,[14] the late nineteenth century is central to an understanding of the role of ideology in class struggle. In the late nineteenth century the twin birth of mass market and mass media gave rise to new patterns of hegemony. At a time of rising living standards, a home-centred consumerist culture encouraged a positive identification with the existing social system. In turn the commercialisation of the periodical press forced it to identify, represent and articulate consensual interests and values. In the Edwardian years, however, a crisis of hegemony was precipitated by the failure of those undertakings for which consent had been sought, namely an expanding empire and a consumerist economy. The Boer War was a severe blow to the imperial ego, while the stagnant Edwardian economy challenged rising expectations. Amid perceptions of imperial and economic decline, social imperialism was an attempt to recreate a consensus around a single national purpose.

Cultural analysis relates popular science to these shifting patterns of hegemony and the negotiation of consent. In popular periodicals science itself was presented as a commodity, a product not a process, to be consumed not participated in. Science was the new authority, and through a mixture of mystery, specious divinity and beneficence ensured the voluntary servitude of its subjects. A history of inexorable progress had given technology impeccable credentials for a better future, while in the present a plethora of advertisements and articles on industrial processes inextricably linked technology with commodity production. In the Edwardian years, however, there was growing apprehension about technology and applied science expressed, for example, in concern for pollution, health and unemployment. The belief in progress was undermined not by the Great War, but as part of the Edwardian crisis of hegemony. Late-nineteenth-century technology was the realisation of the Enlightenment dream of the subjugation of nature, but the Edwardian years give evidence of a call for a new relationship between ourselves and nature. The narrative anthropomorphism of animal biographies, the campaigns of environmentalist and animal welfare organisations, the origins of nature photography and the birth of the nature study movement, all point to new sensibilities. Moreover, the crisis of hegemony is also seen in the analogical interplay of sex, race and madness. After the Boer War the meaning of 'race' became less an assumption of supremacy and more a fear of degeneration. The return to nature was of imperial importance.

Cultural analysis such as this brings us to a different understanding of what we mean by 'popular science'. We should no longer see the media as a means of communication with popular science as its end product, but rather as a system of representations encompassing what was both popular and scientific. It becomes a forum for negotiations, and not a conduit of messages.

How then do we popularise science or, to use current terminology, improve the public understanding of science?

First, we must make clear the double meaning of 'popularise'. It presupposes that science in its original state is somehow 'unpopular', that it is: 1) not common to the people, and 2) it is disliked. The two are easily conflated, and I suspect that for many of those wishing to 'sell science' a solution to the first of these is taken as a solution to the second. What this approach seeks is not so much the public 'understanding' of science as the public 'approval' of science. One wonders what the response of the science salesmen would be if the public really did understand science, and on that basis decided to reject it.

If we accept that the aim of popularisation is to bring science to greater prominence within common culture, then we still have problems. To change the science you need to change the culture. Parallels with Edwardian Britain are dangerous, but enlightening. The public is still excluded from scientific practice and alienated by esoteric language. Again, a period of complacency and consensus has given way to one of doubt, disillusion and 'crisis'. The 'new Elizabethans' and the 'affluent worker' (who 'never had it so good') have passed into (or for the lucky ones passed through) the years of recession. The 'white heat of technology' has, for many, been forsaken for 'green' alternatives. A return to 'Victorian values' would also have to include a return to a faith in Progress, for then, as now, if the public has nothing to be optimistic about, why on earth should it be optimistic about science?

In 1985 an ad hoc group set up by the Royal Society published a report entitled *The Public Understanding of Science*.[15] Science pervades our society, it said, and our national prosperity depends upon it. Improving the public understanding of science is not a luxury, it declared, but 'an investment in the future'. Science and technology have implications for most public policy issues, and some understanding of the underlying science would also help many personal decisions (for example, about diet, hygiene and vaccination). The recommendations in the report included more science education in school, more science in the media, more scientists in management, more information from industry, more meetings of the Parliamentary and Scientific Committee. More, more, more, but the public understanding of science should not be about more knowledge and more information, like shouting English at foreigners. What is needed is not greater understanding of science as product, but greater involvement in science as process. The popularisation of science should share not only knowledge, but also the power that goes with it – in effect not the popularisation of science but the democratisation of science.

Fine words, but what do they mean?

Popular science should be concerned with the 'everyday' both as an object of research and as the terrain for activity. By focusing on media science in a specific historical period, the most appropriate language has been that of 'hegemony', 'ideology', 'crisis' and 'consent'. But I have always been aware of the sheer messiness of history. It is always possible to find counter-examples, or to pick out an individual and say, 'Where's the hegemony here then?' And yet the wider vision remains, like a character that cannot be contained within a novel's single sentence. The language has served me well so far, but perhaps now it is time to celebrate that messiness. In rejecting the idea that the public passively consumes scientific messages, we should see how the public actively produces its own 'vernacular science' and its own 'democratic epistemologies'.[16] By moving from models of communication to the tactical practices of every-day life,[17] we (as the public) stand a better chance of improving not only the world that we see, but also the world that we create.

Notes

INTRODUCTION

1. Hesketh Pritchard, 'Hunting the guanaco', *Pearson's Magazine*, 1902, vol. 2, pp. 268–72.

1 POPULAR CULTURE

1. For this sense of continuity, see Jose Harris, *Private Lives, Public Spirit: A social history of Britain, 1870–1914* (Oxford, 1993).
2. Taken from Holbrook Jackson, *The 1890s* (original 1913, reprinted London 1988), p. 22.
3. J.B. Priestley, *The Edwardians* (London, 1970), p. 61.
4. Lady Violet Greville, 'Society and its morals', *Cassells's Magazine*, 1909, pp. 384–6.
5. Jackson, op. cit., pp. 22–4.
6. C.F.G. Masterman, *From the Abyss* (1902), extract reprinted in Peter Keating (ed.), *Into Unknown England, 1866–1913: Selections from the social explorers* (London, 1976), p. 241.
7. loc. cit., p. 243.
8. B.S. Rowntree, *Poverty: A study of town life* (1901), reprinted in Keating, op. cit., p. 190.
9. Theodore Andrea Cook, 'After sixty years: a record of progress since 1837', *Cassell's Magazine*, 1897, p. 288.
10. See E.J. Hobsbawm, *Industry and Empire* (Harmondsworth, 1969); and W. Hamish Fraser, *The Coming of the Mass Market, 1850–1914* (London, 1981).
11. Hobsbawm, op. cit., p. 163; and Fraser, op. cit.
12. Richard Shannon, *The Crisis of Imperialism, 1865–1915* (London, 1976), p. 207.
13. See Geoffrey Crossick (ed.), *The Lower Middle Class in Britain, 1870–1914* (London, 1977).
14. Gareth Stedman Jones, 'Working-class culture and working-class politics in London, 1870–1900: notes on the remaking of a working class', *Journal of Social History*, VII (1974), pp. 461–500.
15. James Walvin, *Leisure and Society, 1830–1950* (London, 1978), p. 62.
16. See Walvin, op. cit.
17. P.J. Waller, *Town, City and Nation: England, 1850–1914* (Oxford, 1983), p. 4.
18. See Waller, op. cit., pp. 103–5; Walvin, op. cit., chapter 7; and Fraser, op. cit., pp. 215–16.
19. See T.G. Ashplant, 'London working men's clubs, 1875–1914', and Penelope Summerfield, 'The Effingham arms and the Empire: Deliberate

selection in the evolution of music hall in London', both in Eileen and Stephen Yeo (eds), *Popular Culture and Class Conflict, 1590–1914: Explorations in the history of labour and leisure* (Brighton, 1981). See also Peter Bailey, 'Custom, capital and culture in the Victorian music hall', and John Walton and Robert Poole, 'The Lancashire Wakes in the nineteenth century', both in Robert D. Storch (ed.), *Popular Culture and Custom in Nineteenth-Century England* (London, 1982).

20.   Peter Bailey, *Leisure and Class in Victorian England: Rational recreation and the contest for control, 1830–1885* (London, 1978), p. 182. Bailey also writes: 'mass leisure industries of the present century [are] more formidable agents of social control than anything experienced in Victorian society' (loc. cit.).

21.   Eileen and Stephen Yeo, 'Perceived patterns: competition and licence versus class and struggle', in Eileen and Stephen Yeo (eds), op. cit., p. 293.

22.   Hugh Cunningham, 'Class and leisure in mid-Victorian England', in Bernard Waites, Tony Bennett and Graham Martin (eds), *Popular Culture: Past and present* (London, 1982), pp. 87–9.

23.   Robert Gray, 'Bourgeois hegemony in Victorian Britain', in Tony Bennett, Martin Graham, Colin Mercer and Janet Woollacott (eds), *Culture, Ideology and Social Process: A reader* (Milton Keynes, 1981), pp. 244–7.

24.   See Gareth Stedman Jones, 'Working-class culture and working-class politics in London, 1870–1900: notes on the remaking of a working class', *Journal of Social History*, VII (1974), pp. 461–500.

25.   Nicholas Abercrombie, Stephen Hill and Bryan S. Turner, *The Dominant Ideology Thesis* (London, 1980), p. 119.

26.   Jones, op. cit., p. 499.

27.   Bailey, 'Victorian music hall', op. cit., p. 198.

28.   Summerfield, op. cit., p. 209.

29.   Richard Hoggart, *The Uses of Literacy: Aspects of working-class life with special reference to publications and entertainments* (Harmondsworth, 1981), p. 172.

30.   Robert Roberts, *The Classic Slum: Salford life in the first quarter of the century* (Harmondsworth, 1973), p. 32.

31.   For such critiques and discussions of consumerism in general, see *Theory, Culture and Society* (special issue on consumer culture), vol. 1 (1983), no. 3, especially Mike Featherstone, 'Consumer culture: an introduction', pp. 4–9, and Douglas Kellner, 'Critical theory, commodities and the consumer society', pp. 66–84.

32.   Zygmunt Bauman, 'Industrialism, consumerism and power', *Theory, Culture and Society*, vol. 1 (1983), no. 3, pp. 32–43. Bauman writes: 'Money becomes a makeshift power substituted for the one surrendered in the sphere of production; while the experience of unfreedom generated by the conditions in the workplace is re-projected upon the universe of commodities. Correspondingly, the search for freedom is re-interpreted as the effort to satisfy consumer needs through the appropriation of marketable goods' (p. 38).

33.   Shannon, op. cit., p. 204; and David Chaney, 'The department store as cultural form', *Theory, Culture and Society*, vol. 1 (1983), no. 3, pp. 22–31. On the consumer revolution and the growth of retailing, see also W. Hamish

Fraser, op. cit.; James B. Jeffreys, *Retail Trading in Britain, 1850–1950: A study of trends in retailing with special reference to the development of co-operative, multiple shop and department store methods of trading* (London, 1954); and Rosalind H. Williams, *Dream Worlds: Mass consumption in late-nineteenth-century France* (London, 1982), especially chapter 5, 'The dream world of mass consumption'.

34. Abercrombie et al., op. cit., pp. 123 and 166. This might be construed as a circular argument, their appeal to pragmatism implying that society coheres because it is coherent.

35. See Chapter 9 of this book.

36. John M. MacKenzie, *Propaganda and Empire: The manipulation of British public opinion, 1880–1960* (Manchester, 1984), p. 258.

37. Masterman, *From the Abyss*, in Keating, op. cit., p. 242.

38. Roberts, op. cit., p. 143.

39. Henry Pelling, *Popular Politics and Society in Late Victorian Britain* (2nd edition, London, 1979), especially chapter 5, 'British labour and British imperialism'; Richard Price, *An Imperial War and the British Working Class* (London, 1972).

40. Richard Price, 'Society, status and jingoism: the social roots of lower-middle-class patriotism, 1870–1900', in Crossick, op. cit., pp. 89–112. Price writes: 'Jingoism was the expression of a political morality and value system which briefly tried to halt the disintegration of social and political conventions by demanding the creation of a national patriotic consensus' (p. 95).

41. Alan J. Lee, *The Origins of the Popular Press in England, 1855–1914,* (London, 1976), p. 161.

2 POPULAR PRESS

1. H.J. Perkin, 'The origins of the popular press', *History Today*, 7 (1957), p. 429.

2. Richard D. Altick, *The English Common Reader: A social history of the mass reading public, 1800–1900* (Chicago, 1957).

3. Perkin, loc. cit.

4. On the origins of the popular press, see Alan J. Lee, *The Origins of the Popular Press in England 1855–1914* (London, 1976); Raymond Williams, *The Long Revolution* (London, 1961), especially chapter 3, 'The growth of the popular press'; Raymond Williams, 'The press and popular culture: an historical perspective', in George Boyce, James Curran and Pauline Wingate (eds), *Newspaper History: From the seventeenth century to the present day* (London, 1978), pp. 41–50; Francis Williams, *Dangerous Estate: The anatomy of newspapers* (London, 1957); and G.A. Cranfield, *The Press and Society: From Caxton to Northcliffe* (London, 1978).

5. From Raymond Williams, *Communications* (3rd edition, Harmondsworth, 1976), p. 15.

6. Lady Bell, 'Reading habits in Middlesbrough', extract from *At the Works*, 1907, reprinted in Peter Keating (ed.), *Into Unknown England, 1866–1913: Selections from the sociological explorers* (London, 1976).

7. The figure comes from W. Hamish Fraser, *The Coming of the Mass Market, 1850–1914* (London, 1981), p. 73. Raymond Williams emphasises the importance of Sunday reading, and Alan Lee writes of the new weeklies such as *Tit-Bits, Pearson's Weekly* and *Answers* that 'they were, indeed, more important, economically and culturally, than the more famous political weeklies' (Lee, 'The structure, ownership and control of the press, 1855–1914', in Boyce et al., op. cit., p. 124).

8. Francis Williams, op. cit., p. 129.

9. Raymond Williams, *Long Revolution*, op. cit., p. 202.

10. On the economic reorganisation of the press, see Alan Lee, 'The structure, ownership and control of the press', op. cit.; Raymond Williams, *Long Revolution*, op. cit.; and also Raymond Williams, *Communications*, op. cit., p. 18.

11. Lee, *Origins*, op. cit., p. 216.

12. Quoted in Q.D. Leavis, *Fiction and the Reading Public* (London, 1965), p. 179.

13. Quoted in Lee, *Origins*, op. cit., p. 118.

14. ibid., p. 120.

15. ibid., p. 121.

16. Quoted, ibid., p. 189.

17. For the new journalism, see Lee, *Origins*, op. cit., pp. 117–30; and Joel H. Wiener (ed.), *Papers for the Millions: The new journalism in Britain, 1850 to 1914* (Westport, 1988). See also Leavis, *op. cit.*, pp. 180–2; J.O. Baylen, 'Politics and the "new journalism"', *Victorian Periodicals Review*, XX (1987), pp. 126–41; and John Goodbody, '"The Star": its role in the new journalism', *Victorian Periodicals Review*, XX (1987), pp. 141–50.

18. Quoted, ibid., p. 219.

19. Joanne Shattock and Michael Wolff (eds), *The Victorian Periodical Press: Samplings and soundings* (Leicester, 1982), p. xv.

20. See Lee, *Origins*, p. 189.

21. James Curran, 'The press as an agency of social control: an historical perspective', in Boyce et al., op. cit., p. 72. For the promotion of the cult of the home and self-help by the press, see Peter Roger Mountjoy, 'The working-class press and working-class Conservatism', in Boyce et al., op. cit., pp. 265–80.

22. 'The cheap popular magazine', *Practical Advertising*, 1902, p. li.

23. loc. cit.

24. As with the title of the book edited by Shattock and Wolff, op. cit.

25. Sidney Dark, *The Life of Sir Arthur Pearson* (London, 1922), p. 6.

26. Entry for Cyril Arthur Pearson in *Dictionary of National Biography*.

27. See Dark, op. cit.

28. See Michael Rosenthal, *The Character Factory: Baden-Powell and the origins of the Boy Scout movement* (New York, 1986), pp. 81–7.

29. Barbara Quinn Schmidt, entry for *Pearson's Magazine* in Alvin Sullivan (ed.), *British Literary Magazines: The Victorian and Edwardian Age* (London, 1984), pp. 310–13.

30. 'The hundredth number of *Pearson's Magazine*', *Pearson's Magazine*, 1904, vol. 1, p. 347.

31. 'The prevalence of insanity', *Pearson's Magazine*, 1906, vol. 1, pp. 135–46; 'The waste of infant life', *Pearson's Magazine*, 1906, vol. 1, pp. 2–15; Lord Roberts, 'How to make a nation of marksmen', *Pearson's Magazine*, 1906, vol. 1, p. 479.

32. 'With the editor's compliments', *Pearson's Weekly*, 26 July 1890, p. 1.

33. C. Arthur Pearson, '1,000th edition', *Pearson's Weekly*, 16 September 1909, p. 221.

34. See Schmidt, op. cit; 'The smell of this paper kills influenza', *Pearson's Weekly*, 13 February 1892; and Dark, op. cit., pp. 57–9.

35. 'Answers to correspondents', *Tit-Bits*, 13 April 1912, p. 127.

36. See '*Tit-Bits* makes another record', *Tit-Bits*, 14 September 1912, p. 6.

37. 'The romance and reality of a crematorium', *Tit-Bits*, 5 October 1895, p. 2; 'Celebrated people whose mothers have been buried alive', *Tit-Bits*, 25 January 1902, p. 419.

38. Quoted in Simon Nowell-Smith, *The House of Cassell, 1848–1958* (London, 1958), p. 22.

39. ibid, p. 121.

40. 'Greybeards' was the term used by Pemberton. See Nowell-Smith, op. cit., p. 121.

41. 'The humorous side of wearing an artificial leg', *Cassell's Saturday Journal*, 1893, p. 148.

42. Nowell-Smith, op. cit., p. 131.

43. 'A glance-back over one thousand weeks', *Cassell's Saturday Journal*, 26 November 1902, p. 228.

44. 'Workers at work', *Cassell's Saturday Journal*, series started 16 August 1913; 'For all who toil', start of 'Workers' page', *Cassell's Saturday Journal*, 1908.

45. 'The world as it is', *Cassell's Saturday Journal*, 11 February 1911 to 17 August 1912, thereafter called 'If Christ came to London'.

46. Sydney Smith, *Donald Macleod of Glasgow: A memoir and a study* (London, 1926), p. 110.

47. For Macleod as editor, see Smith, op. cit, chapter XI, pp. 109–21.

48. Quoted, ibid., p. 82.

49. 'The editor' (Donald Macleod), 'An editorial retrospect', *Good Words*, 1904, p. 80.

50. ibid.

51. Smith, op. cit, p. 117.

52. See *Good Words*, 1901, p. 621.

53. Macleod MSS, National Library of Scotland, file 9827, letter 225.

54. Macleod, loc. cit.

55. In 'A foreword' to the new magazine, Macleod wrote: '...the demand has increased for what is merely amusing or sensational, in preference – if not to the exclusion – of what is instructive or serious'. The new taste was for 'snapshot' literature and 'swift electric thrills of sensational interest'. He believed, however, that there were still 'masses of the population' who would appreciate the literature that *Good Words* had on offer: 'The original aim of the magazine may be better fulfilled in the present day by appealing to the great body of the people through methods of publication adapted to their requirements, while maintaining the literary excellence and the broad,

healthy, and Christian tone which has hitherto characterised *Good Words*.' (*Good Words and Sunday Magazine*, 5 May 1906, p. 2.) He may have been right. An editorial two weeks later claimed a circulation figure of 600 000 for the first issue of the new magazine (*Good Words and Sunday Magazine*, 19 May 1906, p. 54).

56. 'Jubilee of the Cottager and Artisan', *Cottager and Artisan*, 1910, p. 136.
57. Dr Thain Davidson, 'Life is for work', *Cottager and Artisan*, 1900, p. 117.
58. Robert Blatchford, 'The great announcement', *Clarion*, 8 November 1912, p. 3.
59. 'Nunquam' (Robert Blatchford), *Clarion*, 12 December 1891, p. 1.
60. Robert Blatchford, *My Eighty Years* (London, 1931), p. 199. Blatchford also wrote: 'I am ready to sacrifice Socialism for the sake of England; but never to sacrifice England for the sake of Socialism', ibid., p. 202. Deian Hopkin describes Blatchford as 'a political maverick and clearly more of a journalist than a politician' (from Deian Hopkin, 'The socialist press in Britain, 1890–1910', in George Boyce et al., op. cit., p. 297.
61. See entry for Robert Blatchford in *Dictionary of Labour Biography*. Hopkin claims the *Clarion* to be 'the most commercially successful socialist paper' (Hopkin, op. cit., p. 299).
62. 'Nunquam' (Robert Blatchford), 'A straight talk', *Clarion*, 11 June 1892, p. 7.
63. Robert Blatchford, 'Twenty years after', *Clarion*, 6 December 1912, p. 4.
64. Stanley Harrison, *Poor Men's Guardians: A record of the struggles for a democratic newspaper press, 1763–1973* (London, 1974), p. 171.
65. Alvar Ellegard, *Darwin and the General Reader: The reception of Darwin's theory of evolution in the British periodical press, 1859–1872* (Göteborg, 1958).
66. F.E. Baily, 'The crushing of the middle class', *Pearson's Magazine*, 1912, vol. 2, pp. 382–91.
67. Sally Mitchell, entry for *Good Words* in Sullivan, op. cit., pp. 145–9.
68. 'Popular papers: "Tit-Bits"', *Pearson's Weekly*, 10 January 1891, p. 391.

3 THE POPULARISATION OF SCIENCE

1. A. Neil Lyons, 'The riddle of the universe, not according to Haeckel', *Clarion*, 8 December 1905, p. 5.
2. See Rosalind H. Williams, *Dream Worlds: Mass consumption in late-nineteenth-century France* (London, 1982); W. Hamish Fraser, *The Coming of the Mass Market, 1850–1914* (London, 1981); John Walton, *The English Seaside Resort: A social history, 1750–1914* (Leicester, 1983).
3. *Pearson's Magazine*, July 1911.
4. 'At the zoo', *Cottager and Artisan*, 1912, pp. 37–8; Percy Collins, 'Mimicking nature', *Cassell's Magazine*, 1912, pp. 675–81.
5. 'The elevation of the masses', *Clarion*, 28 March 1902.
6. F.G. Aflalo, 'The Naples aquarium', *Good Words*, 1898, p. 757. See also W.L. Alden, 'From China to Peru', *Pearson's Magazine*, 1900, vol. 2, pp. 342–3.

7. Rachel Low and Roger Manvell, *The History of the British Film, 1896–1906* (London, 1948); Rachel Low, *The History of the British Film, 1906–1914* (London, 1948). For the ideological function of early cinema, see Roy Armes, *A Critical History of British Cinema* (London, 1978); and Michael Chanan, *The Dream that Kicks: The prehistory and early years of cinema in Britain* (London, 1980).

8. Age is taken as at the time of first contribution for one of the eight magazines. Contributors may, of course, have been writing before then, and many continued to do so afterwards.

9. The most notable exception being Camille Flammarion who was 67 when he first wrote for *Cassell's Magazine* in 1909.

10. The main reference works used were *Dictionary of National Biography, Dictionary of Scientific Biography, Who Was Who,* and the *British Museum Catalogue.*

11. George Gissing, *New Grub Street* (1891), and see the introduction by Bernard Bergonzi in the Penguin edition (Harmondsworth, 1968).

12. 'How I write my Pearson's Weekly articles', *Pearson's Weekly,* 17 December 1903, p. 419.

13. 'Books writers write from' by 'one of the staff', *Pearson's Weekly,* 11 May 1905, p. 807.

14. John T. Carrington, 'Science in some magazines', *Science Gossip,* 1897, p. 114.

15. W.T. Stead, 'My system', *Cassell's Magazine,* August 1906, p. 297.

16. Frank Banfield, 'Mr. A.F. Yarrow at Poplar', *Cassell's Magazine,* April 1897, p. 471.

17. 'A few popular errors', *Pearson's Weekly,* 25 July 1891, p. 5; 'Popular delusions', *Tit-Bits,* 18 August 1894, p. 356; 'Popular errors on medical subjects', *Tit-Bits,* 24 August 1895, p. 369.

18. James Nairn, 'X-rays in the Edison laboratory', *Good Words,* 1897, pp. 50–4; Robert Machray, 'By cable, from shore to shore', *Pearson's Magazine,* 1897, vol. 2, pp. 323–8; Walter George Bell, 'The greatest telescope on earth', *Pearson's Magazine,* 1897, vol. 2, pp. 210–13.

19. A.W. Rucker, 'Underground mountains', *Good Words,* 1900, pp. 44–7, 122–7 and 191–6; Professor Thorpe, 'Phosphorous and phosphorescence', *Good Words,* 1891, pp. 249–51 and 306–10; Mrs Percy Frankland, 'Natural mineral waters and bacteria', *Good Words,* 1898, pp. 843–6.

20. 'Aniline birds', *Cassell's Magazine,* 1900, vol. 1, p. 495.

21. Correspondence, *Pearson's Weekly,* 14 August 1897, p. 144; T.W. Wilkinson, 'Cave exploring in England', *Good Words,* 1902, p. 437.

22. Advertisement for the *Harmsworth Popular Science, Clarion,* 13 March 1914, p. 3.

23. E. Kay Robinson, 'The way with weeds', *Good Words,* 1902, p. 423.

24. John J. Ward, 'Glimpses into plant structure', part of the series 'Minute marvels of nature', *Good Words,* 1902, p. 136.

25. Ralph Abercromby, 'Signs in the sky', *Good Words,* 1890, p. 518.

26. R.B. Suthers, 'The fairyland of science', review of the *Harmsworth Popular Science, Clarion,* 23 January 1914, p. 2.

27. Professor Andrew Gray, 'Present-day leaders of science: Lord Kelvin', *Good Words,* 1900, p. 29.

28. R. Blatchford, review of Kropotkin's *Mutual Aid*, *Clarion*, 12 December 1902, p. 3.

29. Robert Blatchford, 'Is Darwin played out?', review of Sir E. Ray Lankester's *Science from an Easy Chair*, *Clarion*, 31 January 1913, p. 3. 'Britain's greatest benefactor', *Clarion*, January 1907: The top three were Darwin with 136 votes, Caxton 103 and Cromwell 52; Stephenson, Professor Simpson and James Watt all came in the top ten.

30. 'I sub-edit a daily paper', *Pearson's Weekly*, 11 August 1904, p. 100.

31. Louis Elkind, 'Radium and its possibilities', *Cassell's Magazine*, April 1904, p. 586.

32. Professor G.G. Henderson, 'Present-day leaders of science: Professor James Dewar', *Good Words*, 1900, p. 765.

33. *Pearson's Weekly*, 17 December 1898, p. 389.

34. Advertisement for *Science History of the Universe*, *Clarion*, 9 February 1912, p. 3.

35. 'Science for the unscientific', *Pearson's Weekly*, 17 November 1894, p. 284. There were a total of 41 articles in the series which appeared every fortnight until January 1896.

36. 'Playing tricks with science' aimed to 'provide readers with simple and inexpensive means of providing an evening entertainment at once diverting and instructive', and included how to make a simple harmonograph and how to lift a plate with a radish (*Pearson's Magazine*, 1907, vol. 1, p. 158); Archibald Williams, 'After-dinner science', *Pearson's Magazine*, 1906, vol. 1, pp. 33–40.

37. See, for example, A.J. Meadows, 'Access to the results of scientific research: developments in Victorian Britain', in A.J. Meadows (ed.), *Development of Science Publishing in Britain* (Oxford, 1980), pp. 61–2. There could, of course, be an ideological utility of science to meet the varying concerns of each magazine (the support of religion in *Good Words*, the undermining of religion in the *Clarion*, the spread of empire in *Pearson's Magazine*). This should be made clear in other chapters but see also Emma Marie Caillard, 'The fourth state of matter', *Good Words*, 1894, p. 95; Harry Lowerison, 'Knowledge is power', *Clarion*, 19 January 1912, p. 3; Ray Stannard Baker, 'The romance of Christmas Island', *Pearson's Magazine*, 1902, vol. 1, p. 266.

38. M. Griffith, 'An electric eye', *Pearson's Magazine*, 1896, vol. 2, pp. 752–3.

39. Alfred T. Story, 'Harnessing the stars', *Pearson's Magazine*, 1896, vol. 2, p. 585.

40. Richard Yeo, 'Scientific method and image of science, 1831–1891', in Roy Macleod and Peter Collins (eds), *The Parliament of Science: The British Association for the Advancement of Science, 1831–1981* (Northwood, 1981) p. 67.

41. Marcus Tindal, 'Kumatology', *Pearson's Magazine*, 1901, vol. 2, p. 10.

42. 'Science for the unscientific', *Pearson's Weekly*, 17 November 1894, p. 284.

43. Emma Marie Caillard, 'Matter', *Good Words*, 1894, p. 382.

44. Sir Robert Ball, 'Copernicus', *Good Words*, 1895, p. 254.

45. J. Holt Schooling, 'The divining rod', *Pearson's Magazine*, 1897, vol. 1, pp. 304–5.

46. Richard Yeo, 'Scientific method and the rhetoric of science in Britain, 1830–1917', in John A. Schuster and Richard R. Yeo (eds), *The Politics and Rhetoric of Scientific Method; Historical studies* (Dordrecht, 1986), pp. 272–3. For professionalisation of science, see D.S.L. Cardwell, *The Organisation of Science in England* (London, 1957); Hilary Rose and Steven Rose, *Science and Society* (Harmondsworth, 1969); and Morris Berman, 'Hegemony and the amateur tradition in British science', *Journal of Social History*, (1975), pp. 33–43.

47. Richard Yeo, 'Science and intellectual authority in mid-century Britain: Robert Chambers and "Vestiges of the Natural History of Creation"', *Victorian Studies*, 28 (1984), pp. 5–31. In 1913 Professor Bickerton praised the broad approach of Harry Lowerison at the *Clarion*: 'We want to be in contact with nature and in tune with the infinite. Scientists have their faults, one is vicious specialisation. They lack the cosmic consciousness...' (Professor Bickerton, 'Science and socialism', *Clarion*, 17 January 1913, p. 3).

48. Susan Sheets-Pyenson, 'Popular science periodicals in Paris and London: the emergence of a low scientific culture', *Annals of Science*, 42 (1985), p. 563.

49. ibid., p. 555. Sheets-Pyenson borrows the terms from H. Perkin, *The Origins of Modern British Society, 1780–1880* (London, 1969), p. 428.

50. See Chapter 1 of this book.

51. 'Science a monopoly', *Science Gossip*, 1897, p. 327. See David Elliston Allen, *The Naturalist in Britain: A social history* (London, 1976); A.G. Tansley, 'The early history of modern plant ecology in Britain', Journal of Ecology, 35 (1947), pp. 130–8; and W.H. Pearsall, 'The development of ecology in Britain', *Journal of Ecology*, supplement 1964, pp. 1–12.

4 IMAGES

1. Rudolph de Cordova, 'The microbe of death', *Pearson's Magazine*, 1897, vol. 2, pp. 464–74; W.L. Alden, 'The purple death', *Cassell's Magazine*, 1895, p. 115.

2. W.L. Alden, 'The earthquaker', *Pearson's Magazine*, 1907, vol. 2, p. 396.

3. John G.E. Leech, 'The microbe of love', *Pearson's Magazine*, 1902, vol. 2, p. 374.

4. John N. Raphael, 'Up above: the story of the sky folk', *Pearson's Magazine*, 1912, vol. 2, pp. 710–60.

5. 'The greatest discovery of the century', *Pearson's Weekly*, 16 June 1894, p. 754.

6. ibid. For the identification of women with vivisected animals, see Coral Lansbury, 'Gynaecology, pornography and the anti-vivisection movement', *Victorian Studies*, 28 (1985) pp. 413–37.

7. E.E. Kellett, 'The lady automaton', *Pearson's Magazine*, 1901, vol. 1, p. 666.

8. loc. cit.

9. L.T. Meade and Robert Eustace, 'The blue laboratory', *Cassell's Magazine*, May 1897, p. 573.

10.   ibid., p. 575.

11.   Professor Andrew Gray, 'Present-day leaders of science: Lord Kelvin', *Good Words*, 1900, p. 29. For Kelvin (and Huxley) as household names, see, for example, 'A martyr to science', a joke about a butcher's son who sets up his own laboratory at home. His mother wonders if he might be a "Uxley somed'y' and his angry father refers to him as 'me Lord Kelvin', *Tit-Bits*, 11 August 1906, p. 493.

12.   'Stories of Lord Kelvin', *Tit-Bits*, 9 April 1910, p. 75; 'The joyful inventor', *Cassell's Saturday Journal*, 1 January 1908, p. 414; 'Biography by anecdote, Lord Kelvin', *Cassell's Magazine*, March 1907, pp. 426–7.

13.   'Workers and their work, Lord Kelvin', *Pearson's Weekly*, 30 March 1895, p. 599.

14.   'People we hear about', *Cassell's Saturday Journal*, 10 April 1907, p. 757.

15.   'Workers and their work', loc. cit.

16.   Donald Macleod, 'The Right Honourable Lord Kelvin', *Good Words*, 1896, pp. 378–88.

17.   Herbert C. Fyfe, 'The first traverse of Africa', *Pearson's Magazine*, 1900, vol. 2, pp. 418–24.

18.   Sir Ernest Shackleton, 'The making of an explorer', *Pearson's Magazine*, 1914, vol. 2, pp. 138–42.

19.   Ejnar Mikkelsen, 'Lost in the Arctic', *Pearson's Magazine*, 1912, vol. 2, pp. 506–20.

20.   'Doctors' experiments upon themselves', *Cassell's Saturday Journal*, 8 January 1902, p. 357.

21.   David A. Hollinger, 'Inquiry and uplift: late-nineteenth-century American academics and the moral efficacy of scientific practice', in Thomas L. Haskell (ed.), *The Authority of Experts: Studies in history* (Bloomington, 1984), p. 142.

22.   Dr J.G. McPherson, 'Numbering the dust', *Good Words*, 1891, p. 755.

23.   'England's roll of fame', *Tit-Bits*, 19 January 1907, p. 450; 'Workers and their work, Sir John Lubbock', *Pearson's Weekly*, 9 January 1892, p. 391.

24.   Julius L.F. Vogel, 'Photographing electricity', *Pearson's Magazine*, 1899, vol. 2, p. 643.

25.   Herbert N. Casson, 'At last we can fly', *Pearson's Magazine*, 1907, vol. 2, p. 98; Alder Anderson, 'Analysing motion', *Pearson's Magazine*, 1902, vol.1, pp. 502–9.

26.   See, for example, Professor Dobbie, 'Present-day leaders of science, Professor William Ramsay', which concludes: 'In all his work he has thought little of personal gain and much of the advancement of science', *Good Words*, 1900, p. 136.

27.   'A great genius of the day', *Cassell's Saturday Journal*, 19 February 1902, p. 474; 'Marconi the magician', *Tit-Bits*, 25 March 1905, p. 11.

28.   F.M. Holmes, 'A famous working man: the story of James Brindley, the canal engineer', *British Workman*, 1897, p. 12.

29.   'Nansen, the Arctic hero', *British Workman*, 1897, p. 40.

30.   Alice Salzman, 'Labour conquers all things', *British Workman*, 1897, p. 47.

31.   See I. Bernard Cohen, 'The fear and distrust of science in historical perspective: some first thoughts', in Andrei S. Markovits and Karl W. Deutsch

(eds), *Fear of Science – Trust in Science: Conditions for change in the climate of opinion* (Cambridge, Mass., 1980), pp. 29–58.

32. Meade and Eustace, op. cit., p. 567.

33. 'Excursions to the heavens, a chat with Sir Norman Lockyer', *Cassell's Saturday Journal*, 8 December 1897, p. 254.

34. Chauncey Montgomery M'Govern, 'The new wizard of the west', *Pearson's Magazine*, vol. 1, pp. 470–6.

35. 'In the public eye' appeared in *Pearson's Magazine*, 'People of importance' in *Pearson's Weekly*, and 'People we hear about' in *Cassell's Saturday Journal*. There were many more, including 'Representative men at home' in *Cassell's Saturday Journal*, and 'In the arena' in *Cassell's Magazine* as well as 'Personal Tit-Bits' in *Tit-Bits*.

36. E.R. Punshon, 'Professor Kenyon's engagement', *Cassell's Magazine*, May 1907, p. 702. This story also appeared anonymously in *Cassell's Saturday Journal*, 26 August 1910, p. 13, under the title 'The professor's engagement'. The professor should not be confused with another Professor Kenyon in the George Griffith story 'A corner in lightning' which appeared in *Pearson's Magazine* in 1898.

37. 'The Whatnot', 'Spiritualism and things: a chat with Dr Russell Wallace', *Clarion*, 22 January 1898, p. 29.

38. Arthur Conan Doyle, 'A study in scarlet' (1887), reprinted in *The Complete Sherlock Holmes Long Stories* (London, 1929), pp. 12–13.

39. Arthur Conan Doyle, 'The sign of four' (1880), reprinted in *The Complete Sherlock Holmes Long Stories* (London, 1929), p. 136.

40. Jacques Futrelle, 'Professor van Dusen's problems', *Cassell's Magazine*, December 1907, pp. 1–10, and several in 1908; 'The mystery of Prince Otto', *Cassell's Magazine*, July 1912, pp. 1–13; 'Wraiths of the storm', *Cassell's Saturday Journal*, 11 September 1909, p. 500.

41. Futrelle, 'Professor van Dusen's problems', op. cit., p. 2.

42. ibid. See also 'The mystery of Prince Otto', op. cit., p. 1.

43. Futrelle, 'Professor van Dusen's problems', op. cit., pp. 3 and 9.

44. See Cohen, op. cit., p. 55: 'Basically, there is a fear and dislike of science because it seems like a juggernaut, something inhuman, something impersonal, something that affects the scientists themselves and makes them dehumanised and impersonal.' Contrast this with the 'moral efficacy of scientific practice' of Hollinger below.

45. Futrelle, 'The mystery of Prince Otto', op. cit., p. 2.

46. 'Scientific detectives of to-day', *Cassell's Saturday Journal*, series began 14 May 1902.

47. 'Science as Sherlock Holmes', *Cassell's Saturday Journal*, 18 April 1906, p. 773.

48. Brian Wynne, 'Physics and psychics: science, symbolic action and social control in late Victorian England', in Barry Barnes and Steven Shapin (eds), *Natural Order: Historical studies of scientific culture* (London, 1979), p. 174.

49. John Munro, 'Is the end of the world near?', *Cassell's Magazine*, May 1898, p. 563.

50. 'The strangest man in the world', *Tit-Bits*, 4 July 1903, p. 350.

51. Colin Russell, *Science and Social Change, 1700–1900* (London, 1983), p. 257.

52. Michael Worboys, 'The British Association and empire: science and social imperialism', in Macleod and Collins, op. cit., pp. 170–87.

53. Frank M. Turner, 'Public science in Britain, 1880–1919', *Isis*, 71 (1980), pp. 589–608.

54. Quoted, ibid., p. 602. Of the British Science Guild, Turner writes: 'By 1912 the Guild had a membership of 900 and was clearly a conservative, social imperialist pressure group seeking to combine the intellectual prestige of science with the political attraction of efficiency and empire' (p. 602).

55. See G.R. Searle, *The Quest for National Efficiency: A study in British politics and political thought, 1899–1914* (Berkeley, 1971); Bernard Semmel, *Imperialism and Social Reform: English social-imperial thought, 1895–1914* (London, 1960); and Robert Scally, *The Origins of the Lloyd George Coalition: The politics of social-imperialism, 1900–1918* (Princeton, 1975).

56. Hollinger, op. cit., p. 147.

57. Étienne de La Boétie, *The Politics of Obedience: The discourse of voluntary servitude*, translated by Harry Kurz (Montreal, 1975).

58. See Patrick Joyce, *Work, Society and Politics: The culture of the factory in later Victorian England* (London, 1982).

59. 'Dangle' (Alex M. Thompson), 'Uses of science', *Clarion*, 30 December 1910, p. 7.

5 SCIENCE AND RELIGION

1. Professor Sir Hector C. Cameron, 'Present-day leaders of science: Lord Lister', *Good Words*, 1900, pp. 516–22; Professor Sydney Young, 'Present-day leaders of science: William Henry Perkin', *Good Words*, 1900, pp. 256–61; Professor Dobbie, op. cit.; J.D. Cormack, 'Edison', *Good Words*, 1901, pp. 157–63; Sir Robert Ball, 'Isaac Newton', *Good Words*, 1895, pp. 53–7 and 109–15.

2. Rev. O.J. Vignoles, 'The home of a naturalist', *Good Words*, 1893, p. 97.

3. Gertrude Bacon, 'The most wonderful observatory in the world', *Good Words*, 1901, p. 89.

4. Rev. O.J. Vignoles, op. cit., p. 97.

5. Mona Caird, 'Scientific popery', *Clarion*, 29 December 1894, p. 6. Caird was calling for scepticism over the claims for a new anti-toxin treatment for diphtheria. The rejection of a new scientific priesthood and the abandonment of the Christian faith left many like Sidgwick, Myers and Butler 'between science and religion'. See Frank M. Turner, *Between Science and Religion: The reaction to scientific naturalism in late Victorian England* (London, 1974).

6. Edward Carpenter, 'Vivisection', *Clarion*, 1 December 1894, p. 8; Edith Carrington, 'Vivisection by women and children', *Clarion*, 17 February 1894, p. 8.

7. Mona Caird, 'Vivisection', *Clarion*, 10 November 1894, p. 7.

8. Richard D. French, *Anti-vivisection and Medical Science in Victorian Society* (London, 1975), p. 230.

9. Owen Chadwick, *The Victorian Church* (London, 1966), pt II, p. 35.
10. Frederic Douglas How, 'The Marquis of Salisbury', *Good Words*, 1902, p. 414.
11. 'The religious value of the first chapters of Genesis', *Good Words*, 1897, p. 350.
12. Chadwick, loc. cit.
13. Frank M. Turner, 'Public science in Britain, 1880–1919', *Isis*, 71 (1980), pp. 589–608. On the 'conflict' of science and religion, see also Frank M. Turner, *Between Science and Religion: The reaction to scientific naturalism in late Victorian England* (London, 1974), and 'The Victorian conflict between science and religion: a professional dimension', *Isis*, 69 (1978), pp. 356–76.
14. Susan Budd, 'The loss of faith: reasons for unbelief among members of the secular movement in England, 1850–1950', *Past and Present*, 36 (1967), p. 125. See also Susan Budd, *Varieties of Unbelief: Atheists and agnostics in English society, 1850–1960* (London, 1977).
15. 'To correspondents', *Family Herald*, 9 January 1897, p. 156.
16. F. le Gros Clark, *Paley's Natural Theology: Revised to harmonize with modern science* (London, 1885).
17. ibid., pp. 9 and 27.
18. T.F. Manning, 'God in trifles', *Good Words*, 1899, pp. 684–5.
19. ibid., p. 683.
20. John Hedley Brooke, 'The natural theology of the geologists: some theological strata', in L.J. Jordanova and Roy Porter (eds), *Images of the Earth: Essays in the history of the environmental sciences* (Chalfont St Giles, 1979), pp. 39–64.
21. John J. Ward, 'Glimpses into plant structure', *Good Words*, 1902, p. 136; Robert Ball, 'The sun', *Good Words*, 1890, p. 629.
22. Rev. B.G. Johns, 'The trout of the chalk stream', *Good Words*, 1892, pp. 166–171; Rev. Robert C. Nightingale, 'A muddy corner', *Good Words*, 1899, pp. 307–11.
23. Rev. Hugh Macmillan, 'The cranberry', *Good Words*, 1902, p. 665. Throughout the second half of the nineteenth century Macmillan published numerous books highlighting the harmony between the natural and the spiritual world and using scientific research to illustrate moral and spiritual truths – books with titles like *Bible Teachings in Nature*, *The Ministry of Nature*, and *The Sabbath of the Fields*, together with prolific contributions to scientific and religious periodicals. In 1897 he gave the Gunning Lectures at Edinburgh University on the subject of science and revelation, and in his last years wrote a number of articles for *Good Words*.
24. Rev. Hugh Macmillan, 'The globe flower', *Good Words*, 1902, p. 328.
25. W.E. Gladstone, 'On the recent corroborations of Scripture from the regions of history and natural science', *Good Words*, 1890, p. 676.
26. ibid., p. 677.
27. loc. cit.
28. loc. cit.
29. ibid., p. 678.
30. Emma Marie Caillard, 'On the use of science to Christians', *Good Words*, 1896, p. 52.

31. ibid.
32. ibid., p. 605.
33. ibid.
34. ibid.
35. Henry Drummond, *Natural Law in the Spiritual World* (London, 1883).
36. Caillard, op. cit.
37. ibid.
38. ibid.
39. ibid.
40. A.E. Fletcher, 'Science and Christianity', *Clarion*, 4 March 1910, p. 2.
41. Robert Blatchford, 'Jovian noddings', *Clarion*, 21 October 1904, p. 1.
42. R. Blatchford, 'In the library', *Clarion*, 23 January 1903, p. 3.
43. R. Blatchford, 'In the library', *Clarion*, 30 January 1903, p. 5.
44. A.M. Thompson, preface to Robert Blatchford, *My Eighty Years* (London, 1931), p. ix.
45. R. Blatchford, 'Science and religion', *Clarion*, 13 February 1903, p. 5.
46. R. Blatchford, 'The universe and its creator', *Clarion*, 17 April 1903, p. 1.
47. R. Blatchford, 'Science and religion', *Clarion*, 13 February 1903, p. 5.
48. R. Blatchford, 'In the library', *Clarion*, 30 January 1903, p. 5.
49. ibid.
50. ibid.
51. John Kent, *From Darwin to Blatchford: The role of Darwinism in Christian apologetics, 1875–1910* (London, 1966).
52. Blatchford's position has much in common with German evolutionary socialism. See Alfred Kelly, *The Descent of Darwin: The popularisation of Darwinism in Germany, 1860–1914* (Carolina, 1981), and Hugh MacLeod, 'Religion in the British and German labour movements, *c.* 1890–1914', *Bulletin of the Society for the Study of Labour History*, vol. 51 (1986), pt 1, pp. 25–35.
53. John Laurent, 'Science, society and politics in late-nineteenth-century England: a further look at mechanics' institutes', *Social Studies of Science*, vol. 14 (1984), p. 598.
54. Correspondence to 'Britain's greatest benefactor', *Clarion*, 11 January 1907, p. 2.
55. 'England's roll of fame', *Tit-Bits*, started 8 December 1906, prizes announced 16 March 1907; 'Britain's greatest benefactor', *Clarion*, result published 4 January 1907.
56. The fallacy is pointed out by Alfred Kelly in relation to the concept of struggle. See Kelly, op. cit.
57. Adrian Desmond, 'Artisan resistance and evolution in Britain, 1819–1848', *Osiris*, (1987), no. 3, pp. 102–3.
58. Laurent, op. cit., p. 606.
59. Correspondence to 'Britain's greatest benefactor', *Clarion*, 11 January 1907, p. 2.
60. Harry Lowerison, 'A nature-education', *Clarion*, 22 September 1894, p. 2; R. Blatchford, review of *Mutual Aid*, *Clarion*, 12 December 1902, p. 3.
61. R.B. Suthers, 'Socialism and the unfit', *Clarion*, 16 November 1906, p. 2, and 21 December 1906, p. 7.

62. See Logie Barrow, *Independent Spirits: Spiritualism and English plebeian culture, 1850–1910* (London, 1986), and 'The socialism of Robert Blatchford and the "Clarion"' (Unpublished Ph.D. thesis, University of London, 1975).

6 NATURE

1. Rev. Hugh Macmillan, 'The cranberry', *Good Words*, 1902, p. 663.
2. ibid., p. 664.
3. 'A lesson from the hills', *Cottager and Artisan*, 1892, pp. 7–8; 'A leaf from the Book of Nature', *Cottager and Artisan*, 1914, p. 30.
4. 'A dazzling light', *Cottager and Artisan*, 1892, p. 24.
5. 'Drink and the sensitive plant', *British Workman*, 1897, p. 31.
6. Rev. Robert C. Nightingale, 'Of some birds with little song', *Good Words*, 1897, p. 464.
7. ibid.
8. Rev. John Isabell, 'A chapter about flies', *Cottager and Artisan*, 1902, p. 83.
9. Rev. John Isabell, 'A chapter about spiders', *Cottager and Artisan*, 1902, pp. 99–100; 'A chapter on earwigs', 1904, p. 62.
10. Frank Marshall White, 'One day with a working ant', *Pearson's Magazine*, 1902, vol. 1, pp. 27–32; 'One day with a busy spider', *Pearson's Magazine*, 1902, vol. 1, pp. 287–93; 'A day in a bee-hive', *Pearson's Magazine*, 1902, vol. 1, pp. 604–11.
11. Burbidge, op. cit., p. 463; John Fyvie, 'Wild bees in a London garden', *Good Words*, 1905, p. 312.
12. J. Brand, 'Animals as criminals', *Pearson's Magazine*, 1896, vol. 1, p. 664.
13. Geoffrey Winterwood, 'Bufo of the jewelled head', *Good Words*, 1894, p. 690.
14. 'The settlers', *Cottager and Artisan*, 1896, p. 21.
15. William Davenport Hulbert, 'The story of the beaver', *Pearson's Magazine*, 1901, vol. 2, pp. 189–202.
16. William Davenport Hulbert, 'Pointers from a porcupine quill', *Pearson's Magazine*, 1900, vol. 2, pp. 513–22.
17. S.L. Bensusan, *Wild-life Stories: Stories from a home county* (London, 1907), p. vii.
18. ibid., p. viii.
19. S.L. Bensusan, 'The autobiography of a partridge', *Pearson's Magazine*, 1902, vol. 2, pp. 298–304; 'The life story of a hedgehog', *Pearson's Magazine*, 1906, vol. 2, pp. 51–7; 'The biography of a bat', *Pearson's Magazine*, 1906, vol. 1, pp. 177–83.
20. 'Sparks from our anvil', *Pearson's Magazine*, 1909, vol. 1, p. 38.
21. S.L. Bensusan, 'The life story of a golden eagle', *Pearson's Magazine*, 1908, vol. 2, pp. 282–9; 'The story of Rip, a weasel', *Pearson's Magazine*, 1908, vol. 2, pp. 552–9; 'The raven', *Pearson's Magazine*, 1907, vol. 2, pp. 293–300; 'The life story of a roebuck', *Pearson's Magazine*, 1906, vol. 2, pp. 409–15; 'The life story of a magpie', *Pearson's Magazine*, 1905, vol. 1, pp. 541–6; 'The barn owl', *Pearson's*

Magazine, 1905, vol. 2, pp. 403–9; 'The life story of a pheasant', *Pearson's Magazine*, 1904, vol. 2, pp. 420–7; 'The life story of a porcupine', *Pearson's Magazine*, 1905, vol. 1, pp. 321–27; 'The hare's life story', *Pearson's Magazine*, 1904, vol. 2, pp. 298–304; 'The life story of a wild boar', *Pearson's Magazine*, 1904, vol. 2, pp. 101–6; 'The life story of a fox', *Pearson's Magazine*, 1904, vol. 2, pp. 526–33; 'Jack the otter', *Pearson's Magazine*, 1907, vol. 2, pp. 416–23; 'The story of a foxhound', *Pearson's Magazine*, 1906, vol. 2, pp. 501–6.

22. Charles G.D. Roberts, 'Babes of the wild', *Cassell's Magazine*, series began in September 1911 and appeared each month until, and including, February 1912.

23. Editorial note to William J. Long, 'Kingfisher's kindergarten', *Pearson's Magazine*, 1905, vol. 2, p. 546. The note also referred to Long as 'probably the greatest living authority on Natural History in America, [and] is certainly the most popular writer on the wild life of the American woods'.

24. Hulbert, 'The story of the beaver', op. cit., p. 198 (emphasis added).

25. John Berger, 'Animals as metaphor', *New Society*, 10 March 1977, pp. 504–5. 'Until the nineteenth century, however, anthropomorphism was integral to the relations between man and animal and was an expression of their proximity. Anthropomorphism was an expression of the continuous use of animal metaphor' (p. 505).

26. Keith Thomas, *Man and the Natural World: Changing attitudes in England, 1500–1800* (London, 1983).

27. ibid., p. 298.

28. ibid., p. 91.

29. Gillian Beer, *Darwin's Plots: Evolutionary narrative in Darwin, George Eliot and nineteenth-century fiction* (London, 1983). See also Gillian Beer, 'The "Face of Nature": anthropomorphic elements in the language of the "Origin of Species"', in L.J. Jordanova (ed.), *Languages of Nature: Critical essays on science and literature* (London, 1986), pp. 39–64.; D.R. Crocker, 'Anthropomorphism: bad practice, honest prejudice?', *New Scientist*, 16 July 1981, pp. 159–62. Interestingly ethology has its origins in the early years of this century; see John R. Durant, 'Innate character in animals and man: a perspective on the origins of ethology', in Charles Webster (ed.), *Biology, Medicine and Society, 1840–1940* (Cambridge, 1981), pp. 157–92.

30. Crocker, op. cit., p. 162.

31. Thomas, op. cit., pp. 15 and 70.

32. ibid., p. 265.

33. ibid., p. 169.

34. For a comprehensive catalogue of cruelty, see E.S. Turner, *All Heaven in a Rage* (London 1964), a history of the establishment and activities of the RSPCA.

35. ibid., p. 172.

36. David Elliston Allen, *The Naturalist in Britain: A social history* (London, 1976), p. 232; Bruce Campbell, 'Birds in boxes', *The Countryman*, winter 1970/1, pp. 264–272. Flora Thompson also has a passing reference to farm labourers shaking out the crumbs from their lunches for the birds to eat, Flora Thompson, *Lark Rise to Candleford* (Harmondsworth, 1973; original 1939–45), p. 56.

37. 'Is cruelty to animals decreasing?', *Cassell's Saturday Journal*, 9 August 1893, p. 924.
38. For nature study, see E.W. Jenkins, 'Science, sentimentalism and social control? The nature study movement in England and Wales, 1899–1914', *History of Education*, vol. 10 (1981), no. 1, pp. 33–43. The relationship of what David Allen calls 'vitalism' to both nature study and animal biographies warrants further research. It was through the efforts of Patrick Geddes and J. Arthur Thomson, both vitalists, that nature study was first added to the school curriculum. See Allen, op. cit., pp. 200–2.
39. Thompson, op. cit., pp. 152–3. As a caveat to modern perceptions of 'new sensibilities' it is worth noting Thompson's comment on the 1880s that: 'Ordinary country people at that time, though not actively cruel to animals, were indifferent to their sufferings' (p. 152).
40. Allen, op. cit., p. 230.
41. 'Deer as photographers', *Cassell's Magazine*, August 1897, p. 335.
42. Alder Anderson, 'Hunting with the camera', *Pearson's Magazine*, 1902, vol. 1, p. 130.
43. Allen, op. cit., pp. 233–5 and 206.
44. 'Flowers, bees and poultry', *Cassell's Magazine*, December 1895, p. 80.
45. 'From all quarters', *Cassell's Saturday Journal*, 10 July 1907, p. 1061.
46. See Colin Russell, *Science and Social Change, 1700–1900* (London, 1983), pp. 181–6.
47. John Ranlett, 'Checking nature's desecration: late Victorian environmental organization', *Victorian Studies*, vol. 26 (1983), no. 2, p. 198.
48. ibid., pp. 205–8.
49. S.L. Bensusan, 'The Selborne sanctuary', *Pearson's Magazine*, 1912, vol. 1, pp. 465 and 476.
50. M. Tindal, 'A paradise for big game', *Pearson's Magazine*, 1910, vol. 2, pp. 624–7; Linda Gardiner, 'Our ally the bird', *Pearson's Magazine*, 1905, vol. 1, pp. 425–30.
51. H. Hesketh Pritchard, 'Slaughtered for fashion', *Pearson's Magazine*, 1914, vol. 1, pp. 256–67.
52. See Chapter 5 of this book.
53. Allen, op. cit.
54. ibid., pp. 204–5.
55. ibid., p. 204.
56. ibid., pp. 205–6.
57. Robert Blatchford, 'The love of nature', *Clarion*, 1 March 1912, p. 1.
58. F.G. Aflalo, 'The case of the beasts and the birds', *Good Words*, 1898, p. 459.
59. French, op. cit., pp. 236 and 374.
60. Jerome Bump, review of *The Rural Tradition* by W.J. Keith, *Victorian Studies*, 20 (1976), p. 97. Bump describes the 'rural tradition' as 'the city-dwellers' facile substitute for the rural experience' (p. 97).
61. See Thomas, op. cit., pp. 243–54.
62. Allen, op. cit., pp. 224–6; Pamela Horn, *The Changing Countryside in Victorian and Edwardian England and Wales* (London, 1984), p. 225.
63. Thomas, op. cit., p. 251.
64. Horn, op. cit., p. 224.

65. Martin J. Wiener, *English Culture and the Decline of the Industrial Spirit, 1850–1980* (Cambridge, 1981).
66. John Berger, 'Vanishing animals', *New Society*, 31 March 1977, p. 664. For the explosion in pet ownership, see John Walton, 'Mad dogs and Englishmen: the conflict over rabies in late Victorian England', *Journal of Social History*, vol. 13, no. 2, pp. 219–39, and Harriet Ritvo, 'Pride and pedigree: the evolution of the Victorian dog fancy', *Victorian Studies*, vol. 29 (1986), pp. 227–53. Ritvo writes: 'The prize winning pedigree dogs of the late nineteenth century seemed to symbolise simply the power to manipulate and the power to purchase – they were emblems of status and rank as pure commodities' (pp. 244–5).
67. French, op. cit., pp. 373–7.
68. See Roderick Nash, *Wilderness and the American Mind* (revised edition, London, 1973).
69. 'Sparks from our anvil', *Pearson's Magazine*, 1907, vol. 1, p. 14.
70. Jack London, 'The Nature Man', *Cassell's Magazine*, December 1908, p. 51.
71. ibid., p. 53.
72. Nash, op. cit., pp. 141–2.
73. See Allen, op. cit., p. 229.
74. Harry Lowerison, 'A nature talk', *Clarion*, 4 August 1894, p. 2.
75. Marcus Woodward, 'The nature cure', *Pearson's Magazine*, 1905, vol. 1, p. 562.
76. See Chapters 1 and 2 of this book.
77. John Hedley Brooke, 'The natural theology of the geologists: some theological strata', in L.J. Jordanova and Roy Porter (eds), *Images of the Earth: Essays in the history of the environmental sciences* (Chalfont St Giles, 1979), p. 39.
78. See Robert M. Young, 'Natural theology, Victorian periodicals and the fragmentation of a common context', in Colin Chant and John Fauvel (eds), *Darwin to Einstein: Historical studies on science and belief* (Harlow, 1980), pp. 69–107. Of the demise of natural theology, Young writes: 'Theology was no longer the context; it was but one element in a fragmented culture.... What remained common was popularization and uncertain generalization' (p. 96).

7 EVOLUTION

1. Peter Bowler, *Theories of Human Evolution: A century of debate, 1844–1944* (Oxford, 1987), p. 41. See also Peter Bowler, *The Eclipse of Darwinism: Anti-Darwinian evolutionary theories around 1900* (Baltimore, 1983).
2. Peter Bowler, 'Darwinism and the argument from design: suggestions for a revaluation', *Journal of the History of Biology*, vol. 10 (1977), p. 42.
3. James R. Moore, *The Post-Darwinian Controversies: A study of the Protestant struggle to come to terms with Darwin in Great Britain and America, 1870–1900* (Cambridge, 1979), p. 218.

4. John Kent, *From Darwin to Blatchford: The role of Darwinism in Christian apologetics* (London, 1966), p. 28; and John Durant, editor's introduction to *Darwinism and Divinity: Essays on evolution and religious belief* (Oxford, 1985).

5. See Neal C. Gillespie, *Charles Darwin and the Problem of Creation* (Chicago, 1979).

6. Moore, op. cit., p. 240.

7. ibid., p. 239.

8. ibid., p. 15.

9. Durant, op. cit., p. 20. See also Robert M. Young, 'The impact of Darwin on conventional thought', in Anthony Symondson (ed.), *The Victorian Crisis of Faith* (London, 1970), pp. 13–35.

10. 'To correspondents', *Family Herald*, 9 January 1897, pp. 125–6.

11. Owen Chadwick, *The Victorian Church* (London, 1966), pt II, pp. 23–4; and Kent, op. cit., p. 37.

12. 'E.S.', 'Evolution', *British Workman*, 1892, p. 14; 'The seeker after truth', *Good Words and Sunday Magazine*, 1907, p. 369.

13. 'Heredity and moral freedom', *Good Words*, 1897, pp. 125–6.

14. W.E. Gladstone, 'On the recent corroborations of Scripture from the regions of history and natural science', *Good Words*, 1890, p. 679.

15. F.G. Aflalo, 'Monkeys at the zoo', *Good Words*, 1901, p. 560.

16. How, op. cit., pp. 420–41.

17. Rev. Hugh Macmillan, 'In a nutshell', *Good Words*, 1902, p. 768.

18. ibid., p. 769.

19. ibid., p. 770.

20. 'The religious value of the first chapters of Genesis', *Good Words*, 1897, pp. 352–3.

21. 'The seeker after truth', *Good Words and Sunday Magazine*, 1907, p. 289.

22. Alvar Ellegard, *Darwin and the General Reader: The reception of Darwin's theory of evolution in the British periodical press, 1859–1872* (Göteborg, 1958), p. 98.

23. ibid., p. 9.

24. ibid., pp. 24–9.

25. See Peter Bowler, *Theories of Human Evolution: A century of debate, 1844–1944* (Oxford, 1987), p. 14.

26. 'The religious value of the first chapters of Genesis', *Good Words*, 1897, p. 352.

27. Emma Marie Caillard, 'On the use of science to Christians', *Good Words*, 1896, p. 103.

28. ibid.

29. For recapitulation, see Stephen Jay Gould, *Ontogeny and Phylogeny* (London, 1977), especially pp. 115–66, and Stephen Jay Gould, *The Mismeasure of Man* (London, 1981), especially pp. 113–45.

30. Nancy Stepan, 'Race and gender: the role of analogy in science', *Isis*, 77 (1986), p. 264.

31. ibid.

32. 'Such a busy day', *Cassell's Saturday Journal*, 11 August 1897, p. 996.

33. 'The fireside of the future', *Pearson's Weekly*, 1 October 1892, p. 161.

34. Brian Harrison, 'Women's health and the women's movement in Britain, 1840–1940', in Charles Webster (ed.), *Biology, Medicine and Society, 1840–1940* (Cambridge, 1981), p. 24. Harrison also writes: 'Doctors offered vigorous intellectual resistance to the campaign for women's suffrage', and 'the doctors' arguments merely reinforced a preconception which was usually formulated in an unscientific manner' (pp. 27 and 29).

35. Caroll Smith-Rosenberg and Charles Rosenberg, 'The female animal: medical and biological views of woman and her role in nineteenth-century America', *Journal of American History*, 60 (1973–4), p. 333.

36. Barbara Ehrenreich and Deidre English, *For Her Own Good: 150 years of the experts' advice to women* (London, 1979), pp. 124 and 127.

37. 'The gatherer', *Cassell's Magazine*, July 1892, p. 508. The report came from a meeting of the Medical Society of London.

38. 'Questions worth answering', *Pearson's Weekly*, 9 July 1892, p. 804.

39. 'Are women becoming bald?', *Tit-Bits*, 29 March 1890, p. 400.

40. 'The ugliest women', *Pearson's Weekly*, 23 December 1893, p. 362.

41. 'Ugliest women on earth', *Pearson's Weekly*, 13 November 1902, p. 302; 'Beauty v brains', *Tit-Bits*, 13 September 1902, p. 592; 'All for all', *Cassell's Saturday Journal*, 10 December 1902, p. 290. The *Tit-Bits* story noted: 'A physician with wide experience among the insane has come to the conclusion...that Nature makes palpable differences between male and female brains. And he fears that the tendency of too much education in intellectual women is to make them lose beauty.'

42. S.S. Buckman, 'Our descent from monkeys', *Pearson's Magazine*, 1902, vol. 1, pp. 369–78; and 1903, vol. 2, pp. 555–63. Buckman, 1902, p. 369. For recapitulation, see Stephen Jay Gould, *Ontogeny and Phylogeny* (London, 1977), especially pp. 115–66, and Stephen Jay Gould, *The Mismeasure of Man* (London, 1981), especially pp. 113–45.

43. 'All for all', *Cassell's Saturday Journal*, 1907, p. 449.

44. S.S. Buckman, 'Our descent from monkeys', *Pearson's Magazine*, 1902, vol. 1, p. 371. See also S.S. Buckman, 'Our descent from monkeys', *Pearson's Magazine*, 1903, vol. 2, pp. 555–63.

45. Herbert Ward, 'A day in a Central African village', *Cassell's Magazine*, June 1897, pp. 67–8.

46. Joseph Conrad, *Heart of Darkness* (Harmondsworth, 1973, original 1902), p. 48.

47. Nancy Stepan, *The Idea of Race in Science: Great Britain, 1800–1960* (London, 1982), p. 83.

48. Brian Street, 'Reading the novels of empire: race and ideology in the classic "tale of adventure"', in David Dabydean (ed.), *The Black Presence in English Literature* (Manchester, 1985), p. 98.

49. Herbert C. Fyfe. 'The first traverse of Africa', *Pearson's Magazine*, 1900, vol. 2, p. 421.

50. 'Evolution confirmed', *Clarion*, 23 September 1899, quoted in L.J.W. Barrow, 'The socialism of Robert Blatchford and "The Clarion"' (unpublished Ph.D. thesis, University of London, 1975), p. 421.

51. *Clarion*, 2 September 1893 and 25 April 1902.

52. Sander L. Gilman, *Difference and Pathology: The stereotypes of sexuality, race and madness* (New York, 1985), p. 18.

53.   'All for all', *Cassell's Saturday Journal*, 12 November 1902, p. 198; 'Tit-bits of general information', *Tit-Bits*, 11 January 1902, p. 376; 'All for all', *Cassell's Saturday Journal*, 14 May 1902, p. 724. For laughing Persians, see also 'All for all', *Cassell's Saturday Journal*, 10 April 1907, p. 770, and 'Tit-bits of general information', *Tit-Bits*, 8 February 1902, p. 472.

54.   See, for example, 'Girl with a skin which changes colour', *Tit-Bits*, 13 December 1902, p. 275; 'Can a negro's skin be bleached?', *Cassell's Saturday Journal*, 2 August 1905, p. 1010; 'How negroes' skin can be turned white', *Pearson's Weekly*, 22 April 1893, p. 636. There were others. Only in fiction have I come across anyone turning from white to black. The man is subsequently rejected by fiancée, friends, colleagues and society at large. See Albert Bigelar Paine, 'The black hand', *Pearson's Magazine*, 1903, vol. 2, p. 637.

55.   'Answers to correspondents', *Tit-Bits*, 5 June 1897, p. 185; and 'Making negroes into white men', *Tit-Bits*, 29 May 1897, p. 166.

56.   Nancy Stepan, *The Idea of Race in Science: Great Britain, 1800–1960* (London, 1982).

57.   Gilman, op. cit., p. 37.

58.   Brian V. Street, *The Savage in Literature: Representations of 'primitive' society in English fiction, 1858–1920* (London, 1975), pp. 2–4.

59.   Brian Street, 'Reading the novels of empire: race and ideology in the classic "tale of adventure"', in David Dabydean (ed.), *The Black Presence in English Literature* (Manchester, 1985), p. 98.

60.   'Are we an aggressive race?', *Pearson's Weekly*, 21 October 1899, p. 245.

61.   For a Lamarckian explanation of racial supremacy, see 'Questions worth answering', *Pearson's Weekly*, 14 May 1892, p. 676. The question asked was: 'Why should the inhabitants of temperate regions be mentally and physically superior to those of warmer and pleasanter zones?' Using the assumption from evolutionary theory that the organs which develop are those which are most frequently used, the magazine explains that in the temperate regions people need to work harder to get the necessaries of life: 'This constant exercise of the faculties has strengthened and enlarged them, and has resulted in the production of races of men superior, mentally and physically, to those of countries where less demand is made upon individual exertion.'

62.   Gould, *Ontogeny*, op. cit., p. 126.

63.   Street, *Savage in Literature*, op. cit., p. 68.

64.   See Norman Etherington, *Theories of Imperialism: War, conquest and capital* (London, 1984), pp. 72–4. For assumptions of supremacy built upon ethnocentric classifications, see Christine Bolt, *Victorian Attitudes to Race* (London, 1971).

65.   Captain Guy Burrows, 'Where men eat men', *Pearson's Magazine*, 1899, vol. 1, p. 377.

66.   'Negro art', *Cassell's Magazine*, January 1897, pp. 220–1.

67.   'They use stone hatchets', *Cassell's Saturday Journal*, 10 September 1902, p. 2.

68.   'From far and near', *Tit-Bits*, 13 April 1912, p. 128.

69.   Elizabeth Fee, 'Nineteenth-century craniology: the study of the female skull', *Bulletin of the History of Medicine*, 53 (1979), pp. 415–33. Fee writes:

'craniology served to legitimize and reinforce existing relations between the sexes: the dominance of men, defined as more intelligent and more advanced on an evolutionary scale, and the corresponding subordination of women' (p. 433). See also Elizabeth Fee, 'The sexual politics of Victorian social anthropology', in Colin Chant and John Fauvel (eds), *Darwin to Einstein: Historical studies on science and belief* (Harlow, 1980), p. 196.

70. George W. Stocking Jr, *Victorian Anthropology* (New York, 1987), pp. 201, 204 and 205.
71. 'The big-hearted race of the future', *Tit-Bits*, 1910, p. 449.
72. 'The legs of the coming race', *Pearson's Weekly*, 1895, p. 205.
73. H.G. Wells, 'The future is as fixed and determinate as the past', *Cassell's Magazine*, 1913, p. 83.
74. ibid., p. 85.
75. Advertisement for *Science History of the Universe*, *Clarion*, 23 August 1912, p. 5.

8 PROGRESS

1. Patrick Parrinder, *H.G. Wells: The critical heritage* (London, 1972), pp. 2–6.
2. ibid.; and John Batchelor, *H.G. Wells* (Cambridge, 1985), p. 4.
3. H.G. Wells, 'The war of the worlds', *Pearson's Magazine*, 1897; 'The food of the gods', *Pearson's Magazine*, 1904; 'The invisible man: a grotesque romance', *Pearson's Weekly*, 1897.
4. Krishan Kumar, *Utopia and Anti-Utopia in Modern Times* (Oxford, 1987), p. 181.
5. 'The novelist as prophet', *Family Herald*, 1899, p. 670.
6. Alex M. Thompson, 'In the library', *Clarion*, 8 April 1904, pp. 3, and 15 April 1904, p. 3; H.G. Wells, 'On Mr Alex M. Thompson', *Clarion*, 22 April 1904, p. 3.
7. Umberto Eco, 'Science fiction and the art of conjecture', *Times Literary Supplement*, 2 November 1984, p. 1257.
8. ibid.
9. I.F. Clarke, *The Pattern of Expectation, 1644–2001* (London, 1979), p. 213.
10. Ernest Lee Tuveson, *Millennium and Utopia: A study in the background of the idea of Progress* (Gloucester, Massachusetts, 1972), p. 201.
11. Carl L. Becker, *The Heavenly City of the Eighteenth-Century Philosophers* (New Haven, 1932), p. 129.
12. Kumar, op. cit., p. 220.
13. Batchelor, op. cit., p. 28.
14. Tuveson, op. cit., p. xii.
15. Frederick Gregory, 'The impact of Darwinian evolution on Protestant theology in the nineteenth century', in David C. Lindberg and Ronald L. Numbers (eds), *God and Nature: Historical essays on the encounter between Christianity and science* (London, 1986), p. 379.
16. Quoted in J.W. Burrow, *Evolution and Society: A study in Victorian social theory* (Cambridge, 1966), p. 275.

17. ibid., pp. 273–7. For the idea of Progress, see also J.B. Bury, *The Idea of Progress: An inquiry into its origins and growth* (New York, 1955), and John Passmore, *The Perfectibility of Man* (London, 1970).

18. 'Modern inventions', *Cottager and Artisan*, 1906, p. 11.

19. 'Everybody's business', *Cassell's Saturday Journal*, 6 July 1898, p. 908.

20. Chauncey M'Govern, 'A visit to a balloon farm', *Pearson's Magazine*, 1902, vol. 1, p. 595.

21. *Cassell's Saturday Journal*, 13 February 1907, p. 549.

22. 'The romance of flying machines', *Tit-Bits*, 13 April 1907, p. 82; 'Can balloons ever be steered?', *Cassell's Saturday Journal*, 9 November 1892, p. 142; 'Will battles be fought in the air?', *Cassell's Saturday Journal*, 19 December 1894, p. 262; 'Shall we ever fly to business?', *Pearson's Weekly*, 18 April 1907, p. 697; 'Shall we ever fly to New York?', *Tit-Bits*, 9 July 1910, p. 394; 'Will man conquer the air?', *Pearson's Weekly*, 21 July 1900, p. 24; 'When shall we fly?', *Pearson's Weekly*, 26 September 1907, p. 218; 'When will we fly?', *Pearson's Weekly*, 30 May 1896, p. 755; 'Shall we ever be able to fly?', *Cassell's Saturday Journal*, 16 March 1898, p. 552.

23. Herbert C. Fyfe, 'Signalling through space', *Pearson's Magazine*, 1899, vol. 2, p. 117.

24. Cleveland Moffett, 'Seeing by wire', *Pearson's Magazine*, 1899, vol. 2, pp. 490–6; C. Montgomery M'Govern, 'Talking along a beam of light', *Pearson's Magazine*, 1900, vol. 2, pp. 326–9; Chauncey M'Govern and F.S. Livingstone, 'Talking through the earth', *Pearson's Magazine*, 1901, vol. 2, pp. 97–100; 'H.H.', 'Steering torpedoes by wireless telegraphy', *Good Words*, 1902, p. 376; 'The latest scientific marvel', *Tit-Bits*, 20 November 1909, p. 226.

25. 'The electric telegraph', *Cottager and Artisan*, 1897, p. 64. This was the final part of a five-part series on the electric telegraph.

26. 'The new photography', *Clarion*, 11 April 1896, p. 118; 'The future of the new photography', *Cassell's Magazine*, 1896, vol. 1, pp. 506–8; 'All for all', *Cassell's Saturday Journal*, 10 November 1897, p. 179. Note also 'Photographing the skeleton', in 'The gatherer' of *Cassell's Magazine*, March 1896, which reported: 'Vienna journals announce that Professor Roentgen, of Würzburg, has made a discovery which is likely to be of much practical importance in the medical arts' (p. 348).

27. 'Radium revolutioniser', *Pearson's Weekly*, 25 February, 1909, p. 700; 'We want more radium', *Pearson's Weekly*, 21 March 1914, p. 1006; 'Making black men white', *Pearson's Weekly*, 7 April 1904, p. 735.

28. A.S.M. Hutchinson, 'The riddle of radium', *Pearson's Magazine*, 1903, vol. 2, pp. 496–9.

29. Charles E. Benham, 'The modern philosophers stone', *Cassell's Magazine*, June 1910, p. 133; Athol Maude, 'The new elixir of life', *Pearson's Magazine*, 1902, vol. 1, pp. 328–31.

30. 'Liars cured by machinery', *Tit-Bits*, 14 September 1907, p. 620; 'Scientific and useful', *Family Herald*, 6 February 1897, p. 222. Professor Mosso's work was also reported elsewhere.

31. 'From lightning flashes', *Cassell's Saturday Journal*, 12 November 1902, p. 193.

32. 'Living in an electric current', *Cassell's Saturday Journal*, 5 October 1898, p. 64; 'Shall we ever see by wire?', *Cassell's Magazine*, June 1896, p. 589.

33. *Clarion*, 11 December 1897, p. 392.

34. C. Montgomery M'Govern, 'Tapping the sun's strength', *Pearson's Magazine*, 1900, vol. 2, pp. 598–600; E.H. Rydall, 'The sun – a servant', *Pearson's Magazine*, 1902, vol. 1, pp. 74–5.

35. William McClean, 'The longest trestle bridge in the world', *Pearson's Magazine*, 1904, vol. 2, p. 611; 'The force of the future', *Tit-Bits*, 19 January 1901, p. 424.

36. See, for example, Charles L. Sanford, 'Technology and culture at the end of the nineteenth century: the will to power', in Melton Kranzberg and Carroll W. Pursell Jr. (eds), *Technology in Western Civilisation: vol. I. The emergence of modern industrial society: Earliest times to 1900* (Oxford, 1967), p. 727.

37. Robert Machray, 'The terrible trades of Sheffield', *Pearson's Magazine*, 1897, vol. 1, p. 292.

38. John Passmore, *The Perfectibility of Man* (London, 1970), p. 262. Note also that Humphrey Jennings uses the building of Pandaemonium as the metaphor for the coming of industrialisation throughout his book *Pandaemonium, 1660–1886: The coming of the machine as seen by contemporary observers* (London, 1985).

39. Alton Telford, 'The king of the coming age', *British Workman*, December 1897, pp. 90–1. See also 'W.S.S.', 'The engineer', *Cottager and Artisan*, 1897, p. 110.

40. Richard Kerr, FGS, FRAS, 'Wireless telegraphy', *Cassell's Magazine*, July 1906, p. 213.

41. 'Telegraphy as it is and was', *Cottager and Artisan*, 1902, p. 48. This was the second and concluding part of a two-part article.

42. 'Radium and its discoverers', *Cassell's Saturday Journal*, 12 October 1904, p. 104.

43. 'By aeroplane to the moon', *Pearson's Weekly*, 24 September 1908, p. 255; 'Inventions for the millennium', *Cassell's Saturday Journal*, 6 November 1901, p. 185; 'Railways on the housetops', *Pearson's Weekly*, 12 August 1899, p. 75; 'Pills as food', *Pearson's Weekly*, 28 July 1900, p. 37; 'The edge of the future', *Clarion*, 24 June 1893, p. 2. See also 'Getting about in A.D.1920', *Pearson's Weekly*, 16 May 1907, p. 769; 'Roadways of the future', *Pearson's Weekly*, 1 September 1910, p. 185; 'Trains running at 200 miles an hour', *Cassell's Saturday Journal*, 9 May 1900, p. 722.

44. 'The year 2000', *Cassell's Magazine*, 1894, p. 720.

45. loc. cit.

46. 'Britain a hundred years hence: a peep into 1997', *Tit-Bits*, 9 January 1897, p. 270.

47. 'How London will look in 1998', *Pearson's Weekly*, 29 January 1898, p. 471.

48. 'A Christmas house party a hundred years hence', *Pearson's Weekly*, 12 December 1907, p. 403.

49. Richard Hoggart, *The Uses of Literacy: Aspects of working-class life with special reference to publications and entertainments* (Harmondsworth, 1958), pp. 190–1.

50. Rosalind H. Williams, *Dream Worlds: Mass consumption in late-nineteenth-century France* (London, 1982), pp. 9–10, and note especially chapter 5, 'The dream world of mass consumption'.

51. ibid., p. 84.

52. For the impact of illuminations, see James Walvin, *Leisure and Society, 1830–1950* (London, 1978), pp. 75–6. American-style pleasure beaches were also dependent upon advances in mechanical and electrical power.

53. Mike Featherstone, 'Consumer culture: an introduction', *Theory, Culture and Society*, vol. 1 (1983), no. 3, p. 5.

54. See Chapters 1 and 3 of this book. On media as commodities, see Robert Dunn, 'Television, consumption and the commodity form', *Theory, Culture and Society*, vol. 1 (1983), no. 3, pp. 49–64.

55. E. Traynor, 'How phonograph records are made', *Cassell's Magazine*, 1909, p. 445; G.R. Fleming, 'How linoleum is made', *Good Words*, 1897, pp. 748–51; 'How soap is made', *Cottager and Artisan*, 1910, p. 93.

56. H.J.W. Dam, 'In a dynamite factory', *Pearson's Magazine*, 1897, vol. 2, pp. 146–54; Frank Lamburn, 'How our army is clothed', *Pearson's Magazine*, 1896, vol. 1, pp. 518–23; Mark Potter, 'The birth of a battleship', *Cassell's Magazine*, January 1909, p. 265; D. Theodore Timins, 'A visit to a gun factory', *Cassell's Magazine*, September 1900, p. 464.

57. See Peter Roger Mountjoy, 'The working-class press and working-class Conservatism', in George Boyce, James Curran and Pauline Wingate (eds), *Newspaper History: From the seventeenth century to the present day* (London, 1978), pp. 265–80. Mountjoy says of the *British Workman* and *Cottager and Artisan* that: 'The accent on the painstaking learning of useful skills and the minute regulation of everyday life, is absolutely in tune with the self-help concern with utility, industry and duty' (p. 277).

58. 'Sunlight at last', *Clarion*, 23 July 1892, p. 6; R.B. Suthers, 'The mysteries of soap', *Clarion*, 11 April 1913, p. 7.

59. Sidney Pollard, *The Idea of Progress: History and society* (Hamondsworth, 1971), p. 150.

60. Richard Hoggart, op. cit., p. 171.

61. Standish Meacham, *A Life Apart: The English working class, 1890–1914* (London, 1977), p. 199.

62. Adrian Desmond, 'Artisan resistance and evolution in Britain, 1819–1848', *Osiris*, second series, vol. 3 (1987), p. 88.

63. Kumar, op. cit., p. 45.

9 NEW MENTALITIES

1. For a full statistical breakdown, see P. Broks, 'Science and the popular press: a cultural analysis of British family magazines, 1890–1914' (Lancaster Ph.D., 1988).

2. Quoted in Samuel Hynes, *The Edwardian Turn of Mind* (London, 1968), pp. 133–4.

3. ibid., p. 132. Hynes also quotes Wells: 'The first decade of the twentieth century was for the English a decade of badly strained optimism.' For Wells

the major causes of this were the disillusion following the Boer War and the discontent of women (Hynes, p. 7).

4. Michael Rosenthal, *The Character Factory: Baden-Powell and the origins of the Boy Scout movement* (New York, 1986), p. 3; G.R. Searle, *The Quest for National Efficiency: A study in British politics and political thought, 1899–1914* (Berkeley, 1971), p. 34.

5. Bernard Porter, 'The Edwardians and the empire', in Donald Read (ed.), *Edwardian England* (London, 1982), pp. 128–44.

6. Searle, op. cit., p. 54.

7. Bernard Semmel, *Imperialism and Social Reform: English social-imperial thought, 1895–1914* (London, 1960), p. 24.

8. Robert J. Scally, *The Origins of the Lloyd George Coalition: The politics of social-imperialism* (London, 1975), p. 22. The frustration of social-imperialists may be associated with the marginal social status of lower-middle-class jingoists (see Richard N. Price, 'Society, status and jingoism: the social roots of lower-middle class patriotism, 1870–1900', in Geoffrey Crossick, *The Lower Middle Class in Britain, 1870–1914* (London, 1977), pp. 89–112). For lower-middle-class frustration, see also Geoffrey Crossick, 'The emergence of the lower middle class in Britain: a discussion', in Crossick, *The Lower Middle Class in Britain, 1870–1914* (London, 1977), pp. 21–7.

9. W. Hamish Fraser, *The Coming of the Mass Market, 1850–1914* (London, 1981), pp. 17–18.

10. T.R. Gourvish, 'The standard of living, 1890–1914', in Alan O'Day (ed.), *The Edwardian Age: Conflict and stability, 1900–1914* (London, 1979), p. 29.

11. Taken from Keith Burgess, *The Challenge of Labour: Shaping British society, 1850–1930* (London, 1980), p. 114.

12. ibid.

13. ibid., p. 80.

14. John K. Walton, *Lancashire: A social history, 1558–1939* (Manchester, 1987), p. 292; Standish Meacham, *A Life Apart: The English working class, 1890–1914* (London, 1977), p. 215.

15. Burgess, op. cit., pp. 80–1 and 116.

16. Paul Thompson, *The Edwardians: The remaking of British society* (London, 1984), p. 271.

17. Burgess, op. cit., pp. 116–22.

18. Thompson, op. cit., p. 274. See also the rest of Thompson's chapter on the crisis, pp. 252–75.

19. 'Is a revolution coming?', *Cassell's Saturday Journal*, 30 March 1912, p. 3; Ben Tillet, 'The great unrest', *Clarion*, 1912, series of articles in January; Captain Frank Shaw, 'The world in revolt', *Cassell's Saturday Journal*, 1909, serial story started in May; 'No coal – no nuffin'', *Pearson's Weekly*, 1 February 1912, p. 775. These are only a few of many such pieces.

20. Burgess, op. cit., p. 113.

21. W.L. Alden, 'From China to Peru', *Pearson's Magazine*, 1900, vol. 2, pp. 116–17.

22. 'You're booked for a violent death', *Pearson's Weekly*, 6 September 1913, p. 279.

23. *Pearson's Weekly*, 25 August 1910, cover, p. III.

24. Ellen S. Gaskell, 'Chemicalised foods', *Clarion*, 17 October 1902, p. 1.
25. 'When electricity runs amok', *Pearson's Weekly*, 14 March 1907, p. 617; '1914 ailments', *Pearson's Weekly*, 18 April 1914, p. 1111.
26. 'Our canopy of coal', *Pearson's Magazine*, 1913, vol. 1, pp. 373–6; 'Petrologia', *Pearson's Weekly*, 12 September 1907, p. 190.
27. W.L. Alden, 'From China to Peru', *Pearson's Magazine*, 1900, vol. 2, p. 568; 'The modern plague', *Pearson's Weekly*, 10 April 1897, p. 636.
28. Harold Perkin, *The Age of the Automobile* (London, 1976), p. 52. *Cassell's Saturday Journal* reported in 1905 that: 'There are few questions before the public at the present moment which give rise to so much animated discussion as that which some folks describe as the motor nuisance', in 'Are motorists getting more disliked?', *Cassell's Saturday Journal*, 28 June 1905, p. 881.
29. Perkin, op. cit., p. 52.
30. 'Perils of London's streets', *Tit-Bits*, 19 August 1912, p. 599.
31. Quoted in Perkin, op. cit., p. 53.
32. G.M. Mackness, 'The future of motoring', *Cassell's Magazine*, August 1909, p. 422.
33. 'Are motorists getting more disliked?', loc. cit.
34. Walden Fawcett, 'Wonders of the transportation world', *Pearson's Magazine*, 1902, vol. 1, p. 61.
35. 'You're booked for a violent death', *Pearson's Weekly*, 6 September 1913, p. 279.
36. M. Blatchford, 'A matter of machinery', *Clarion*, 13 September 1907, p. 7.
37. 'Why flurry, scurry, or hurry?', *Cassell's Saturday Journal*, 5 September 1900, p. 1081; 'What it is coming to', 1 July 1903, p. 909; 'The benefactor?', 1 June 1912, p. 17.
38. See Chapter 6 of this book.
39. Quoted in Anthony S. Wohl, op. cit, p. 331. For fears of deterioration, see Wohl, chapter 12. See also G.R. Searle, *Eugenics and Class in Britain, 1900–1914* (Leyden, 1976), chapter 3; Michael Rosenthal, *The Character Factory: Baden-Powell and the origins of the Boy Scout movement* (New York, 1986), chapter 5; John Springhall, *Youth, Empire and Society: British youth movements, 1883–1940* (London, 1977), pp. 57–64.
40. C.F.G. Masterman, 'The heart of empire', quoted in Wohl, op. cit., p. 336.
41. Nikolas Rose, *The Psychological Complex: Psychology, politics and society in England, 1869–1939* (London, 1985), p. 53.
42. Searle, op. cit., p. 30.
43. 'You're booked for a violent death', *Pearson's Weekly,* 6 September 1913, p. 279.
44. Andrew T. Scull, *Museums of Madness: The social organisation of insanity in nineteenth-century England* (London, 1979), p. 225.
45. 'The insane do not shed tears', *Pearson's Weekly*, 25 February 1893, p. 497; 'Strange experiences of madmen', *Cassell's Saturday Journal*, 7 November 1891, p. 163; 'Their queer hallucinations', *Cassell's Saturday Journal*, 11 August 1897, p. 993; 'Strange forms of sickness', *Tit-Bits*, 2 January 1897, p. 257.
46. Forbes Winslow, 'Is insanity on the increase?', *Cassell's Saturday Journal*, 14 March 1894, p. 502.

47. J. Holt Schooling, 'We shall all be mad in AD2301', *Pearson's Weekly*, 13 November 1897, p. 274.
48. Forbes Winslow, 'Is insanity on the increase?', *Pearson's Weekly*, 4 May 1905, p. 781.
49. 'The prevalence of insanity', *Pearson's Magazine*, 1906, vol. 1, p. 135. The article was headed by a letter to the editor from Forbes Winslow, who wrote: 'I am of opinion that degeneration and how to contend with it are the most important questions of the present day. It is the duty of everyone to aid in the prevention of this calamity. Our one aim in life should be to improve the intellectual, moral, and physical condition of man, to prevent his degeneration, and to establish, if possible, his regeneration.'
50. ibid., p. 137.
51. C.G. Crosley, 'The problem of the feebleminded', *Pearson's Magazine*, 1912, vol. 1, p. 275.
52. ibid., p. 274.
53. ibid.
54. See Stepan, *Idea of Race*, op. cit., p. 121, and David Barker, 'How to curb the fertility of the unfit: the feebleminded in Edwardian Britain', *Oxford Review of Education*, 9 (1983), pp. 197–211.
55. G.R. Searle, 'Eugenics and class', in Webster, op. cit., p. 238.
56. Searle, *Eugenics and Politics*, op. cit., p. 18. See also Michael Freeden, 'Eugenics and progressive thought: a study in ideological affinity', *Historical Journal*, 22 (1979), p. 647.
57. C.W. Saleeby, 'Worry – the disease of the age', *Cassell's Magazine*, January–June 1907.
58. Victor Fisher, 'Socialism and eugenics', *Clarion*, 16 May 1912, p. 5.
59. For a discussion of Fabians and eugenics, see Searle, 'Eugenics and class', op. cit., pp. 240–2.
60. Donald MacKenzie, 'Eugenics in Britain', *Social Studies of Science*, 6 (1976), p. 501.
61. Donald MacKenzie, 'Karl Pearson and the professional middle class', *Annals of Science*, 36 (1979), p. 125.
62. For the Eugenics Laboratory and Eugenics Education Society, and the debate between MacKenzie and Searle, see Searle, 'Eugenics and class', op. cit., and *Eugenics and Politics*, op. cit.; and MacKenzie, 'Eugenics in Britain', op. cit., 'Karl Pearson', op. cit., together with Donald MacKenzie, 'Sociobiologies in competition: the biometrician–Mendelian debate', in Webster, op. cit., pp. 243–8, and MacKenzie's review of Searle's *Eugenics and Politics* in *British Journal for the History of Science* (1978), pp. 89–91. Considering the Mendelism of the Eugenics Education Society, the statement of Greta Jones that 'eugenics was brought into sharp conflict with Mendelism' is unacceptable. See Greta Jones, *Social Darwinism and English Thought: The interaction between biological and social theory* (Brighton, 1980), p. 117.
63. Searle, *Eugenics and Politics*, op. cit., p. 12, and 'Eugenics and class', op. cit. By way of explication, Searle writes: 'In short, medical men may have been one of the largest group within the Eugenics Society, but they comprised only a small minority of the profession as a whole' ('Eugenics and class', p. 226).

64. See, for example, Jayne Woodhouse, 'Eugenics and the feebleminded: the parliamentary debate of 1912–1914', *History of Education*, 11 (1982), pp. 127–37.
65. See Chapters 1 and 6 of this book.

CONCLUSION

1. See S. Hilgartner, 'The dominant view of popularisation: conceptual problems, political uses', *Social Studies of Science*, 20 (1990), pp. 519–39.
2. See Stuart Hall, 'The rediscovery of "ideology": return of the repressed in media studies', in Micheal Gurevitch, Tony Bennett, James Curran and Janet Woollacott, *Culture, Society and the Media* (London, 1982).
3. See, for example, G. Philo, *Seeing and Believing: The influence of television* (London, 1990); H. Collins, *Television: Policy and culture* (London, 1990); and A. Goodwin and G. Whannel, *Understanding Television* (London, 1990).
4. Christopher Dornan, 'Science and scientism in the media', *Science as Culture*, Vol. 1 (1989), no. 7, pp. 101–21.
5. Steven Shapin and Barry Barnes, 'Science, nature and control: interpreting mechanics' institutes', *Social Studies of Science* (1977), p. 55.
6. ibid., p. 60.
7. ibid., p. 64.
8. Roger Cooter, *The Cultural Meaning of Popular Science: Phrenology and the organisation of consent in nineteenth-century Britain* (Cambridge, 1984), pp. 165 and 98.
9. ibid., p. 85.
10. Adrian Desmond, 'Artisan resistance and evolution in Britain, 1819–1848', *Osiris*, second series, vol. 3 (1987), p. 78. See also Richard Johnson, '"Really Useful Knowledge": radical education and working-class culture', in John Clarke, Chas Critcher and Richard Johnson, *Working-Class Culture: Studies in history and theory* (London, 1979), pp. 75–102.
11. Cooter, op. cit., pp. 117, 152 and 183–9.
12. John Laurent, 'Science, society and politics in late-nineteenth-century England: a further look at mechanics' institutes', *Social Studies of Science*, 14 (1984), p. 586.
13. See Chapter 1 of this book.
14. As is claimed by Nicholas Abercrombie, Stephen Hill and Bryan S. Turner, *The Dominant Ideology Thesis* (London, 1980).
15. Royal Society, *The Public Understanding of Science* (London, 1985).
16. Neil Ryder, 'Vernacular science: something to rely on in your actions?', in P.J. Black and A.M. Lucas, *Children's Informal Ideas* (London, 1987). 'Democratic epistemologies' is a term coined by Logie Barrow in *Independent Spirits: Spiritualism and English plebeians, 1850–1910* (London, 1986).
17. Michel de Certeau, *The Practice of Everyday Life*, translated by Steven F. Rendall (California, 1984).

Bibliography

Information on contributors is scarce. Anyone carrying out research in the field may find the following checklist of signed articles of some help.

SIGNED ARTICLES CITED IN THE TEXT

ABERCROMBY, Ralph, 'Signs in the sky', *Good Words*, 1890, pp. 518–21, and 735–6.

AFLALO, F.G., 'The case of the beasts and the birds', *Good Words*, 1898, pp. 459–62.

——, 'Monkeys at the zoo', *Good Words*, 1901, pp. 559–61.

——, 'The Naples aquarium', *Good Words*, 1898, pp. 756–62.

ALDEN, W.L., 'The earthquaker', *Pearson's Magazine*, 1907, vol. 2, pp. 395–8.

——, 'From China to Peru', *Pearson's Magazine*, 1900, vol. 2, pp. 116–17.

——, 'From China to Peru', *Pearson's Magazine*, 1900, vol. 2, pp. 342–3.

——, 'From China to Peru', *Pearson's Magazine*, 1900, vol. 2, pp. 567–8.

——, 'The purple death', *Cassell's Magazine*, 1895, pp. 112–19.

——, 'Wisdom let loose', *Pearson's Magazine*, 1896, vol. 1, p. 420.

ANDERSON, Alder, 'Analysing motion', *Pearson's Magazine*, 1902, vol. 1, pp. 502–9.

——, 'Hunting with the camera', *Pearson's Magazine*, 1902, vol. 1, pp. 130–5.

BACON, Gertrude, 'The most wonderful observatory in the world', *Good Words*, 1901, pp. 85–92.

BADEN-POWELL, Lieutenant-General Sir Robert, 'Workers or shirkers', *Pearson's Magazine*, 1911, vol. 2, p. 361.

BAILY, F.E., 'The crushing of the middle class', *Pearson's Magazine*, 1912, vol. 2, pp. 382–91.

BAKER, Ray Stannard, 'The romance of Christmas Island', *Pearson's Magazine*, 1902, vol. 1, pp. 260–6.

BALL, Sir Robert S., 'Copernicus', *Good Words*, 1895, pp. 252–8.

——, 'Isaac Newton', *Good Words*, 1895, pp. 53–7 and 109–15.

——, 'The sun', *Good Words*, 1890, pp. 244–7, 467–70, 553–7 and 626–9.

BANFIELD, Frank, 'Mr. A.F. Yarrow at Poplar', *Cassell's Magazine*, April 1897, pp. 469–79.

BELL, Walter George, 'The greatest telescope on earth', *Pearson's Magazine*, 1897, vol. 2, pp. 210–13.

BENHAM, Charles E., 'The modern philosopher's stone', *Cassell's Magazine*, June 1910, p. 133.

BENSUSAN, S.L., 'The autobiography of a partridge', *Pearson's Magazine*, 1902, vol. 2, pp. 298–304.

——, 'The barn owl', *Pearson's Magazine*, 1905, vol. 2, pp. 403–9.

——, 'The biography of a bat', *Pearson's Magazine*, 1906, vol. 1, pp. 177–83.

——, 'The hare's life story', *Pearson's Magazine*, 1904, vol. 2, pp. 298–304.

——, 'Jack the otter', *Pearson's Magazine*, 1907, vol. 2, pp. 416–23.

——, 'The life story of a fox', *Pearson's Magazine*, 1904, vol. 2, pp. 526–33.

——, 'The life story of a golden eagle', *Pearson's Magazine*, 1908, vol. 2, pp. 282–9.

——, 'The life story of a hedgehog', *Pearson's Magazine*, 1906, vol. 2, pp. 51–7.

——, 'The life story of a magpie', *Pearson's Magazine*, 1905, vol. 1, pp. 541–6.

——, 'The life story of a pheasant', *Pearson's Magazine*, 1904, vol. 2, pp. 420–7.

——, 'The life story of a porcupine', *Pearson's Magazine*, 1905, vol. 1, pp. 321–7.

——, 'The life story of a roebuck', *Pearson's Magazine*, 1906, vol. 2, pp. 409–15.

——, 'The life story of a wild boar', *Pearson's Magazine*, 1904, vol. 2, pp. 101–6.

——, 'The raven', *Pearson's Magazine*, 1907, vol. 2, pp. 293–300.

——, 'Red deer stalking', *Pearson's Magazine*, 1902, vol. 2, p. 425.

——, 'The Selborne sanctuary', *Pearson's Magazine*, 1912, vol. 1, pp. 465 and 476.

——, 'The story of a foxhound', *Pearson's Magazine*, 1906, vol. 2, pp. 501–6.

——, 'The story of Rip, a weasel', *Pearson's Magazine*, 1908, vol. 2, pp. 552–9.

BICKERTON, Professor, 'Science and socialism', *Clarion*, 17 January 1913, p. 3.

BIRD, Rev. T., 'Some self-burying seeds', *Good Words*, 1899, p. 273.

BLATCHFORD, M. ('Mont Blong'), 'A matter of machinery', *Clarion*, 13 September 1907, p. 7.

BLATCHFORD, Robert ('Nunquam'), 'A straight talk', *Clarion*, 11 June 1892, p. 7.

——, 'The great announcement', *Clarion*, 8 November 1912, p. 3.

——, 'In the library', *Clarion*, 23 January 1903, p. 3.

——, 'In the library', *Clarion*, 30 January 1903, p. 5.

——, 'Is Darwin played out?', review of Sir E. Ray Lankester's *Science from an Easy Chair*, *Clarion*, 31 January 1913, p. 3.

——, 'Jovian noddings', *Clarion*, 21 October 1904, p. 1.

——, 'The love of nature', *Clarion*, 1 March 1912, p. 1.

——, Review of Kropotkin's *Mutual Aid*, *Clarion*, 12 December 1902, p. 3.

——, 'Science and religion' (later 'Religion and science'), *Clarion*, series started 13 February 1903, p. 5.

——, 'A straight talk', *Clarion*, 11 June 1892, p. 7.

——, 'Twenty years after', *Clarion*, 6 December 1912, p. 4.

——, 'The universe and its creator', *Clarion*, 17 April 1903, p. 1.

BRAND, J., 'Animals as criminals', *Pearson's Magazine*, 1896, vol. 1, pp. 664–5.

BUCKMAN, S.S., 'Our descent from monkeys', *Pearson's Magazine*, 1902, vol. 1, pp. 369–78.

——, 'Our descent from monkeys', *Pearson's Magazine*, 1903, vol. 2, pp. 555–63.

BURBIDGE, Frederick, 'Under the blossom', *Good Words*, 1892, pp. 463–8.

BURROWS, Captain Guy, 'Where men eat men', *Pearson's Magazine*, 1899, vol. 1, pp. 376–81.

CAILLARD, Emma Marie, 'The fourth state of matter', *Good Words*, 1894, pp. 92–5.

——, 'Matter', Good Words, 1894, pp. 379–83.

——, 'On the use of science to Christians', *Good Words*, 1896, pp. 52–3, 102–3, 398–400, 570–2, 604–6 and 253–4.

CAIRD, Mona, 'Scientific popery', *Clarion*, 15 December 1894, p. 2.

——, 'Scientific popery', *Clarion*, 29 December 1894, p. 6.

——, 'Vivisection', *Clarion*, 10 November 1894, p. 7.

CAMERON, Professor Sir Hector C., 'Present-day leaders of science: Lord Lister', *Good Words*, 1900, pp. 516–22.

CARPENTER, Edward, 'Vivisection', *Clarion*, 1 December 1894, p. 8.

CARRINGTON, Edith, 'Vivisection by women and children', *Clarion*, 17 February 1894, p. 8.

CARRINGTON, John T., 'Science in some magazines', *Science Gossip*, 1897, p. 114.

CASSON, Herbert N., 'At last we can fly', *Pearson's Magazine*, 1907, vol. 2, pp. 94–9.

COLLINS, Percy, 'Mimicking nature', *Cassell's Magazine*, 1912, pp. 675–81.

de CORDOVA, Rudolph, 'The microbe of death', *Pearson's Magazine*, 1897, vol. 2, pp. 464–74.

CORMACK, J.D., 'Edison', *Good Words*, 1901, pp. 157–63.

CROSLEY, C.G., 'The problem of the feebleminded', *Pearson's Magazine*, 1912, vol. 1, pp. 273–8.

DALE, Darley, 'Trap-door spiders' tunnels', *Good Words*, 1903, pp. 750–2.

DAM, H.J.W., 'In a dynamite factory', *Pearson's Magazine*, August 1897, pp. 146–54.

DAVIDSON, Dr Thain, 'Life is for work', *Cottager and Artisan*, 1900, p. 117.

DOBBIE, Professor, 'Present-day leaders of science: Professor William Ramsay', *Good Words*, 1900, pp. 130–6.

'E.S.', 'Evolution', *British Workman*, 1892, p. 14.

ELKIND, Louis, 'Radium and its possibilities', *Cassell's Magazine*, April 1904, p. 586.

FAWCETT, Walden, 'Wonders of the transportation world', *Pearson's Magazine*, 1902, vol. 1, pp. 61–4.

FISHER, Victor, 'Socialism and eugenics', *Clarion*, 16 May 1912, p. 5.

FLEMING, G.R., 'How linoleum is made', *Good Words*, November 1897, pp. 748–51.

FLETCHER, A.E., 'Science and Christianity', *Clarion*, 4 March 1910, p. 2.

FRANKLAND, Mrs Percy, 'Half an hour with the microbes', *Good Words*, 1894, pp. 266–70.

——, 'Louis Pasteur: a sketch', *Good Words*, 1897, pp. 490–4.

——, 'Natural mineral waters and bacteria', *Good Words*, 1898, pp. 843–6.

FUTRELLE, Jacques, 'Professor van Dusen's problems', *Cassell's Magazine*, December 1907, pp. 1–10, and several in 1908.

——, 'The mystery of Prince Otto', *Cassell's Magazine*, July 1912, pp. 1–13.

——, 'Wraiths of the storm', *Cassell's Saturday Journal*, 11 September 1909, p. 500.

FYFE, Herbert C., 'The first traverse of Africa', *Pearson's Magazine*, 1900, vol. 2, pp. 418–24.

——, 'Signalling through space', *Pearson's Magazine*, 1899, vol. 2, pp. 114–22.

FYVIE, John, 'Wild bees in a London garden', *Good Words*, 1905, pp. 312–15.

GARDINER, Linda, 'Our ally the bird', *Pearson's Magazine*, 1905, vol. 1, pp. 425–30.

GASKELL, Ellen S., 'Chemicalised foods', *Clarion*, 17 October 1902, p. 1.

GLADSTONE, W.E., 'On the recent corroborations of Scripture from the regions of history and natural science', *Good Words*, 1890, pp. 676–85.

GRAY, Professor Andrew, 'Present-day leaders of science: Lord Kelvin', *Good Words*, 1900, pp. 27–35.

GRIFFITH, George, 'A corner in lightning', *Pearson's Magazine*, 1898, vol. 1, pp. 264–71.

GRIFFITH, M., 'An electric eye', *Pearson's Magazine*, 1896, vol. 2, pp. 752–3.

'H.H.', 'Steering torpedoes by wireless telegraphy', *Good Words*, 1902, p. 376.

HENDERSON, Professor G.G., 'Present-day leaders of science: Profesor James Dewar', *Good Words*, 1900, pp. 765–71.

HOLMES, F.M., 'A famous working man: the story of James Brindley, the canal engineer', *British Workman*, 1897, p. 12.

HOW, Frederic Douglas, 'The Marquis of Salisbury', *Good Words*, 1902, pp. 414–21.

HULBERT, William Davenport, 'Pointers from a porcupine quill', *Pearson's Magazine*, 1900, vol. 2, pp. 513–22.

——, 'The story of the beaver', *Pearson's Magazine*, 1901, vol. 2, pp. 189–202.

HUTCHINSON, A.S.M., 'The riddle of radium', *Pearson's Magazine*, 1903, vol. 2, pp. 496–9.

ISABELL, Rev. John, 'A chapter about flies', *Cottager and Artisan*, 1902, p. 83.

——, 'A chapter about spiders', *Cottager and Artisan*, 1902, pp. 99–100.

——, 'A chapter on earwigs', *Cottager and Artisan*, 1904, p. 62.

JOHNS, Rev. B.G., 'The trout of the chalk stream', *Good Words*, 1902, pp. 166–71.

KELLETT, E.E., 'The lady automaton', *Pearson's Magazine*, 1901, vol. 1, pp. 663–75.

KERR, Richard, 'Wireless telegraphy', *Cassell's Magazine*, July 1906, pp. 208–13.

LAMBURN, Frank, 'How our army is clothed', *Pearson's Magazine*, 1896, vol. 1, pp. 518–23.

LEECH, John G.E., 'The microbe of love', *Pearson's Magazine*, 1902, vol. 2, pp. 373–8.

LONDON, Jack, 'The Nature Man', *Cassell's Magazine*, 1908, pp. 51–8.

LOWERISON, Harry, 'Knowledge is power', *Clarion*, 19 January 1912, p. 3.

——, 'A nature-education', *Clarion*, 22 September 1894, p. 2.

——, 'A nature talk', *Clarion*, 4 August 1894, p. 2.

LYONS, A. Neil, 'The riddle of the universe, not according to Haeckel', *Clarion*, 8 December 1905, p. 5.

MACHRAY, Robert, 'By cable, from shore to shore', *Pearson's Magazine*, 1897, vol. 2, pp. 323–8.

——, 'The terrible trades of Sheffield', *Pearson's Magazine*, March 1897, pp. 290–8.

MACHRAY, Robert and BROWNE, J. Arthur, 'The army of the interior', *Pearson's Magazine*, 1899, vol. 1, pp. 521–5.

MACKNESS, G.M., 'The future of motoring', *Cassell's Magazine*, August 1909, p. 422.

MACLEOD, Rt Rev. Donald, 'An editorial retrospect', *Good Words*, 1904, p. 80.

——, 'A foreword', *Good Words and Sunday Magazine*, 5 May 1906, p. 2.

——, 'The Right Honourable Lord Kelvin', *Good Words*, 1896, pp. 378–88.

MACMILLAN, Rev. Hugh, 'The cranberry', *Good Words*, 1902, pp. 661–6.

——, 'The globe flower', *Good Words*, 1902, pp. 328–33.

——, 'Grass of Parnassus', *Good Words*, 1898, pp. 673–7.

——, 'In a nutshell', *Good Words*, 1902, pp. 766–70.

——, 'The secret of a weed's plain heart', *Good Words*, 1895, pp. 302–6.

MANNING, T.F., 'God in trifles', *Good Words*, 1899, pp. 683–6.

MAUDE, Athol, 'The new elixir of life', *Pearson's Magazine*, 1902, vol. 1, pp. 328–31.

McLEAN, William, 'The longest trestle bridge in the world', *Pearson's Magazine*, 1904, vol. 2, pp. 611–14.

McPHERSON, Dr J.G., 'Numbering the dust', *Good Words*, 1891, pp. 754–8.

MEADE, L.T. and EUSTACE, Robert, 'The blue laboratory', *Cassell's Magazine*, May 1897, pp. 562–75.

M'GOVERN, Chauncey Montgomery, 'The new wizard of the west', *Pearson's Magazine,* vol. 1, pp. 470–6.

——, 'Talking along a beam of light', *Pearson's Magazine*, 1900, vol. 2, pp. 326–9.

——, 'Tapping the sun's strength,' *Pearson's Magazine*, 1900, vol. 2, pp. 598–600.

——, 'A visit to a balloon farm', *Pearson's Magazine*, 1902, vol. 1, pp. 594–9.

M'GOVERN, Chauncey and LIVINGSTONE, F.S., 'Talking through the earth', *Pearson's Magazine*, 1901, vol. 2, pp. 97–100.

MIKKELSEN, Ejnar, 'Lost in the Arctic', *Pearson's Magazine,* 1912, vol. 2, pp. 506–20.

MOFFETT, Cleveland, 'Seeing by wire', *Pearson's Magazine*, 1899, vol. 2, pp. 490–6.

MUNRO, John, 'Is the end of the world near?', *Cassell's Magazine*, May 1898, pp. 562–6.

MYERS, A. Walter, 'The most costly animals at the zoo', *Cassell's Magazine*, May 1902, pp. 705–9.

NAIRN, James, 'X-rays in the Edison laboratory', *Good Words*, 1897, pp. 50–4.

NIGHTINGALE, Rev. Robert C., 'A muddy corner', *Good Words*, 1899, pp. 307–11.

——, 'Of some birds with little song', *Good Words*, 1897, pp. 461–7.

PAINE, Albert Bigelar, 'The black hand', *Pearson's Magazine*, 1903, vol. 2, p. 637.

PEARSON, C. Arthur, '1,000th edition', *Pearson's Weekly*, 16 September 1909, p. 221.

POTTER, Mark, 'The birth of a battleship', *Cassell's Magazine*, January 1909, p. 265.

PRITCHARD, Hesketh, 'Hunting the guanaco', *Pearson's Magazine*, 1902, vol. 2, pp. 268–72.

——, 'Slaughtered for fashion', *Pearson's Magazine*, 1914, vol. 1, pp. 256–67.

PUNSHON, E.R., 'Professor Kenyon's engagement', *Cassell's Magazine*, May 1907, p. 702. This story also appeared anonymously in *Cassell's Saturday Journal*, 26 August 1910, p. 13, under the title 'The professor's engagement'.

RAPHAEL, John N., 'Up above: the story of the sky folk', *Pearson's Magazine*, 1912, vol. 2, pp. 710–60.

ROBERTS, Charles G.D., 'Babes of the wild', *Cassell's Magazine*, series from September 1911 to February 1912.

Lord ROBERTS, 'How to make a nation of marksmen', *Pearson's Magazine*, 1906, vol. 1, p. 479.

ROBINSON, E. Kay, 'The way with weeds', *Good Words*, 1902, pp. 422–4.

RUCKER, A.W., 'Underground mountains', *Good Words*, 1900, pp. 44–7, 122–7 and 191–6.

RYDALL, E.H., 'The sun – a servant', *Pearson's Magazine*, vol. 1, 1902, pp. 74–5.

SALEEBY, C.W., 'Worry – the disease of the age', *Cassell's Magazine*, January–June 1907.

SALZMAN, Alice, 'Labour conquers all things', *British Workman*, 1897, p. 47.

SCHLESINGER, Kathleen and GENIAUX, Charles, 'Hypnotism – a science', *Pearson's Magazine*, 1900, vol. 2, pp. 220–7.

SCHOOLING, J. Holt, 'The divining rod', *Pearson's Magazine*, 1897, vol. 1, pp. 304–5.

——, 'We shall all be mad in AD2301', *Pearson's Weekly*, 13 November 1897, p. 274.

SHACKLETON, Sir Ernest, 'The making of an explorer', *Pearson's Magazine*, 1914, vol. 2, pp. 138–42.

SHAW, Captain Frank, 'The world in revolt', *Cassell's Saturday Journal*, serial story started in May 1909.

STEAD, W.T., 'My system', *Cassell's Magazine*, August 1906, pp. 292–7.

STORY, Alfred T., 'Harnessing the stars', *Pearson's Magazine*, 1896, vol. 2, pp. 585–92.

SUTHERS, R.B., 'The fairyland of science', review of *Harmsworth Popular Science*, *Clarion*, 23 January 1914, p. 2.

——, 'The mysteries of soap', *Clarion*, 11 April 1913, p. 7.

——, 'Socialism and the unfit', *Clarion*, 16 November 1906, p. 2, and 21 December 1906, p. 7.

TELFORD, Alton, 'The king of the coming age', *British Workman*, December 1897, pp. 90–1.

THORPE, Professor, 'Phosphorous and phosphorescence', *Good Words*, 1891, pp. 249–51 and 306–10.

THOMPSON, Alex M. ('Dangle'), 'In the library', *Clarion*, 8 April 1904, p. 3, and 15 April 1904, p. 3.

——, 'The microbe craze', *Clarion*, 14 April 1911, p. 5.

——, 'Uses of science', *Clarion*, 30 December 1910, p. 7.

THOMSON, Rev. John Scoular, 'The big white diver and the gay young porpoise', *Good Words*, 1904, pp. 692–7.

TILLETT, Ben, 'The great unrest', *Clarion*, series started in January 1912.

TIMINS, D. Theodore, 'A visit to a gun factory', *Cassell's Magazine*, September 1900, p. 464.

TINDAL, Marcus, 'Kumatology', *Pearson's Magazine*, 1901, vol. 2, pp. 10–17.

——, 'A paradise for big game', *Pearson's Magazine*, 1910, vol. 2, pp. 624–7.

TRAYNOR, E., 'How phonograph records are made', *Cassell's Magazine*, March 1909, p. 445.

VERNEY, Sir Edmund, 'On the track of the microbe', *Good Words*, 1899, pp. 208–12.

VIGNOLES, Rev. O.J., 'The home of a naturalist', *Good Words*, 1893, pp. 95–101.

VOGEL, Julius L.F., 'Photographing electricity', *Pearson's Magazine*, 1899, vol. 2, pp. 642–8.

'W.S.S.', 'The engineer', *Cottager and Artisan*, 1897, p. 110.

WARD, Herbert, 'A day in a Central African village', *Cassell's Magazine*, June 1897, pp. 64–9.

WARD, John J., 'Glimpses into plant structure', part of the series 'Minute marvels of nature', *Good Words*, 1902, pp. 127–36.

WELLS, H.G., 'The food of the gods', serialised in *Pearson's Magazine*, 1904.

——, 'The future is as fixed and as determinate as the past', *Cassell's Magazine*, July 1913, pp. 79–85.

——, 'The invisible man: a grotesque romance', serialised in *Pearson's Weekly*, 1897.

——, 'On Mr Alex M. Thompson', *Clarion*, 22 April 1904, p. 3.

——, 'The war of the worlds', serialised in *Pearson's Magazine*, 1897.

WHITE, Frank Marshall, 'A day in a beehive', *Pearson's Magazine*, 1902, vol. 1, pp. 604–11.

——, 'One day with a busy spider', *Pearson's Magazine*, 1902, vol. 1, pp. 287–93.

——, 'One day with a working ant', *Pearson's Magazine*, 1902, vol. 1, pp. 27–32.

WILKINSON, T.W., 'Cave exploring in England', *Good Words*, 1902, p. 437.

WILLIAMS, Archibald, 'After-dinner science', *Pearson's Magazine*, 1906, vol. 1, pp. 33–40.

WINSLOW, Forbes, 'Is insanity on the increase?, *Pearson's Weekly*, 4 May 1905, p. 781.

WINTERWOOD, Geoffrey, 'Bufo of the jewelled head', *Good Words*, 1894, pp. 684–90.

WOODWARD, Marcus, 'The nature cure', *Pearson's Magazine*, 1905, vol. 1, pp. 562–6.

YOUNG, Professor Sydney, 'Present-day leaders of science: William Henry Perkin', *Good Words*, 1900, pp. 256–61.

SECONDARY SOURCES

ABERCROMBIE, Nicholas, HILL, Stephen and TURNER, Bryan S., *The Dominant Ideology Thesis* (London, 1980).

ALLEN, David Elliston, *The Naturalist in Britain: A social history* (London, 1976).

ARMES, Roy, *A Critical History of British Cinema* (London, 1978).

ALTICK, Richard D., *The English Common Reader: A social history of the mass reading public, 1800–1900* (Chicago, 1957).

BAILEY, Peter, *Leisure and Class in Victorian England: Rational recreation and the contest for control, 1830–1885* (London, 1978).

BARNES, Barry, *Scientific Knowledge and Sociological Theory* (London, 1974).

BARNES, Barry and SHAPIN, Steven (eds), *Natural Order: Historical studies of scientific culture* (London, 1979).

BARROW, Logie, *Independent Spirits: Spiritualism and English plebeians, 1850–1910* (London, 1986).

BATCHELOR, John, *H.G. Wells* (Cambridge, 1985).

BECKER, Carl. L., *The Heavenly City of the Eighteenth-Century Philosophers* (New Haven, 1932).

BEER, Gillian, *Darwin's Plots: Evolutionary narrative in Darwin, George Eliot and nineteenth-century fiction* (London, 1983).

BENNETT, Tony, MARTIN, Graham, MERCER, Colin and WOOLLACOTT, Janet (eds), *Culture, Ideology and Social Process: A reader* (Milton Keynes, 1981).

BERELSON, Bernard, *Content Analysis in Communication Research* (original 1952, reprinted New York, 1971).

BIDDISS, Michael D., *The Age of the Masses: Ideas and society in Europe since 1870* (Harmondsworth, 1977).

BLACK, P.J. and LUCAS, A.M. (eds), *Children's Informal Ideas* (London, 1987).

BLATCHFORD, Robert, *My Eighty Years* (London, 1931).

BOGGS, Carl, *Gramsci's Marxism* (London,1976).

BOLT, Christine, *Victorian Attitudes to Race* (London, 1971).

BOWLER, Peter, *The Eclipse of Darwinism: Anti-Darwinian evolutionary theories around 1900* (Baltimore, 1983).

——, *Theories of Human Evolution: A century of debate, 1844–1944* (Oxford, 1987).

BOYCE, George, CURRAN, James and WINGATE, Pauline (eds), *Newspaper History: From the seventeenth century to the present day* (London, 1978).

BRAND, Jeanne L., *Doctors and the State: The British medical profession and government action in public health, 1870–1912* (Baltimore, 1965).

BRITISH ASSOCIATION FOR THE ADVANCEMENT OF SCIENCE, *Science and the Media: Report of a study group* (London, 1976).

BROWN, Lucy, *Victorian News and Newspapers* (Oxford, 1985).

BUDD, Susan, *Varieties of Unbelief: Atheists and agnostics in English society, 1850–1960* (London, 1977).

BURGESS, Keith, *The Challenge of Labour: Shaping British society, 1850–1930* (London, 1980).

BURROW, J.W., *Evolution and Society: A study in Victorian social theory* (Cambridge, 1966).

BURY, J.B., *The Idea of Progress: An inquiry into its origins and growth* (New York, 1955).

CARDWELL, D.S.L., *The Organisation of Science in England* (London, 1957).

de CERTEAU, Michel, *The Practice of Everyday Life*, translated by Steven F. Rendall (California, 1984).

CHADWICK, Owen, *The Victorian Church* (London, 1966).

CHANAN, Michael, *The Dream that Kicks: The prehistory and early years of cinema in Britain* (London, 1980).

CHANT, Colin, and FAUVEL, John (eds), *Darwin to Einstein: Historical studies on science and belief* (Harlow, 1980).

CHRISTIAN, Harry (ed.), *The Sociology of Journalism and the Press*, Sociological Review Monograph 29 (Keele, 1980).

CLARKE, I.F., *The Pattern of Expectation, 1644–2001* (London, 1979).

CLARKE, John, CRITCHER, Chas and JOHNSON, Richard (eds), *Working-Class Culture: Studies in history and theory from the Centre for Contemporary Cultural Studies* (London, 1979).

COLEY, Noel and MARTIN, Graham, *Science, Technology and Popular Culture*, Open University course U203 'Popular culture', block 6, units 26 and 27 (Milton Keynes, 1982).

COOTER, Roger, *The Cultural Meaning of Popular Science: Phrenology and the organisation of consent in nineteenth-century Britain* (Cambridge, 1984).

CRANFIELD, G.A., *The Press and Society: From Caxton to Northcliffe* (London, 1978).

CROSSICK, Geoffrey (ed.), *The Lower Middle Class in Britain, 1870–1914* (London, 1977).

DABYDEEN, David (ed.), *The Black Presence in English Literature* (Manchester, 1985).

DARK, Sidney, *The Life of Sir Arthur Pearson* (London, 1922).

DURANT, John (ed.), *Darwinism and Divinity: Essays on evolution and religious belief* (Oxford, 1985).

EHRENREICH, Barbara and ENGLISH, Deidre, *For Her Own Good: 150 years of the experts' advice to women* (London, 1979).

ELLEGARD, Alvar, *Darwin and the General Reader: The reception of Darwin's theory of evolution in the British periodical press* (Göteborg, 1958).

ETHERINGTON, Norman, *Theories of Imperialism: War, conquest and capital* (London, 1984).

FRASER, W. Hamish, *The Coming of the Mass Market, 1850–1914* (London, 1981).

FRENCH, Richard D., *Anti-vivisection and Medical Science in Victorian Society* (London, 1975).

GILLESPIE, Neal C., *Charles Darwin and the Problem of Creation* (Chicago, 1979).

GILMAN, Sander L., *Difference and Pathology: The stereotypes of sexuality, race and madness* (New York, 1985).

GOULD, Stephen Jay, *The Mismeasure of Man* (London, 1981).

——, *Ontogeny and Phylogeny* (London, 1977).

GRAMSCI, Antonio, *Selections from the Prison Notebooks*, edited and translated by Quinton Hoare and Geoffrey Nowell Smith (London, 1971).

——, *Selections from Cultural Writings*, edited by David Forgacs and Geoffrey Nowell Smith (London, 1985).

GRAY, Robert, *The Aristocracy of Labour in Nineteenth-Century Britain, c. 1850–1900* (London, 1981).

GUREVITCH, Michael, BENNETT, Tony, CURRAN, James and WOOLLA-COTT, Janet (eds), *Culture, Society and the Media* (London, 1982).

HALL, Stuart, HOBSON, Dorothy, LOWE, Andrew and WILLIS, Paul (eds), *Culture, Media, Language: Working papers in cultural studies, 1972–1979* (London, 1980).

HALLER, John S. and HALLER, Robin M., *The Physician and Sexuality in Victorian America* (New York, 1977).

HARRIS, Jose, *Private Lives, Public Spirit: A social history of Britain, 1870–1914* (Oxford, 1993).

HARRISON, Stanley, *Poor Men's Guardians: A record of the struggles for a democratic newspaper press, 1763–1973* (London, 1974).

HASKELL, Thomas L. (ed.), *The Authority of Experts: Studies in history* (Bloomington, 1984).

HOGGART, Richard, *The Uses of Literacy: Aspects of working-class life with special reference to publications and entertainments* (Harmondsworth, 1981).

HOLTON, Gerald and BLANPIED, William (eds), *Science and its Public: The changing relationship* (Boston, 1976).

HORN, Pamela, *The Changing Countryside in Victorian and Edwardian England and Wales* (London, 1984).

HYNES, Samuel, *The Edwardian Turn of Mind* (London, 1968).

JEFFREYS, James B., *Retail Trading in Britain, 1850–1950: A study of trends in retailing with special reference to the development of co-operative, multiple shop and department store methods of trading* (London, 1954).

JENNINGS, Humphrey, *Pandaemonium, 1660–1886: The coming of the machine as seen by contemporary observers* (London, 1985).

JOLL, James, *Gramsci* (London, 1977).

JONES, Greta, *Social Darwinism and English Thought: The interaction between biological and social theory* (Brighton, 1980).

JONES, Greta, CONNELL, Ian and MEADOWS, Jack, *The Presentation of Science by the Media* (Primary Communications Research Centre, University of Leicester, 1978).

JORDANOVA, L.J. (ed.), *Languages of Nature: Critical essays on science and literature* (London, 1986).

JORDANOVA, L.J. and PORTER, Roy (eds), *Images of the Earth: Essays in the history of the environmental sciences* (Chalfont St Giles, 1979).

JOYCE, Patrick, *Work, Society and Politics: The culture of the factory in later Victorian England* (London, 1982).

KEATING, Peter (ed.), *Into Unknown England, 1866–1913: Selections from the sociological explorers* (London, 1976).

KELLY, Alfred, *The Descent of Darwin: The popularisation of Darwinism in Germany, 1860–1914* (Carolina, 1981).

KENT, John, *From Darwin to Blatchford: The role of Darwinism in Christian apologetics, 1875–1910* (London, 1966).

KRANZBERG, Melton and PURSELL, Carroll W. (eds), *Technology in Western Civilisation: vol. I. The emergence of modern industrial society: Earliest times to 1900* (Oxford, 1967).

KRIEGHBAUM, Hillier, *Science and the Mass Media* (London, 1968).

KRIPPENDORF, Klaus, *Content Analysis: An introduction to its methodology* (London, 1980).

KUMAR, Krishan, *Utopia and Anti-Utopia in Modern Times* (Oxford, 1987).

de La BOÉTIE, Étienne, *The Politics of Obedience: The discourse of voluntary servitude*, translated by Harry Kurz (Montreal, 1975).

LEAVIS, Q.D., *Fiction and the Reading Public* (London, 1965).

LEE, Alan J., *The Origins of the Popular Press in England, 1855–1914* (London, 1976).

LOW, Rachel, *The History of the British Film, 1906–1914* (London, 1948).

LOW, Rachel and MANVELL, Roger, *The History of the British Film, 1896–1906* (London, 1948).

LOWE, Marian and HUBBARD, Ruth (eds), *Woman's Nature: Rationalisations of inequality* (Oxford, 1983).

MacCORMACK, Carol P. and STRATEHRN, Marilyn (eds), *Nature, Culture and Gender* (Cambridge, 1980).

MacKENZIE, John M., *Propaganda and Empire: The manipulation of British public opinion, 1880–1960* (Manchester, 1984).

MACLEOD, Roy and COLLINS, Peter (eds), *The Parliament of Science: The British Association for the Advancement of Science, 1831–1981* (Northwood, 1981).

MANSBRIDGE, Albert, *An Adventure in Working-Class Education, being the Story of the Workers' Educational Association, 1903–1915* (London, 1920).

MARKOVITS, Andrei S. and DEUTSCH, Karl W. (eds), *Fear of Science – Trust in Science: Conditions for change in the climate of opinion* (Cambridge, Mass., 1980).

McQUAIL, Denis, *Analysis of Newspaper Content*, Royal Commission on the Press, Cmnd 6810–14 (London, 1977).

MEACHAM, Standish, *A Life Apart: The English working class, 1890–1914* (London, 1977).

MEADOWS, A.J. (ed.), *Development of Science Publishing in Europe* (Oxford, 1980).

MERCHANT, Carolyn, *The Death of Nature: Women, ecology and the scientific revolution* (New York, 1980).

MORRELL, Jack and THACKRAY, Arnold, *Gentlemen of Science: Early years of the British Association for the Advancement of Science* (Oxford, 1981).

MOORE, James R., *The Post-Darwinian Controversies: A study of the Protestant struggle to come to terms with Darwin in Great Britain and America, 1870–1900* (Cambridge, 1979).

NASH, Roderick, *Wilderness and the American Mind* (London, 1973).

NELKIN, Dorothy, *Selling Science: How the press covers science and technology* (New York, 1987).

NOWELL-SMITH, Simon, *The House of Cassell, 1848–1958* (London, 1958).

O'DAY, Alan (ed.), *The Edwardian Age: Conflict and stability, 1900–1914* (London, 1979).

PARRINDER, Patrick, *H.G. Wells: The critical heritage* (London, 1972).

—— (ed.), *Science Fiction: A critical guide* (London, 1979).

PASSMORE, John, *The Perfectibility of Man* (London, 1970).

PELLING, Henry, *Popular Politics and Society in Late Victorian Britain* (2nd edition, London, 1979).

PERKIN, Harold, *The Age of the Automobile* (London, 1976).

——, *The Origins of Modern British Society, 1780–1880* (London, 1969).

PHILMUS, Robert and HUGHES, David (eds), *H.G. Wells: Early writings in science and science fiction* (California, 1975).

POLLARD, Sidney, *The Idea of Progress: History and society* (Harmondsworth, 1971).

PRICE, Richard, *An Imperial War and the British Working Class* (London, 1972).

READ, Donald (ed.), *Edwardian England* (London, 1982).

ROBERTS, Robert, *The Classic Slum: Salford life in the first quarter of the century* (Harmondsworth, 1973).

ROSE, Hilary and ROSE, Steven, *Science and Society* (Harmondsworth, 1969).

ROSE, Nikolas, *The Psychological Complex: Psychology, politics and society in England, 1869–1939* (London, 1985).

ROSENTHAL, Michael, *The Character Factory: Baden-Powell and the origins of the Boy Scout movement* (New York, 1986).

ROTHSTEIN, Theodore, *From Chartism to Labourism* (original 1929, reprinted London, 1983).

ROYAL SOCIETY, *The Public Understanding of Science* (London, 1985).

RUSSELL, Colin, *Science and Social Change, 1700–1900* (London, 1983).

SASSOON, Anne Showstack, *Gramsci's Politics* (2nd edition, London, 1987).

SCALLY, Robert J., *The Origins of the Lloyd George Coalition: The politics of social-imperialism* (London, 1975).

SCULL, Andrew T., *Museums of Madness: The social organisation of insanity in nineteenth-century England* (London, 1979).

SEARLE, G.R., *Eugenics and Class in Britain, 1900–1914* (Leyden, 1976).

——, *The Quest for National Efficiency: A study in British politics and political thought, 1899–1914* (Berkeley, 1971).

SEMMEL, Bernard, *Imperialism and Social Reform: English social-imperial thought, 1895–1914* (London, 1960).

SEYMOUR-URE, Colin, *Science and Medicine and the Press*, Royal Commission on the Press, part B, section 1 (London, 1977).

SHANNON, Richard, *The Crisis of Imperialism, 1865–1915* (London, 1976).

SHATTOCK, Joanne and WOLFF, Michael (eds), *The Victorian Periodical Press: Samplings and soundings* (Leicester, 1982).

SILVERSTONE, Roger, *Framing Science: The making of a BBC documentary* (London, 1985).

SMITH, F.B., *The People's Health, 1830–1910* (London, 1979).

SMITH, Sydney, *Donald Macleod of Glasgow: A memoir and a study* (London, 1926).

SPRINGHALL, John, *Youth, Empire and Society: British youth movements, 1883–1940* (London, 1977).

STEPAN, Nancy, *The Idea of Race in Science: Great Britain, 1800–1960* (London, 1982).

STOCKING, George W., *Victorian Anthropology* (New York, 1987).

STORCH, Robert D. (eds), *Popular Culture and Custom in Nineteenth-Century England* (London, 1982).

STREET, Brian V., *The Savage in Literature: Representations of 'primitive' society in English fiction, 1858–1920* (London, 1975).

STRINATI, Dominic, *An Introduction to Theories of Popular Culture* (London, 1995).

SULLIVAN, Alvin (ed.), *British Literary Magazines: The Victorian and Edwardian age* (London, 1984).

SUTHERLAND, Gillian, *Ability, Merit and Measurement: Mental testing and English education* (Oxford, 1984).

SYMONDSON, Anthony (ed.), *The Victorian Crisis of Faith* (London, 1970).

THOMAS, Keith, *Man and the Natural World: Changing attitudes in England, 1500–1800* (London, 1983).

THOMPSON, Kenneth, *Beliefs and Ideologies* (London, 1986).

THOMPSON, Paul, *The Edwardians: The remaking of British society* (London, 1984).

THOMSON, Flora, *Lark Rise to Candleford* (Harmondsworth, 1973).

TURNER, E.S., *All Heaven in a Rage* (London 1964).

——, *Boys Will Be Boys* (London, 1975).

——, *The Shocking History of Advertising* (London, 1952).

TURNER, Frank M., *Between Science and Religion: The reaction to scientific naturalism in late Victorian England* (London, 1974).

TUVESON, Ernest Lee, *Millennium and Utopia: A study in the background of the idea of Progress* (Gloucester, Massachusetts, 1972).

WAITES, Bernard, BENNETT, Tony and MARTIN, Graham (eds), *Popular Culture: Past and present* (London, 1982).

WALTON, John K., *The English Seaside Resort: A social history, 1750–1914,* (Leicester, 1983).

——, *Lancashire: A social history, 1558–1939* (Manchester, 1987).

WALVIN, James, *Leisure and Society, 1830–1950* (London, 1978).

WEBSTER, Charles (ed.), *Biology, Medicine and Society, 1840–1940* (Cambridge, 1981).

WELLS, H.G., *The Shape of Things to Come* (London, 1933; Corgi edition, 1967).

WIENER, Joel H., *Papers for the Millions: The new journalism in Britain, 1850 to 1914* (Westport, 1988).

WIENER, Martin, *English Culture and the Decline of the Industrial Spirit, 1850–1980* (Cambridge, 1981).

WILLIAMS, Francis, *Dangerous Estate: The anatomy of newspapers* (London, 1957).

WILLIAMS, Raymond, *Communications* (Harmondsworth, 1976).

——, *The Long Revolution* (London, 1961).

WILLIAMS, Rosalind H., *Dream Worlds: Mass consumption in late-nineteenth-century France* (London, 1982).

WOHL, Anthony S., *Endangered Lives: Public health in Victorian Britain* (London, 1983).

YEO, Eileen and YEO, Stephen (eds), *Popular Culture and Class Conflict, 1590–1914: Explorations in the history of labour and leisure* (Brighton, 1981).

Index